IMMIGRATION THE WORLD OVER

IMMIGRATION THE WORLD OVER

Statutes, Policies, and Practices

James P. Lynch
and
Rita J. Simon

ROWMAN & LITTLEFIELD PUBLISHERS, INC.
Lanham • Boulder • New York • Oxford

ROWMAN & LITTLEFIELD PUBLISHERS, INC.

Published in the United States of America
by Rowman & Littlefield Publishers, Inc.
A Member of the Rowman & Littlefield Publishing Group
4501 Forbes Boulevard, Suite 200, Lanham, Maryland 20706
www.rowmanlittlefield.com

P.O. Box 317, Oxford OX2 9RU, United Kingdom

British Library Cataloguing in Publication Information Available

Library of Congress Cataloging-in-Publication Data

Lynch, James P. (James Patrick), 1949–
Immigration the world over : statutes, policies, and practices / James P. Lynch and Rita J. Simon.
p. cm.
Includes bibliographical references and index
ISBN 0-7425-1877-9 (cloth : alk. paper) — ISBN 0-7425-1878-7 (paper : alk. paper)
1. Emigration and immigration law. 2. Emigration and immigration. I. Simon, Rita James. II. Title
K3275 .L96 2003
342'.082—dc21

2002011276

Printed in the United States of America

∞™ The paper used in this publication meets the minimum requirements of American National Standard for Information Sciences—Permanence of Paper for Printed Library Materials, ANSI/NISO Z39.48-1992.

Contents

List of Tables vii

Introduction 1

Part I: Country Descriptions

1 Immigration in the United States 11

2 Immigration in Canada 55

3 Immigration in Australia 87

4 Immigration in Great Britain 123

5 Immigration in France 147

6 Immigration in Germany 171

7 Immigration in Japan 189

Part II: Cross-National Comparisons

8 Comparative Immigration Policy 209

9 Criminal Involvement among Immigrants and Natives across Countries 227

10 Public Opinion toward Immigrants 239

11 Social Integration of Immigrants in Host Societies 251

Conclusion 269

Index 273

About the Authors 291

Tables

1.1	Allocation of Permanent Residence Visas, Fiscal Year 1995	20
1.2	Increase in U.S. Population by Component of Change, 1810–1989	21
1.3	The Leading "Sender" States, 1820–1989	22
1.4	Percentage Distribution of Permanent Legal Immigration to the United States by Region of Last Residence, 1821–1830 and 1981–1990	23
1.5	Refugee Status Applications Filed and Approved and Refugees Admitted by Selected Nationality, Fiscal Year 1991	24
1.6	Immigration to the United States, Fiscal Years 1821–1995	25
1.7	Rates of Naturalization for Legal Aliens by Class of Admission	26
1.8	Percentage Naturalized by the End of Fiscal Year 1991 for the Immigration Cohort Aged 16 Years Old and over in 1977 by Country of Birth	27
1.9	Estimates of Undocumented Aliens in the United States by Country of Birth	29
1.10	Marital Status and Gender Distribution of Immigrant Admissions, 1995, and U.S. Population, 1990, by Age Group	31
1.11	Education Characteristics by Gender between Immigrants and U.S. Natives in 1970, 1980, and 1990	32

1.12 English Language Ability of Recent Immigrants, 1990 33

1.13 Occupational Distribution of Aliens Admitted under the Preference System in Fiscal Years 1972, 1976, 1978, 1983, and 1988 34

1.14 Labor-Market Characteristics of Legal Immigrants, Recent Immigrants, and Natives for Persons 16 Years Old and over, 1980 36

1.15 Occupation, Immigrants Aged 21 to 65 Years at Admission to Permanent Residence, Fiscal Years 1977, 1982, and 1994 Cohorts 37

1.16 Estimated Incarceration Rates by Citizenship Status and Offense 41

1.17 Estimated Offending Rates (per 100,000) by Citizenship Status and Type of Crime, 1992–1993 42

1.18 Immigrants Who on Balance Have Been a Good Thing or Bad Thing for This Country, 1982 44

1.19 Public Opinion on Immigrants by Ethnicity, 1985–1993 45

1.20 Should U.S. Immigration Be Kept at Its Present Level, Increased, or Decreased? 47

2.1 Selection Criteria for Independent Immigrants 59

2.2 Immigration to Canada, 1946–2000 62

2.3 Immigration to Canada by Country or Geographical Area of Last Permanent Residence, since 1946 63

2.4 Number and Country of Origin of Immigrants to Canada, 1981–1991 64

2.5 Percent Distribution of Admissions by Region and Year of Admission 65

2.6 Admissions by Class and Year 66

2.7 Admission of Refugees by Category, since 1980 67

2.8 Age Structure of the Immigrant and Native Populations 70

2.9 Persons Attending School As a Percentage of All Persons by Age Group and Gender, 1996 72

2.10 Proportion of Men and Women 15 and Older Who Immigrated between 1991 and 1996 and Are Able to Speak English or French, 1996 73

2.11 Occupations of Employed Persons 25 to 64 Years of Age by Gender, 1996 74

2.12 Skill Levels of Jobs of University Graduates 25 to 64 Years of Age by Gender and Immigration Status, 1996 74

2.13 Level of Income by Gender and Immigration Status, 1996 75

2.14 Income by Sources, Average Immigrant, and Nonimmigrant Households, Canada, 1990 77

2.15 Taxes Paid, Average Immigrant and Nonimmigrant Households, Canada, 1990 78

2.16 Net Public Treasury Effect of Immigration on Nonimmigrant Households, Canada, 1990 79

2.17 Should Canadian Immigration Be Kept at Its Present Level, Increased, or Decreased? 81

3.1 Net Immigration and Population Growth, Australia, 1788–1920 88

3.2 Net Immigration by Periods, Annual Averages 89

3.3 Eligibility Components and Categories of Settler Arrivals, 1990–1991 and 1991–1992 93

3.4 Program Planning Levels, 1991–1992 and 1992–1993 94

3.5 Net Immigration by Periods: Annual Averages and Percentage Distribution 99

3.6 Birthplace of Settler Arrivals by Regions, 1989–1999 100

3.7 Civilian Labor Force by Birthplace 104

3.8 Occupational Distributions, Average for 1979–1983 105

3.9 Australian and Migrant Occupational Distributions 106

3.10 Mean Weekly Earnings of Full-Time Employees, by Birthplace 107

3.11 Self-Employment and Employer Status, by Sex, Birthplace, and Period of Residence, South Australia, June 1981 108

3.12 Imprisonment Rates per 100,000 for Age 17 and Older by Birthplace, Australia, 1971 111

3.13 Prisoners by Birthplace, 1985 112

3.14 Stock Incarceration Rates (per 1,000), All Offenses, by Country of Birth, 1992–1997 112

3.15 Prison Inmates by Country of Origin and Offense 113

3.16 Offense-Specific Stock Incarceration Rates per 1,000 by Country of Birth, Australia, 1992, 1995, and 1997 114

3.17 Attitudes toward Ethnic Groups, 1947 115

3.18 Attitudes toward Admitting Non-European Immigrants by Year 116

3.19 Public Opinion Poll of Numbers of Immigrants Allowed to Enter Australia 117

3.20 Should Australia Encourage Immigrants from the Following Countries? 118

4.1 Estimated Net Immigration from the New Commonwealth, 1953–1962 128

4.2 Immigration to the United Kingdom from the New Commonwealth, 1962–1991 129

4.3 Asylum Applications, 1979–1999 130

4.4 Change in Stock of Foreign Population in Great Britain, 1984–1990 133

4.5 Distribution of National, Foreign, and Total Employment between the Eleven Major Industry Divisions in Great Britain, 1991 136

4.6 Victimization Reporting Rates by Ethnic Group 138

4.7 Should Britain Allow More, Less, or the Same Amount of Settlement? 140

4.8 British Attitudes toward Particular Groups, 1991 141

5.1 Evolution of the Foreign Population in France, 1921–1990 149

5.2 Total Fertility Rates (per 1,000), 1982–1985 157

5.3 Percentage of Pupils Who Are Foreign Born 158

5.4 Estimated Offenses by Citizenship and Types of Crime, France, 1991 159

5.5 Sentencing Following Trial, Percentage of Unsuspended Prison Sentences (with or without Partial Suspension) for At Least One Year, According to Immigrant Status, 1991 161

5.6 Percentage of Admissions by Pretrial Detention and Breakdown of Summary Trials by Offense, 1993 162

5.7	Foreign Prison Populations by Nationality, January 1, 1995	162
5.8	Ratios of Processing Rates for Foreigners and Citizens by Stage of Processing and Whether Violations of Immigration Laws Are Included or Excluded	163
5.9	Proportion of Police Matters Involving Foreigners by Whether Immigration Offenses Are Included or Excluded by Year	163
5.10	French Attitudes toward Particular Groups, 1994	167
6.1	Employed Foreigners in Germany by Economic Activities, 1996	175
6.2	Share of Foreigners in Total Employment in Germany, 1983 and 1991	179
6.3	Distribution of National, Foreign, and Total Employment between the Eleven Major Industry Divisions in 1991 in Germany	180
6.4	Contributions to Social Security Insurance, Tax Payments, and Transfers, Deutsche Marks per Average Household, 1984	181
6.5	Estimates of Offending by Citizenship and Type of Crime, Germany, 1985	181
6.6	Age-Specific Analysis by Citizenship and Gender of Total Suspects for Germany, 1984 and 1990	182
6.7	German Attitudes toward Foreigners, 1989	184
6.8	German Attitudes toward Particular Groups of Foreigners, 1989	185
7.1	Residence Statuses and Authorized Activity, Japan	191
7.2	Estimates of Unauthorized Visa Overstayers, by Nationality, 1990–1993	199
7.3	Percentage Distribution of Offenses for Foreigners and Japanese Citizens	200
8.1	Dimensions of Immigrant Policy by Nation	220
8.2	A Typology of Immigration Policies	221
9.1	Incarceration Ratios for Immigrants and Nonimmigrants by Nation and Year	230

9.2 Criminal Involvement Ratios for Immigrants and Nonimmigrants by Type of Offense, Nation, and Year 231

9.3 Offense-Specific Stock Incarceration Rates per 1,000 by Country of Birth, Australia, 1992, 1995, 1997 232

9.4 Estimated Offenses by Citizenship and Types of Crime, France, 1991 233

9.5 Estimates of Offending by Citizenship and Type of Crime, Germany, 1985 234

9.6 U.S. Incarceration Rates and Ratios for Aliens and Citizens by Types of Offense, 1991 234

11.1 Social Integration of Immigrants by Nation 260

Introduction

Scholarly debates over immigration policy are conducted mainly in terms of the effect of that policy on labor markets and economic measures of productivity. Of principal concern is the fit between the labor-market needs of a given nation and the composition of people immigrating to that country. Debates over the displacement of indigenous workers are equally prevalent. While the economic and labor-force implications of immigration and immigration policy are important, they are not the only standards against which to measure the effects of these policies. The impact of immigration and immigration policy on other institutions in society should also be considered.

Outside of scholarly debate, economic concerns give way to anxieties about the effect of immigrants on other institutions. The extent to which immigrants, and particularly illegal immigrants and their children, contribute to welfare dependency or to the strain on local and state educational and health resources is a recurrent theme, particularly in the popular press. Less frequently, references are made to the long-term effects of immigration and related fertility patterns on political institutions. The participation of immigrants in criminal activities also figures largely in the press, as does their presence in correctional institutions. Although the specific content of treatments may vary, when considered outside a scholarly context, the underlying theme is the same—immigration has a disruptive and negative effect on major social institutions in society. Thus, the implications for policy are clear: restrict immigration.

It is unfortunate that the bulk of debate over the implications of immigration for noneconomic institutions should take place in the media and not in more scholarly forums. The issues surrounding the social impact of immigration are complex and the time constraints on the media preclude dealing with these issues in a sufficiently detailed manner. Moreover, the information necessary to answer many of the questions about the social repercussions of immigration is even less available than those pertaining to economic issues. As a result, the evidence offered to support arguments on both sides of the immigration issue is often derived from anecdotes or case studies. However, neither is sufficient to describe the effects of immigration, especially when these effects are likely to vary so much among people and locations.

A major goal of this book, therefore, is to examine the impact of immigration on largely noneconomic institutions in seven nations using the best available, nationally representative statistical data. The descriptions that emerge will hopefully serve as a check on the more anecdotal evidence offered in the media. But having said this, we must warn our readers that the amount and quality of data available for the seven countries are not uniform. There are wide variations, especially in the sections on criminal involvement and social indicators. In some instances, we had to resort to regional statistics, shorter time periods, less reliable sources, and other less than ideal alternatives, which will become apparent as you move from one country to the next.

Discussions of immigration policy not only suffer from potentially misleading information about immigration's impacts on society, but such discussions also often lead to questionable projections as to what immigration policy can do to shape these effects. Calls for more open or more restrictive immigration policies can, in most cases, only be defended by conjecture or extrapolation. For example, a very restrictive immigration policy oriented toward serving a nation's short-term labor needs can be advocated on the belief that the more restrictive a policy, the higher the quality of those admitted. But, this may be only partly true. It assumes that we can adequately distinguish, a priori, persons who will be nonproductive and socially disruptive from those who will be productive. It further assumes that screening criteria that yield immigrants desirable from a labor-force perspective will also yield them desirable from the perspective of other societal institutions. Likewise, the arguments for completely open immigration policies are equally conjectural with regard to their effects.

To some extent, conjecture is unavoidable in predicting the outcome of immigration policy because one cannot know for certain what will occur until a policy is actually implemented. For example, it is unclear what would happen if the United States were today to implement an exclusively guest-worker policy (in which admissions are restricted to workers who can stay only as long as there is need for their labor), since such a policy has not been followed recently in this nation. If such a policy was ever implemented in the past, it would be useful to assess its effects and to project the implications of future policies. There is some risk in this strategy, however, in that the United States circa 1900 is quite different from the United States in the twenty-first century.

One alternative is to examine the impact of immigration policies in other nations on social institutions and to use this experience to predict the effect in the United States. But this strategy also has limitations as other nations may be sufficiently different from the United States that such comparisons would not be particularly helpful. The social contexts in which these policies are implemented may be too radically different to produce comparable results. The utility of cross-national comparisons of immigration policies as a basis for projection must therefore be assessed on a case-by-case basis. But even when the nations compared are not exactly comparable, cross-national comparisons can be a useful heuristic device for illuminating the potential consequences of policy. Whatever the limitations of cross-national comparisons may be, however, this approach to projecting policy outcomes has not often been used in the case of immigration and it is certainly a better basis for prediction than extrapolation based on media-driven rhetoric, instinct, or "common sense."

This book compares the impact of immigration on major social institutions in seven industrialized democracies: the United States, Canada, Australia, Great Britain, France, Germany, and Japan. These nations were chosen because they are arguably similar in terms of economic development and governance, that is, they are all industrialized democracies. More importantly, they represent a wide range of immigration policies. Australia, Canada, and the United States are often referred to as "immigrant nations" because a substantial proportion of their current population are immigrants or the children of immigrants rather than indigenous people. These nations are accustomed to receiving and accommodating large influxes of immigrants and their official and actual immigration policies reflect that history. Although France does not share the same history of welcoming large numbers of immigrants, it has a less restrictive immigration record than either Great Britain and Germany. Both by policy and self identity, Great Britain and Germany are not immigrant nations. Likewise, Japan is not an immigrant nation as it is the most homogenous and closed society of all the industrialized nations in the world.[1] As a result, there is considerable variation in policies and outcomes not only across, but within the groups of immigrant and nonimmigrant nations. This variability can provide useful insights into the potential effects of specific policies and an understanding of why these outcomes occur in a specific social context.

Our comparison across nations relies heavily on the social indicator data from each nation. Some of the very informative comparisons of two nations that have been done have used much more detailed and nuanced information on the history and politics of the nations compared. This level of detail was not possible for seven nations. We traded detail for a greater variety of immigration policies and outcomes. Moreover, we believe that substantial differences in policy and outcomes should be visible in the social indicators data.

Characterizing Immigration Policy Cross-Nationally

For each country, we describe national immigration policy, by which we mean both the laws and policies that govern admission to a given nation, as well as the institutional arrangements available to accommodate newcomers in that society. Under immigration policy, we address the laws and procedures that determine admission, affect the control of immigrants after admission, and specify the requirements for naturalization. Admission laws and rules specify how many immigrants can be admitted in a given year, the various preferences and exclusions that apply, and the proper procedure required to gain legal admission. Special attention is given to the status of refugees and asylum seekers, as well as to the issue of those who avoid the process entirely through illegal immigration. The policies governing control of immigrants after admission refer to any special duties of legal aliens, such as reporting requirements and restrictions on work, schooling, movement, residence, or property ownership.

Policies that affect the accommodation of immigrants can be divided into direct and indirect policies. Direct policies refer to those actions of the government that are specifically designed to assist immigrants, such as language or vocational training. Indirect policies refer to actions of the government that are not specifically designed to assist immigrants, but do affect the ability of immigrants to live in the host society. The existence of and eligibility for welfare and medical benefits, for example, would be an indirect policy that can affect the accommodation of immigrants in the host society.

In addition to describing formal immigration policy, we will also examine (to the greatest extent possible) the implementation of that policy. So, for example, we examine not only a nation's eligibility requirements for naturalization, but also the rate at which immigrants apply for and are granted citizenship status. Policy and its implementation can be very different.

Finally, we consider institutional arrangements that are not government policies, but are circumstances that affect the ability of immigrants to live and prosper in the host society. Factors such as the size of the particular immigrant group, the length of time that a particular group has had a presence in the host nation, the relative affluence of a group, and the assimilation of prior waves of immigrants from that particular group constitute an important part of the social context of immigration policy. Where these elements of the social context of immigration are conducive to accommodating immigrants, the disruptive effects of immigration to both the immigrants and the host society will likely be minimal and the import of immigrant policy will be slight.

Where the social context of immigration is not conducive, however, the role of immigrant policy can be determinative of whether the accommodation of immigrants is harmonious or disruptive.

Defining Impacts on Major Social Institutions

The effect of immigration and immigration policy will be assessed with regard to three major sets of social institutions that are not directly "economic." The first includes the principal integrative institutions in our society: family, community, and educational and occupational institutions. The second is crime and the third is dependency, for example, welfare. These institutions were chosen, in part, because they are central to the maintenance of society. Broad-based participation in integrative institutions and minimal participation in crime and dependence are conducive to social order. These institutions were also chosen in part because they are topical. Crime and dependency are the two greatest fears regarding immigrants after competition in the labor market. Indeed, these fears may be more prevalent than fears of competition in the labor market because competition will most likely affect only a small group of native-born citizens at the margin of the labor force. It is important to examine the involvement of immigrants in crime and dependency across different nations and under different immigrant policies.

Finally, these institutions were chosen because we believe that they are interconnected. There is reason to believe that the level of participation by immigrants in the major integrative institutions in society will affect the involvement of these groups in crime and dependency. The greater the extent of participation in these integrative institutions, the lower the involvement of immigrants in crime and dependency. This relationship will also be explored in this book.

In addition, we will examine public opinion about immigrants and immigration policy. Public opinion is important because it can influence public policy vis-à-vis immigrants. Public opinion is therefore both a product of institutions of social control and a force that shapes these institutions. If, for example, immigrants participate in these institutions in a fashion similar to native citizens, public opinion about immigrants and immigration policy may take a particular tone and influence certain policy choices. On the other hand, public opinion about immigrants can influence policies that encourage or limit access to these institutions, as in the case where immigrants (both legal and illegal) are barred from the public school systems or from working in the host country. The link between public opinion and the social impact of immigrants is also important because a high level of dependency and criminal involvement for immigrants is likely to induce negative public attitudes about them. In sum, the nature of public opinion in different societies can help us understand the patterns that emerge between immigration policy and the social impact of immigration.

Organization of the Volume

Part I is the heart of the book. It contains seven case studies of the immigration laws and official policies and practices, institutional arrangements, numbers, demographic characteristics, and behaviors of the immigrants who have entered each of the seven countries over the past thirty-plus years. The case studies provide descriptions, to the greatest extent possible, of the marital rates, fertility patterns, age and gender distributions, and the educational and occupational characteristics of past and current immigrants. Each case study also includes data on public opinion toward immigrants, comparisons of crime rates, and the percentage of welfare recipients in immigrant and native-born populations.

Part II is explicitly comparative. It examines similarities and differences in the policies, practices, numbers, and characteristics and behavior of immigrants across the seven countries. On the basis of these comparisons, implications about the roles immigrants play and the contributions, or lack thereof, they make to the host society are drawn.

A Brief Afterthought

Although this book did not appear in print until 2003, we completed our research and writing before the events of September 11, 2001. In the months that followed the deaths of over 3,000 people in New York, Pennsylvania, and Washington, D.C., the United States instituted some changes in immigration practices that focused especially on overseas students seeking to study at American universities and on rounding up for interrogation recent immigrants of Middle Eastern background.

On June 5, 2002, Attorney General John Ashcroft announced that he ordered the Immigration and Naturalization Service (INS) to fingerprint and photograph visitors seeking to enter the United States from five countries where terrorists are known to operate: Syria, Sudan, Libya, Iraq, and Iran. Congress also ordered the INS to establish a system for tracking the entry and exit of all visitors to the United States beginning in 2005. According to Ashcroft, the new registration program is the first phase of that effort.

France is another country in this volume that witnessed changes in matters pertaining to immigration. In France, the dramatic event was the unexpected victory of Jean-Marie Le Pen in the primary election for the French presidency held in May 2002. Le Pen came in second, after the incumbent Jacques

Chirac, in the primary defeating a field of more than ten candidates. Le Pen's campaign was marked by strongly anti-immigrant sentiments and policies that advocated closing French borders to foreigners. What policy implications the Le Pen victory may have is still too early to determine. While Le Pen did not win the election, his strong showing in the first round may force the government to embrace more restrictive immigration policies than it would have otherwise.

These events are not covered in this volume. Hopefully, there will be a second edition and we will be able to give them their due.

Note

1. In the chapters on Germany and Japan, we describe and comment on the very recent changes in laws and policies that have occurred especially in those countries.

PART I

COUNTRY DESCRIPTIONS

1

Immigration in the United States

George III and the British government's rejection of colonial demands for a more open immigration policy to attract newcomers to its shores was one of the causes of the American Revolution. The Declaration of Independence charged the king with attempting to keep the colonies depopulated, refusing to recognize naturalization acts passed by colonial assemblies, and restricting westward settlements. The framers of the U.S. Constitution made the foreign born ineligible for only one office in the federal government, that of the presidency.

In 1790, Congress passed the first federal laws that loosely defined a uniform rule for the naturalization of immigrants: any fully white person who resided for two years within the limits and under the jurisdiction of the United States.[1] In 1801, Congress changed the residency requirement to five years, where it remains today. The federal government kept no official records of immigration until 1820. It was not until 1850 that the U.S. Census Bureau distinguished between foreign- and native-born citizens. By 1864, however, Congress had established a Bureau of Immigration.

During the first 150 years of its existence, the United States welcomed forty million immigrants to its shores. In the opinion of historian Marcus Hansen, most of them came because they sought freedom from the laws and customs of countries that curbed individual economic enterprise.[2] In the cities of Europe, citizens wanted to escape regulations of guild and trade unions; in rural areas, they sought exemption from the traditional restrictions on the transfer of land and the conduct of agriculture. They wanted, in essence, the freedom to buy, sell, bargain, to work or to loaf, and to become rich or remain poor. In the period before the Civil War, the large majority of the immigrants, over 80 percent, were from the northern and western parts of Europe. With the exception of the French and Irish, most were Protestant and most were farmers. The big change came in the 1880s and continued up through World War I, when the large majority of immigrants came from southern and eastern Europe and most were Catholics and Jews. The detailed statistical analysis of which groups came when and the welcome or lack of it they received are described in the following sections of this chapter.

Historical Background and Major Legislation

In 1875, Congress enacted the first federal statute to regulate immigration by preventing the entry of criminals and prostitutes. Prior to 1880, there was very little restriction of immigration into the United States. The period from 1880 to the mid-1960s, however, has been characterized as the "restrictionist era" in U.S. immigration policy. Beginning with the Chinese Exclusion Act of 1882, Congress began to take an active part in the administration and control of immigration. This act suspended the entry of Chinese workers for ten years and barred all foreign-born Chinese from acquiring citizenship.[3] This marked the first time in history that a group was excluded from the United States because of its national characteristics. Three years later, Congress passed the Foran Act, which prohibited the recruitment of unskilled laborers by prepaid passage and advance contracting.[4] In 1888, Congress ordered the deportation of all immigrant contract laborers within one year of entry.

In the two decades between 1896 and 1917, Congress grappled with literacy requirements as a means of restricting immigration. From 1896 until 1910, four literacy bills were debated in Congress, but passed in only one house. Between 1910 and 1917, Congress passed and sent to the president three literacy acts, each of which was vetoed. In 1907, Congress established the Dillingham Commission to study the relationship between literacy, deviance, and the types of immigrants who were likely to make the best citizens. Finally, in 1917, over a presidential veto, the Immigration Act of 1917 was passed, which required proof on the part of immigrants over sixteen years of age that they were able to read and write in some language (their native language, English, or any other). Those who could not meet those requirements were sent back. This same statute also barred Asiatics (defined as persons from India, Indochina, Afghanistan, Arabia, and East India) from entry. Although this ban had nothing to do with literacy, it was nevertheless added to the Immigration Act of 1917.[5]

The Johnson Act of 1921, also known as the Quota Act or the Immigration Act, introduced a system of national quotas. The quota was determined as a percentage of the number of immigrants from the country in question at the time of a designated national census. The annual number of immigrants allowed from each nation was set at 3 percent of the foreign born of that nationality as recorded in the 1910 census. The 1921 act also set an annual limit of 350,000 on all European immigration and set quotas for countries in the Near East, Africa, Australia, and New Zealand. No quotas, however, were imposed on immigrants from nations in the Western Hemisphere.[6]

In 1924, the year the 1921 Quota Act expired, Congress passed another National Quota Act, which set quotas at 2 percent of the foreign born from a given nation in the 1890 census. The new act also provided that, beginning in 1927, the overall European quota limit would be 150,000 proportioned by the distribution of the foreign born in the 1920 census. This latter provision was postponed twice before becoming effective in 1929. The 1924 act also barred from entry all immigrants who were ineligible for citizenship.[7]

In the first two decades of the twentieth century, Congress passed various other pieces of restrictionist legislation that limited groups on the basis of political activities and ideologies, and medical histories. Anarchists and epileptics, for example, were excluded by these measures. Between 1929 and 1939, however, Congress passed very little legislation on immigration, largely because there was so little immigration in those years. In 1932, for example, immigration reached its lowest point since 1831. In fact, more people were leaving the United States than were entering due largely to the worldwide depression.

During World War II, in response to the labor shortage created by the war, Congress established the Bracero Program, which permitted the temporary entrance of foreign agricultural workers from Mexico, British Honduras, Barbados, and Jamaica.[8] In addition, the Chinese Exclusion Act of 1882 was repealed in 1943.[9]

Immediately following the end of World War II, Congress passed the War Brides Act, which admitted approximately 120,000 immigrant wives and children of U.S. servicemen on a nonquota basis.[10] Two years later, Congress also passed the Displaced Persons Act, which admitted 280,000 people over a two-year period.[11] Regular immigration quotas were mortgaged at the rate of 50 percent for as many years as it would take to compensate for the number of persons admitted under the Displaced Persons Act. In 1950, still retaining the mortgage principle, an additional 425,000 displaced persons were admitted over two years.

The Immigration and Nationality Act of 1952 was the first major piece of immigration legislation since the Quota Acts of 1921 and 1924. Known as the McCarran-Walters Act, it changed the formula for annual quotas from any country to one-sixth of 1 percent of the persons of each national origin in the United States as of 1920.[12] It limited immigration from the Eastern Hemisphere to 150,000 annually, but imposed no limits on immigration from the Western Hemisphere. The law removed all racial barriers to immigration and naturalization, broadened classes of immigrants subject to exclusion and deportation, and expanded and strengthened provisions for the exclusion and deportation of other classes of immigrants. In addition, preferences were established for skilled workers and for relatives of U.S. citizens.

The Hungarian Uprising of 1956 sparked the passage of the first of a series of refugee acts that have continued to this day. In 1956, Congress allowed 21,000 Hungarian refugees to enter the United States without regard to quotas.[13] In 1960, following the success of Fidel Castro in establishing a communist government in Cuba, Congress passed the Migration and Refugee Assistance Act. This act facilitated the admission and resettlement of more than 600,000 refugees into the United States.[14] In 1964, Congress ended the Bracero Program that it began in 1942.

The Hart-Celler Act of 1965 eliminated national quotas as a basis for admitting immigrants to the United States. Instead, it established an annual limit of 170,000 immigrants who could enter the United States and a per-country quota of 20,000. Not included in the 170,000 figure were potential immigrants from Western Hemisphere countries. This act set a limit of 120,000 immigrants from the Western Hemisphere, thus allowing for a total admission of 290,000 immigrants a year.[15] The Hart-Cellar Act further established a system whereby visas would be distributed according to a preference list that favored close relatives of U.S. citizens and those with desired occupational skills. Countries in the Western Hemisphere did not have per-country quotas. The act also broadened the definition of refugees to include victims of natural calamities along with people who were victims of religious and political persecution. However, the act also broadened the class of immigrants denied immigration, such as drug and alcohol addicts, the mentally ill, those with physically contagious diseases, criminals, prostitutes, subversives, and some twenty other types of "undesirable" persons.

The 1976 Immigration and Nationality Act extended the per-country limitation of 20,000 immigrants to nations in the Western Hemisphere. Finally, in 1978 Congress amended the act to combine the ceiling for both the Eastern and the Western Hemispheres for a worldwide immigrant limit of 290,000 persons.[16]

The 1970s also witnessed the passage of legislation for the admission and resettlement of refugees, mainly from Southeast Asia, the Soviet Union, and Cuba. "Refugees" are defined in accordance with the UN Convention of 1951 as persons outside their homeland who are unable or unwilling to return because of persecution or fear of persecution.

In 1975, Congress enacted the Indochinese Refugee Resettlement Program, allowing more than 200,000 Indo-Chinese refugees to enter the country. Five years later, Congress passed the Refugee Act of 1980, which established an overall policy for the admission and resettlement of refugees to the United States.[17] The 1980 act created the Office of U.S. Coordination for Refugee Affairs and the Office of Refuge Resettlement in the U.S. Department of Health and Human Services to coordinate internal and domestic refugee programs and to arrange for effective absorption and resettlement of the refugees. The act assumed a normal flow of 50,000 refugees a year. It permitted the president, in consultation with Congress, to increase the annual allocation. In 1980, the level was set at 230,000 admissions. In 1986, the level was 67,000, and in 1990 it was increased to 125,000.

The Refugee Act of 1980 also regulates U.S. policy on individuals seeking asylum. The definition of an asylee conforms to the same criteria and categories of persecution as a refugee. The only difference is the location of the immigrant when he or she applies. For example, a potential asylee is in the United States or at a point of entry whereas a potential refugee is outside the United States. Since the 1980 Refugee Act has been in effect, approximately 67,400 persons have been granted asylum. In 1980, the three major countries from which persons sought asylum were El Salvador, Nicaragua, and Guatemala.

In 1986, Congress passed the Immigration Reform and Control Act, which was designed primarily to reduce illegal immigration. The act forbade employers from hiring illegal immigrants and established a regulatory apparatus that helped employers comply with the law and that detected and punished violators.[18] The act also established an enforcement apparatus to ensure that employers would comply with the laws banning discrimination in hiring on the basis of national origin or citizenship and an appeals process that would give persons suffering from discrimination a channel for redress.

The Immigration Reform and Control Act of 1986 also created a general, albeit temporary, program for legalizing undocumented immigrants who could demonstrate continuous residence in the United States as of January 1, 1982. Under a separate provision, the act also permitted those who worked a minimum of ninety days in the delivery of "seasonal agricultural work (SAW)" between May 1, 1985 and May 1, 1986, to become legal immigrants. The requirements for determining eligibility and processing applications differed markedly between the two programs.[19]

Under terms governing the general legalization program, applicants had to make timely application, maintain a continuous presence in the United States from the time the law was passed, and be admissible in all other ways. Immigrants were also required to apply for temporary resident status in person at newly established, local Immigration and Naturalization Service (INS) legalization offices between May 5, 1987, and May 5, 1988, at which time they had to provide evidence of identity and continuous residence in the United States since 1982. The law required those who received temporary status to return to the INS office in eighteen months to demonstrate an adequate level of English proficiency and citizenship skills, after which they were given permanent resident status (their temporary status expired if they failed to return).

Requirements under the SAW program were considerably more lenient. Applicants who could demonstrate they had worked ninety days or more in designated seasonal agriculture between May 1985 and May 1986 and could demonstrate admissibility as an immigrant were awarded temporary status, which they could adjust to permanent status after two years without fulfilling further requirements. They could apply at any time between June 1987 and November 1988. Because they were not required to maintain continuous residence, immigrants could apply at local domestic legalization offices or at the consular or INS offices in their countries of residence.

In November 1990, Congress passed the most liberal immigration bill since the first Quota Act of 1921. The Immigration Act of 1990 set the overall annual quota at 700,000 for the period 1992 through 1994 and set a permanent annual level of 675,000 immigrants beginning in 1995.[20] The act established a three-track preference system for family-sponsored, employment-based, and diversity immigrants. Diversity immigrants are persons from countries with low sending rates. Of the 675,000 visas, 480,000 would be allocated on the basis of family-preference criteria. The law continues to permit the immediate family (spouse, parents, and children) of U.S. citizens to enter without restriction and without regard to the annual level. After accounting for the entry of unrestricted immediate family, the balance of the family quota (480,000 visas) is then allocated to children and siblings of U.S. citizens and to spouses of permanent immigrants. However, the law guarantees a minimum of 226,000 visas for the latter group, irrespective of the number of immediate family members who enter in the unrestricted category. This number slightly exceeds the approximately 215,000 visas currently issued under the four-family-preference categories. Since those entering as immediate family of U.S. citizens have also exceeded 200,000 in recent years, it is probable that the limit of 480,000 family preference visas will be reached and, in turn, that the 675,000 worldwide ceiling will also be reached.

An additional 195,000 visas are reserved for nonfamily immigrants. One hundred and forty thousand of these are allocated to those who qualify on the basis of their ability to make an economic contribution, including 10,000 visas set aside for entrepreneurs who are prepared to invest $500,000 to $1 million in a U.S. business. In October 2000, new legislation was passed that increased the number of visas available for skilled foreign laborers. The new law increases the number of H-1B temporary visas to 195,000 per year for the next three years and will double the fee charged employers using the program.[21] In contrast to the 1965 act, which set aside 27,000 visas for highly skilled immigrants and an additional 27,000 for either skilled or demonstrably needed unskilled workers, the 1990 act expressly specified high skill levels for 90,000 of those qualifying under the employment preference. Unskilled workers who can demonstrate that no qualified workers are available in the United States for the jobs they will take may qualify for the remaining

50,000 visas. In total, 21 percent of the 657,000 visas will be reserved for individuals who can make an economic contribution. The new statute also makes 55,000 additional diversity visas available for immigrants from countries that have not been well represented in the immigrant pool, particularly European countries. Finally, the 1990 law provides that no single country can use more than 7 percent of those visas reserved for family and economic applicants. Thus, country quotas have effectively been increased from 20,000 to about 47,000.

The 1990 act also gave a statutory basis to the practice under which citizens from areas designated by the attorney general were granted "extended voluntary departure." Under that provision, citizens of specifically designated areas suffering from armed conflict or natural disaster can be granted temporary protective status, permitting them to reside and work in the United States for a period of time. The act gives undocumented Salvadorans protected status for a limited period of time, and reserves the grounds for exclusion and deportation that have been controversial since their enactment in 1952.[22]

Congress passed two pieces of legislation in 1996 that affected immigrants. Following the outrage over the Oklahoma City bombing, Congress passed the Anti-Terrorism and Effective Death Penalty Act (AEDPA) that mandated swift detention and removal of criminal and illegal aliens and of those who could be even tenuously linked to terrorist groups.[23] It also limited hardship waivers and appeal rights for certain alien categories and made many of these changes retroactive. Ironically, the behavior that stimulated these acts were not carried out by aliens (illegal or legal) but by Americans.

Congress also passed laws that made many legal aliens ineligible for important public benefits. In August 1996, President Bill Clinton signed the Personal Responsibility and Work Opportunity Reevaluation Act (PRWORA) into law. The PRWORA, commonly called the welfare act, affected immigrant eligibility for Supplemental Security Income (SSI), Medicaid, food stamps, and other benefits.[24] But in 1997 Congress restored many of the SSI and related benefits to those who were eligible under the earlier law. Later in the same year, Congress passed the Illegal Immigration Reform and Immigrant Responsibility Act (IRIRA), which revamped the enforcement process and extended the AEDPA. The major provisions of the law consisted of the imposition of a deadline for the submission of all asylum applications and the creation of expedited procedures to remove and send back to their countries of nationality people without the required documents who were seeking entry to the United States. The IRIRA also contained an expedited removal provision that took effect on April 1, 1997, that stated that people who want to apply for asylum must file an application with the INS within one year of arriving in the United States.[25] The expedited procedures were designed to remove aliens who arrived in the United

States without proper travel documents or who were suspected of carrying documents that were procured by fraud and who might not be fleeing persecution. A single immigration officer at an airport or other port of entry will screen each member of that class of arriving aliens to determine whether someone intends to apply for asylum or fears persecution. If the officer thinks that the person does not fear persecution, he or she will order that person summarily removed from the United States and bar him or her from reentering for five years, without any further hearing or judicial oversight. Those people arriving who do express fear or want to apply for asylum will immediately be transferred to a detention center, where an asylum officer will conduct an interview to determine whether the person has a "credible fear" of persecution.

If the asylum officer determines that the person does not have a credible fear of persecution, then that person must affirmatively request a review by an immigration judge. There is no right to judicial review. The review before the immigration judge is expedited and limited. That is, the review must be concluded no later than seven days after the credible fear determination and need not even be conducted in person; it can be conducted by telephone or video connection. Asylum seekers cannot present evidence, call witnesses, or be represented by legal counsel at the immigration judge review (although counsel may be present). In many instances, they will not be released from detention until they are granted asylum by an immigration judge.

But only if the asylum officer believes that the person being interviewed does have a credible fear of persecution will that person be permitted to present a claim for asylum. He or she will probably be in detention until asylum is granted.

The removal procedures included in the IRIRA are also being used to bar ordinary business travelers and tourists with valid visas from entering the country. For example, if an immigration officer suspects that someone intends to enter the United States for reasons other than what he or she explained to the U.S. embassy abroad when applying for the visa, the officer can order the person removed. The officer need not prove to any judge or tribunal that suspicions are well founded; the decision is the officer's, subject to a cursory paper review by the supervisor. Finally, the person who is removed, even an executive business traveler who is on a legitimate buying trip and has a valid multiuse visa, will be returned to his or her home country and barred from reentering the United States for five years.

In the words of Peter H. Schuck: "This statute (IRIRA) is the most radical reform of immigration law in decades—or perhaps ever. It thoroughly revamps the enforcement process and extends the AEDPA in ways that even many INS officials find arbitrary, unfair and unadministrable."[26]

To summarize the basic rules governing immigration admission in the United States, we noted that since 1921, the U.S. government has set quotas on the number of immigrants that will be allowed to enter the United States in a given year. Certain classes of people are exempted from quotas. Currently, these include immediate relatives—spouses, parents, and children—of U.S. citizens. Other groups have been exempted by acts of Congress on a one-time basis, for example, Hungarian refugees in 1956. In addition to regular immigrants, provision is made for the admission of refugees. As of 1980, the president, in consultation with Congress, can set annual limits on the number of refugees admitted.

Within the quotas noted earlier, preference is given to certain classes of people. These preferences tell us something about the intent and therefore the restrictiveness of admission policies. The worldwide quotas noted earlier are allocated among three different classes of immigrants: family-sponsored immigrants, employment-based immigrants, and diversity immigrants. Family-sponsored immigrants include the immediate family members of legal resident immigrants. Employment-based immigrants are those in occupations that are beneficial to the U.S. economy. Diversity immigrants are immigrants from countries with low sending rates.

Even after a potential immigrant has met all eligibility requirements in terms of quotas and preferences, he or she may nevertheless be excluded on a number of grounds. Presumably, a nation could have a liberal admissions criteria but exclude a high proportion of those eligible, and thereby have a restrictive admissions policy. In 1990, grounds for exclusion included mental retardation, contagious diseases, criminal convictions, lack of labor certification, the danger of a person becoming a public charge, previous deportation, fraud, illiteracy, politics, or an unsatisfactory application. In 1989, approximately 92,000 applicants for admission were excluded on one of these grounds. The most prevalent reason for exclusion was the likelihood of becoming a public charge. Table 1.1 summarizes the allocation of permanent resident visas in 1995.

Stock and Flow of Immigrants

Table 1.2 shows the increase in U.S. population by births over deaths and by excess of immigrant arrivals over departures between 1810 and 1989. We see that the big increase in immigrants began in the 1830s, reached its peak in the first decade of the twentieth century, fell to its lowest level during the 1930s, and rose again sharply in the 1950s, 1960s, and 1980s. Indeed, during the 1930s the United States lost more people through migration than it gained. Over six million people came to the United States between 1900 and 1910; after that, immigration fell to between two and three million per

Table 1.1 Allocation of Permanent Residence Visas, Fiscal Year 1995

Type of Visa	*1995 Limit*	*1995 Admissions*
Family-sponsored preferences, total	226,000	238,122
1. Unmarried adult children of U.S. citizens	23,400	15,182
2. Spouses, minor children, and unmarried adult children of permanent residents	114,200	144,535
3. Married adult children of U.S. citizens	23,400	20,876
4. Brothers and sisters of U.S. citizens (at least twenty-one years of age)	65,000	57,529
Employment-based preferences, total	146,504	85,336
1. Priority workers	41,858	17,339
2. Professionals with advanced degrees or aliens of exceptional ability	41,858	10,475
3. Skilled workers and professionals, Chinese Student Protection Act, and needed unskilled workers	41,858	50,245
4. Special immigrants	10,465	6,737
5. Employment creation ("investors")	10,465	540
IRCA[a] dependents	0	277
Diversity immigrants	55,000	47,245
Immediate relatives of U.S. citizens	0	220,360
Children born abroad to permanent residents	0	1,894
Refugee and asylee adjustments to permanent residents	0	114,664
Miscellaneous categories (IRCA legalization, Amerasians, and parolees)	0	12,563
Total	427,504	720,461

Source: Data from U.S. Immigration and Naturalization Service (1997: Tables A and 4), as cited in James Smith and Barry Edmonston, eds., *The New Americans* (Washington, D.C.: Natural Academic Press, 1997), 42, table 2.3.

[a]IRCA = Immigration Reform and Control Act of 1986.

decade because of restrictive legislation, the worldwide economic depression in the 1930s, and World War II.

For the first 150 years, between 1810 and 1960, the large majority of immigrants (more than 80 percent) came from Europe. Between 1961 and 1970, the European immigration began to decline and was superseded by people coming from Central and South America, Canada, and the Caribbean. European immigration declined to 18 percent from 1971 to 1980 and to 11 percent from 1981 to 1989. Between 1971 and 1980, immigrants from the Western Hemisphere comprised 44 percent of the total U.S. immigration. Mexico, Cuba, and Canada were the major sources of Western Hemisphere immigrants. In the decades from 1971 to 1989, more people emigrated from Asia (33 percent), mostly from the Philippines, Korea, and China, than from Europe. The rest of

Table 1.2 Increase in U.S. Population by Component of Change, 1810–1989 (thousands per decade)

Period	*Total Increase*	*Natural Increase*[a]	*Net Arrivals*[b]
1821–1830	3,228	3,105	123
1831–1840	4,203	3,710	493
1841–1850	6,122	4,702	1,420
1851–1860	8,251	5,614	2,593
1861–1870	8,375	6,291	2,102
1871–1880	10,377	7,675	2,622
1881–1890	12,792	7,527	4,966
1891–1900	13,047	9,345	3,711
1901–1910	15,978	9,656	6,294
1911–1920	13,738	11,489	2,484
1921–1930	17,064	14,500	3,187
1931–1940	8,894	9,962	−85
1941–1950	19,028	17,666	1,362
1951–1960	28,686	25,446	3,180
1961–1970	23,912	19,894	4,018
1970	2,617	1,812	353
1975	2,165	3,144	1,894
1980	2,582	1,622	960
1985	2,325	1,674	651
1987	2,367	1,685	682
1988	2,409	1,742	667
1989	2,505	1,822	683
Total	210,665	170,083	44,360

Sources: Conrad Taeuber, *The Changing Population of the United States* (New York: Wiley, 1958), 294, table 91; U.S. Department of Commerce, Bureau of the Census, *Historical Statistics of the United States: Colonial Times to 1970* (Washington, D.C.: U.S. Government Printing Office, 1975), 8, 49; U.S. Department of Commerce, Bureau of the Census, *Statistical Abstract of the United States, 1990* (Washington, D.C.: U.S. Government Printing Office, 1990), 9.

[a]Excess of births over deaths.

[b]Excess of immigrant arrivals over departures. Estimated natural increase and estimated net arrivals do not coincide precisely with total increase figures because of imperfect data for births, deaths, and immigration.

the world—for example, Africa, Australia, and New Zealand—accounted for about 2 percent of the immigration to the United States.

Table 1.3 shows the particular countries from which the immigrants arrived in the greatest numbers between 1820 and 1989 and the peak year for each nationality. Except for Ireland, from which the largest influx came prior to the Civil War, European immigrants from the four other largest sending nations (Germany, Italy, Great Britain, and Austria-Hungary) all came in the three decades between 1880 and 1910.

Table 1.4 describes the percentage of immigrants who arrived in the United States from 1820 through 1990 by area of the world.

Table 1.3 The Leading "Sender" States, 1820–1989

Country	*Total*	*Peak Year*
Germany	7,071,000	1882
Italy	5,356,000	1907
Great Britain	5,100,000	1888
Ireland	4,723,000	1851
Austria/Hungary	4,338,000	1907
Canada	4,270,000	1924
Russia	3,428,000	1913
Denmark	369,000	1882
Finland	33,000	1882
Norway	856,000	1882
Sweden	1,283,000	1882
Mexico	3,208,000	1989
Caribbean (including Cuba)	2,590,000	1988
France	783,000	1851
Greece	700,000	1907
China	823,000	1989
Poland	587,000	1921
Portugal	497,000	1907
Japan	455,000	1907
Philippines	455,000	1989
Turkey	409,000	1913
Netherlands	372,000	1882
Korea	611,000	1987
Vietnam	443,000	1984

Sources: American Heritage (New York: Forbes, 1981), 55; U.S. Department of Commerce, Bureau of the Census, *Statistical Abstract of the United States, 1990* (Washington, D.C.: U.S. Government Printing Office, 1990), 10.
Note: All totals have been rounded off.

From 1900 on, the percentage of immigrants from northwest Europe dropped sharply, and from 1961 on, European immigrants comprised only one-third of the total number of immigrants arriving in the United States. Most recently, from 1981–1990 immigrants from the Western Hemisphere countries made up almost 50 percent of the newcomers, followed by Asians who comprised 37 percent. European immigrants, however, represented only 10 percent of the most recent arrivals. As of January 2001, Mexico accounted for 28 percent of all immigrants followed by China, Hong Kong, and Taiwan at 5 percent, the Philippines at 4 percent, and India at 4.5 percent. Table 1.5 reports the number of refugee applications filed and approved and the number of refugees by nationality admitted in 1991.

Table 1.6 summarizes the number of immigrants who entered the United States from 1820 to 1995. The overall number is almost 62.2 million.

Table 1.4 Percentage Distribution of Permanent Legal Immigration to the United States by Region of Last Residence, 1821–1830 and 1981–1990

Years	*Northwest Europe*	*Southeast Europe*[a]	*Asia*[b]	*Other Eastern Hemisphere*	*Canada*[c]	*Mexico*[d]	*Other Western Hemisphere*	*Total*
1821–1830	86.6	2.8	0.0	0.0	2.1	4.4	4.0	100.0
1831–1840	92.5	1.1	0.0	0.0	2.6	1.2	2.5	100.0
1841–1850	95.9	0.3	0.0	0.0	2.5	0.2	1.1	100.0
1851–1860	94.6	0.8	1.6	0.0	2.3	0.1	0.5	100.0
1861–1870	88.8	1.1	2.8	0.0	6.7	0.1	0.5	100.0
1871–1880	75.9	4.9	4.4	0.4	13.6	0.2	0.5	100.0
1881–1890	76.3	13.9	1.3	0.3	7.5	0.0	0.6	100.0
1891–1900	55.9	40.8	2.0	0.1	0.1	0.0	0.9	100.0
1900–1910	37.4	54.6	3.7	0.2	2.0	0.6	1.5	100.0
1911–1920	25.3	50.1	4.3	0.4	12.9	3.8	3.2	100.0
1921–1930	32.0	27.9	2.7	0.4	22.5	11.2	3.2	100.0
1931–1940	38.1	27.6	3.1	0.8	20.5	4.2	5.5	100.0
1941–1950	49.6	10.4	3.6	2.1	16.6	5.9	11.8	100.0
1951–1960	39.6	13.4	6.1	1.1	15.1	12.0	12.8	100.0
1961–1970	18.2	15.7	12.9	1.6	12.4	13.7	25.6	100.0
1971–1980	6.6	11.2	35.3	2.7	3.8	14.2	26.1	100.0
1981–1990	5.2	5.2	37.3	3.0	2.1	22.6	24.6	100.0

Source: U.S. Immigration and Naturalization Service, *Statistical Yearbook of the Immigration and Naturalization Service, 1990* (Washington, D.C.: U.S. Government Printing Office, 1991), 48–51.

Note: Some of the rows do not add up exactly to 100 percent due to rounding.

[a]Northwest Europe includes Austria (and Austria-Hungary when Hungary was not specified), Belgium, Denmark, France, Germany, Ireland, the Netherlands, Norway, Sweden, Switzerland, and the United Kingdom. All other European nations are considered part of southeast Europe. Turkey is included in Asia.

[b]Prior to 1934, migrants from the Philippines were not recorded as immigrants.

[c]From 1820 to 1898, figures for Canada include all British North America. Complete records on the number of immigrants arriving by land from Canada were not kept until 1908.

[d]No data on immigrants from Mexico from 1886 through 1893 are available. Complete records on the number of immigrants arriving by land from Mexico were not kept until 1908.

Table 1.5 Refugee Status Applications Filed and Approved and Refugees Admitted by Selected Nationality, Fiscal Year 1991

Nationality	*Refugee Applications Filed*	*Refugee Applications Approved*	*Refugee Arrivals*
Soviet Union	63,185	57,445	39,116
Vietnam	25,412	25,015	27,441
Laos	8,726	8,425	9,212
Ethiopia	4,916	3,978	3,889
Albania	4,065	1,319	1,354
Iran	3,902	2,577	2,833
Afghanistan	3,174	1,477	1,690
Romania	3,116	2,779	4,803
Iraq	2,701	728	812
Cuba	1,687	2,168	3,910
Other	2,608	2,051	5,169
Total	123,492	107,962	100,229

Source: U.S. Immigration and Naturalization Service, *Statistical Yearbook of the Immigration and Naturalization Service, 1991* (Washington, D.C.: U.S. Government Printing Office, 1992).

In its first year, the Immigration Act of 1990 resulted in the admission of 612,000 immigrants, 141,380 temporary workers, and 101,072 refugees, for a total of 854,452 legal immigrants admitted. In addition, an estimated 400,000 persons entered the country illegally and resided here for some period during the year and 255,000 persons entered legally but stayed in the country longer than permitted by their visa. In sum, approximately 1.5 million immigrants entered the United States in 1990. This constitutes 0.006 percent of the U.S. stock population. In the 1990 Current Population Survey, 14.4 million persons reported being foreign born. It is not clear, however, how accurately this number reflects the immigrant population, because it also includes naturalized citizens. It may actually underestimate immigrants because it will include a certain number of illegal immigrants.

Preliminary reports from the 2000 census indicate that 28.4 million immigrants are living in the United States and that they constitute 10.4 percent of the population. This is the highest proportion of immigrants in seventy years.

Naturalizations

The requirements for naturalization in the United States are relatively limited. Any foreigner who has been lawfully admitted to the United States as a permanent resident can apply for citizenship after five years of residence. Spouses and children of resident immigrants can apply after three years. Ap-

Table 1.6 Immigration to the United States, Fiscal Years 1821–1995

Years	*Number*
1821–1830	143,439
1831–1840	599,125
1841–1850	1,713,251
1851–1860	2,598,214
1861–1870	2,314,824
1871–1880	2,812,191
1881–1890	5,246,613
1891–1900	3,687,564
1901–1910	8,795,386
1911–1920	5,735,811
1921–1930	4,107,209
1931–1940	528,431
1941–1950	1,035,039
1951–1960	2,515,479
1961–1970	3,321,677
1971–1980	4,493,314
1981–1990	7,338,062
1991–1995	5,225,897
Total	62,219,911

Note: The numbers shown are as follows: from 1820 to 1867, figures represent immigrant passengers arrived at seaports; from 1868 to 1892 and 1895 to 1897, immigrants arrived; from 1892 to 1894 and 1898 to 1993, immigrants admitted for permanent residence; and from 1892 to 1903, immigrants entering by cabin class were not counted. Land arrivals were not completely enumerated until 1908.

plicants must also demonstrate the ability to read and write basic English and have a general knowledge of U.S. history and governmental structure. Good moral character is also required, which generally means employment and the absence of serious criminal activity. Applicants must also express the intention to remain in the United States and be at least eighteen years old at the time of filing. Immigrants must remain in the country from the time of filing to the point at which their application is approved.

The relative restrictiveness of U.S. naturalization policies can be assessed in terms of application and approval rates. If a nation's naturalization requirements are difficult to satisfy, then few individuals will apply, even though almost all who apply with the requirements satisfied will be admitted. Conversely, nations with limited requirements and a rigorous postapplication screening may be equally restrictive. It is important, therefore, to examine both the application rate and the acceptance rate of those applications.

Since 1907, more than thirteen million immigrants have been naturalized. The 1990 census reports that more than half of all adult immigrants who arrived before 1985 were citizens by 1989. In the 1980s, an average of 237,572 persons each year applied for naturalization status. In 1991 and 1992, the average was 274,468. But in 1995, 1.2 million persons sought citizenship, and in 1996, 1.1 million persons were sworn in as U.S. citizens. John Miller reports that "Asians and Africans tend to naturalize more quickly than other groups. Canadians and Mexicans tend to wait the longest."[27] The rates of naturalization by class of admission are described in table 1.7.

The number of persons naturalized in 1992 was approximately 240,000. The average denial rate for 1991–1992 was 4.6 percent. The annual denial rate may not be the best indicator of inclusiveness because the number of people applying in a given year can fluctuate widely. The INS tracked a cohort of persons admitted to the United States legally in 1977. As shown in table 1.8, by 1991 34.2 percent of this cohort were naturalized.

Policies for the Control of Immigrants

Once a legal immigrant has been admitted to the United States, there are very few opportunities for the INS to become involved in their lives. Legal

Table 1.7 Rates of Naturalization for Legal Aliens by Class of Admission

Class of Admission	*Percent of Persons Admitted in 1977 Who Were Naturalized by 1991*
Family Preferences	
First	43.1
Second	53.3
Fourth	38.5
Fifth	42.8
Employment Preferences	
Third	64.5
Sixth	39.8
Immediate Relatives	31.7
Refugees	61.2
Western Hemisphere	21.1
Other	33.2

Source: U.S. Immigration and Naturalization Service, *Statistical Yearbook of the Immigration and Naturalization Service, 1992* (Washington, D.C.: U.S. Government Printing Office, 1993).

Table 1.8 Percentage Naturalized by the End of Fiscal Year 1991 for the Immigration Cohort Aged 16 Years Old and over in 1977 by Country of Birth

Country of Birth	*Number Admitted As Permanent Legal Residents*	*Percent Naturalized by End of Fiscal 1991*
Soviet Union	4,535	62.4
Philippines	31,686	60.7
China	14,421	58.1
Korea	19,824	54.3
Guyana	4,115	53.9
India	15,053	49.8
Jamaica	7,896	37.6
Haiti	4,268	35.4
Cuba	57,023	34.6
Colombia	6,138	34.0
Greece	6,577	29.9
Trinidad and Tobago	4,516	25.0
Portugal	6,964	22.7
Ecuador	4,063	22.2
Dominican Republic	8,955	20.5
United Kingdom	8,982	17.0
Mexico	30,967	16.2
Italy	5,843	15.1
Germany	4,899	13.4
Canada	9,000	12.1
Other Nations	96,366	43.9
Total	352,091	34.2

Source: U.S. Immigration and Naturalization Service, *Statistical Yearbook of the Immigration and Naturalization Service, 1992* (Washington, D.C.: Government Printing Office, 1993), 130.

immigrants are free to apply for social security cards and can therefore work legally. There are no residence permits or restrictions on their movement, although they are required to report any change of address to the INS within ten days of that change. There are, however, an increasing number of limitations on the ability of legal immigrants to obtain privileges such as government employment or scholarships, and there are some efforts at the state level to restrict social welfare benefits. It remains to be seen how substantial these limitations will become; but in general, legal immigrants enjoy a great deal of freedom and autonomy in the United States.

The government nevertheless has the right, in certain circumstances, to deport legal immigrants who threaten the public welfare. Grounds for deportation include: entry without inspection or at an unauthorized place;

entry while in an excludable class; marriage fraud; violating conditions of immigrant status (including not reporting moves within ten days); criminal convictions; and reasons of political or national security. While these grounds for deportation are available, it is not clear that the INS has the resources to process those immigrants who are eligible for deportation. In the case of conviction for a serious crime, for example, states are required to report immigrants arrested within thirty days of the arrest so that the INS can begin tracking the case. Failure to report these arrests would threaten the availability of federal funds for drug enforcement activity. Studies in specific localities, however, suggest that either the local police are unwilling to notify the immigration authorities or that, when notified, the INS does not have the resources to process the case. Indeed, it is not clear that the INS can process all of the cases for deportation involving criminal immigrants even after they have served their sentence.

One of the reasons that the INS cannot move more expeditiously to deport legal immigrants (including asylum seekers) is that there is extensive judicial review of any decision made by the agency. For example, deportation of criminal immigrants first requires a hearing before an administrative judge within the INS. This hearing has most of the due process procedural requirements of hearings in judicial courts. Moreover, decisions reached by the administrative judges can be appealed to federal courts. This process is extremely time consuming.

The limited amount of state control and the complexity of deportation procedures may explain why deportation is such a rare event. In 1989, 28,965 persons were deported. Of these, 69 percent were deported for evading inspection (illegal entry); 6,975 for committing crimes; and 938 for other reasons. The total number of deportations equals about 2 percent of the annual estimated flow of immigrants into the United States and 0.2 percent of the estimated stock population. Many more immigrants—about 830,000—agree to leave voluntarily each year. The bulk of these voluntary departures involve persons crossing the Mexican border illegally. Moreover, this figure is based on transactions and not persons. One person can be intercepted and returned a number of times and each return is included in that 830,000 figure. Hence, the rate of deportation for the immigrant population in the United States is quite low.

Illegal Immigrants

One of the two major issues in the current debate on immigration in the United States focuses on persons who are in the country illegally. These persons either entered the country without proper documents or they have overstayed their legal time period. Those in the latter category may be persons who entered as tourists, students, or skilled workers in special industries. In fiscal year 1996, twenty-five million "nonimmigrants" (people on temporary visas) entered the United States. Though most of them go home (19 million tourists and 3.8 million business travelers), hundreds of thousands do not. The main categories of temporary visitors who overstay their visas are students and their families, temporary workers and their families, and exchange workers and their families.

Part of the Internal Security Act of 1950 required all immigrants residing in the United States to register their addresses with the INS every January. But in December 1981, Congress passed a law that eliminated the registration requirement, mostly on the grounds that the cost of registration was too great and generally not worthwhile. However, the capability of being able to estimate the number of illegals in the country increased. Table 1.9 describes the estimates of illegals and their countries of origin as reported in the 1980 census.

In 1995, INS estimates placed the number of illegals in the country at between 3.2 and 3.3 million, with about 200,000 to 300,000 entering per year. More than half of the illegals are from Mexico. The other leading countries are El Salvador and Guatemala.

Table 1.9 Estimates of Undocumented Aliens in the United States by Country of Birth (in thousands)

Country of Birth	*Undocumented Aliens, 1980*
Mexico	1,131
Iran	58
El Salvador	51
Haiti	44
Jamaica	39
United Kingdom	38
Guatemala	28
Cuba	27
Colombia	27
Canada	25
China and Taiwan	25
India	18
Philippines	16
Peru	15
Total	1,542

Source: The 1980 figures for undocumented immigrants are from Robert Warren and Jeffrey S. Passel, "A Count of the Uncountable: Estimates of Undocumented Aliens Counted in the 1980 United States Census," *Demography* 24, no. 3 (August 1987): 380–381.

Demographic and Socioeconomic Characteristics of Immigrants

The 1990 U.S. census data report that the median age of the foreign born who entered the United States between 1980 and 1990 was 28.0 years, and that of the native population was 32.5 years. A more detailed breakdown by age and gender of immigrant admissions in 1995 and the U.S. population in 1990 is shown in table 1.10.

Immigrants are more likely to be of working age than natives—71.4 percent for immigrants compared to 56.4 percent for natives. Only 3.8 percent of immigrants are ages sixty-five or older, compared to 12.7 percent of the total population.

Sixty percent of the immigrants in the United States are married as opposed to 55 percent of the natives, and 8 percent are divorced or separated compared to 11 percent of the natives. Immigrants are more likely to live in family units—76.0 percent compared to 70.2 percent for the native born—and immigrant women bear an average of 2.3 children compared to 1.9 for natives.

Although 37 percent of the immigrant population did not finish high school, compared to 14 percent of the native population, the percentage of immigrants and natives who hold at least a college degree was 26 percent for both groups. In addition, immigrants are twice as likely to hold a doctorate, as are natives. Table 1.11 compares education characteristics by gender of immigrants and natives in 1970, 1980, and 1990.

The National Research Council's 1997 report on the economic, demographic, and fiscal effects of immigration states that "nearly three-fifths of immigrants who arrived in the 1980s reported in the 1990 census that they spoke English well or very well." As shown in table 1.12, the groups with the greatest ability were immigrants from Canada, followed by those from South America, Europe, Asia, and the Caribbean. Among recent immigrants from non-English-speaking countries, 47 percent report that they speak English well or very well within about two years after arrival.

Among males sixteen years and older, 76.9 percent of the immigrants are in the labor force compared to 74.2 percent of the natives. The native-born population is more likely to work for the federal, state, or local government than are immigrants—15.7 versus 9.8 percent—and slightly less than 7 percent of both immigrants and natives are self-employed. But 18 percent of all small businesses have been started by foreigners.

Table 1.13 describes the occupational distribution of immigrants who were admitted under the Family and Employment Preference Systems from 1972 through 1988.

Using 1980 census data, table 1.14 compares the occupational distributions of immigrants who entered the United States between 1970 and 1980 against the distribution of native born.

Table 1.10 Marital Status and Gender Distribution of Immigrant Admissions, 1995, and U.S. Population, 1990, by Age Group (in percent)

Age Group and Marital Status	*Male Immigrants*	*U.S. Population*	*Female Immigrants*	*U.S. Population*
25 to 34 years				
Never married	34.8	36.1	18.8	25.0
Married	63.9	54.0	79.7	60.8
Widowed	0.1	0.2	0.2	0.6
Divorced	1.0	7.3	1.1	9.8
Separated	0.2	2.5	0.2	3.8
35 to 44 years				
Never married	14.5	13.4	10.2	10.0
Married	82.4	71.1	85.4	69.1
Widowed	0.2	0.4	0.8	1.6
Divorced	2.5	12.1	3.2	15.4
Separated	0.4	2.9	0.4	3.9
45 to 54 years				
Never married	5.7	6.8	7.7	5.6
Married	90.3	77.4	82.5	70.3
Widowed	0.6	1.1	4.0	5.2
Divorced	3.1	12.1	5.3	15.7
Separated	0.4	2.7	0.5	3.3
55 to 64 years				
Never married	3.7	0.8	7.5	4.5
Married	90.9	69.0	72.0	66.3
Widowed	2.3	12.5	15.1	15.9
Divorced	2.8	7.5	4.9	11.0
Separated	0.4	6.2	0.5	2.2
65 and older				
Never married	3.7	4.8	9.5	5.5
Married	84.3	73.1	46.1	38.6
Widowed	9.7	13.9	40.5	49.4
Divorced	1.8	4.7	3.6	5.5
Separated	0.4	3.5	0.2	1.0

Sources: Data from U.S. Immigration and Naturalization Service (1997: table 14), and U.S. Bureau of the Census (1993: Population Characteristics, table 34), as cited in James Smith and Barry Edmonston, eds., *The New Americans* (Washington, D.C.: National Academy Press, 1997), 57, table 2.7.

Table 1.15 reports the occupational distribution and average incomes of immigrant cohorts for 1977, 1982, and 1994 by gender.

In 1989, the median household income of immigrants was $28,314 compared to $30,176 for the native born. But the per capita incomes were reversed, with immigrants reporting slightly higher earnings—$15,033 for immigrants

Table 1.11 Education Characteristics by Gender between Immigrants and U.S. Natives in 1970, 1980, and 1990

Group/Variable	*1970*	*1980*	*1990*
Men			
Natives			
Mean	11.4	12.7	13.2
educational attainment (in years)			
% less than high school diploma	40.2	22.7	14.4
% college graduate	15.0	22.9	26.3
All immigrants			
Mean	10.7	11.6	11.6
educational attainment (in years)			
% less than high school diploma	48.9	37.7	37.1
% college graduate	18.2	25.0	26.2
Recent			
immigrants (less than 5 years in the United States)			
Mean	11.1	11.7	11.8
educational attainment (in years)			
% less than high school diploma	46.0	37.5	36.2
% college graduate	27.7	29.6	30.5
Women			
Natives			
Mean	11.1	12.1	12.8
educational attainment (in years)			
% less than high school diploma	40.7	26.0	16.7
% college graduate	9.0	14.3	20.4
All Immigrants			
Mean	9.9	10.9	11.2
educational attainment (in years)			
% less than high school diploma	52.1	39.4	37.4
% college graduate	7.9	14.6	19.3
Recent			
immigrants (less than 5 years in the United States)			
Mean	9.8	10.6	11.2
educational attainment (in years)			
% less than high school diploma	52.8	42.2	37.4
% college graduate	13.0	19.3	24.1

Source: James Smith and Barry Edmonston, eds., *The New Americans* (Washington, D.C.: National Academy Press, 1997), 183, table 5.5.

Note: Tabulations from 1970, 1980, and 1990 Public Use Samples of U.S. Census of Population. Educational attainment for men and relative wages for both men and women are calculated in the sample of those aged twenty-five to sixty-four years who did not reside in group quarters, who were not self-employed, and who were employed in the civilian sector. Educational attainment for women is based on the sample of women aged twenty-five to sixty-four years who did not reside in group quarters.

Table 1.12 English Language Ability of Recent Immigrants, 1990 (in percent)

	Speaks English		
Continent of Origin	*Well or Better*	*Not Well*	*Not at All*
Europe	73.8	17.7	8.6
Asia	63.1	27.2	9.7
Canada	97.4	1.7	0.3
Mexico, Central America	26.2	31.0	41.8
Caribbean	61.1	18.2	20.6
South America	85.8	10.7	3.2
Weighted Total	57.5	26.3	16.2

Source: U.S. Bureau of the Census, *1990 Census of the Population: The Foreign-Born Population of the United States, 1990, CP-3-1* (Washington, D.C.: U.S. Department of Commerce, 1993).

Note: Not surprisingly, immigrants from countries where English is the dominant or an official language (e.g., India and the Philippines) reported that they speak English well. Data also show (see fig. 1.1) that over time and with extended exposure to the new language immigrants who arrived without English skills acquire them. Also note that some of the rows do not add up exactly to 100 percent due to rounding.

compared to $14,367 for the native-born population. The 1990 census reported that 9.0 percent of all immigrant-headed households received welfare compared to 7.4 percent of households headed by natives. A further breakdown of the immigrant-welfare relationship shows the following: In 1989, 4.2 percent of the native population who were fifteen years and older received welfare, as did 2.8 percent of the immigrants who arrived between 1980 and 1990, and 4.9 percent who were admitted before 1980 and were at least fifteen years of age. In contrast, 15.6 percent of the persons who were admitted as refugees received welfare in 1989. Thus, the big distinction among welfare recipients is between those who were admitted as refugees compared to those who entered under the general immigration quotas.

Integration Policies

Historically, the U.S. government has offered very little direct assistance to immigrants. While legal immigrants are eligible for the same social welfare benefits as citizens, these benefits are rather meager relative to those in other industrialized democracies. Most of the assistance given to immigrants in the United States has come from philanthropic organizations and ethnic self-help groups. The only exceptions to this rule have been refugees admitted after World War II.

Major sustenance programs include income support, education, and medical care. We focus on these because they can be construed as providing the

Table 1.13 Occupational Distribution of Aliens Admitted under the Preference System in Fiscal Years 1972, 1976, 1978, 1983, and 1988

	Total Admitted	*Total*	*Professional/ Managerial*	*Sales/ Clerical*	*Craft*	*Laborer/ Farming/ Operator*	*% Service*	*% Not Working*
Relative Preferences								
1972	83,165	100	8.2	3.9	6.9	14.3	5.7	61.0
1976	102,007	100	12.5	5.8	5.1	9.0	3.4	64.1
1978	190,297	100	12.5	6.7	5.0	11.5	4.5	59.9
1983	213,488	100	11.0	6.8	5.6	10.5	6.7	59.4
1988	200,771	100	10.7	7.2	4.5	11.3	7.1	59.3
Employment Preferences								
1972	33,174	100	48.0	3.4	4.6	2.9	7.1	34.0
1976	26,361	100	49.5	3.1	3.1	2.0	4.5	37.7
1978	30,909	100	40.1	3.7	3.2	2.5	6.0	44.5
1983	55,468	100	29.8	4.2	4.5	3.5	9.7	48.2
1988	53,607	100	30.4	4.2	3.5	3.5	11.8	46.6

When the percentage "not working" is deleted, the distributions look like this for fall 1988:

Relative Preferences	*Percent*
Professional/Managerial	20.0
Sales/Clerical	16.2
Craft	12.3
Laborer/Farming/Operator	35.7
Service	15.8
Employment Preferences	
Professional/Managerial	60.2
Sales/Clerical	1.0
Craft	8.2
Laborer/Farming/Operator	9.6
Service	11.0

Sources: James Smith and Barry Edmonston, eds., *The New Americans* (Washington, D.C.: Natural Academy Press, 1997), 93; Immigration and Naturalization Service public use files.

Note: Some of the rows do not add up exactly to 100 percent due to rounding.

Table 1.14 Labor-Market Characteristics of Legal Immigrants, Recent Immigrants, and Natives for Persons 16 Years Old and over, 1980 (in percent)

Occupational Distribution	*Immigrants Entered, 1970–1980*	*Native (from Census)*
White Collar	60.7	53.5
Managers	6.9	10.5
Professionals	14.2	15.4
Sales	6.1	10.1
Clerical	11.4	17.5
Service	18.0	12.7
Farming	4.1	2.9
Blue Collar	39.2	31.0
Craft	11.8	12.9
Operatives	21.1	13.6
Laborers	6.3	4.5

Source: U.S. Bureau of the Census, "Characteristics of the Population, PC80-1-D1-A," in *1980 Census of Population* (Washington, D.C.: U.S. Government Printing Office, 1984), vol. 1, chapter D, part 1.

basic necessities for immigrants while they attempt to assimilate into a society. Income support includes unemployment compensation, Aid to Families With Dependent Children (AFDC), food stamps, and Earned Income Tax Credit. Public education is available to all legal immigrants and their children and, in most places, to illegal immigrants as well. Access to medical care depends to a large extent on the availability of medical insurance. In general, medical insurance is available through one's employer in the United States. Legal immigrants are eligible for medical insurance under Medicare, but illegal immigrants are not. Illegal immigrants can, however, obtain emergency medical care through a hospital emergency room. Eligibility for many of these services can be set by both the federal and state governments and, in the latter case, standards for eligibility can vary widely. Moreover, the benefits received through these programs are not lavish. For example:

- Unemployment compensation. Eligibility set by states. Usually, there are minimum weeks working or minimum earnings requirements. The average benefit was $184 per week with a range across states of from $115 to $310.
- AFDC. Single parents are generally eligible. State and federal governments set eligibility. The average benefit for one adult with two children is $368 per month. The range across states is from $118 to $583.
- Earned Income Tax Credit. This measure allows the working poor to avoid paying federal income taxes on a certain portion of their income

Table 1.15 Occupation, Immigrants Aged 21 to 65 Years at Admission to Permanent Residence, Fiscal Years 1977, 1982, and 1994 Cohorts

		FY 1977 Cohort		*FY 1982 Cohort*		*FY 1994 Cohort*	
Summary Occupation Group	*Average Income ($)*	*Men*	*Women*	*Men*	*Women*	*Men*	*Women*
Managerial and professional speciality occupations	31,199	33.3	30.1	30.3	27.9	32.2	33.2
Technical, sales, and administrative support occupations	18,882	11.8	22.9	12.4	24.4	12.1	21.0
Service occupations	13,751	9.1	19.8	10.3	21.8	14.5	21.7
Farming, forestry, and fishing occupations	13,301	4.9	0.9	6.2	4.1	4.4	3.2
Precision production, craft, and repair occupations	18,254	16.4	1.9	17.7	9.9	11.1	14.9
Operators, fabricators, and laborers	15,599	24.5	24.4	23.1	11.8	25.7	14.9
Percentage reporting occupations		86.6	40.7	77.9	44.1	69.9	38.5
Average occupational earnings, 1979 dollars		21,267	18,888	20,010	18,609	19,648	18,767
Number aged 21 to 65 years		130,011	152,654	173,185	173,201	216,306	266,130

Source: James Smith and Barry Edmonston, eds., *The New Americans* (Washington, D.C.: National Academy Press, 1997), 193, table 5.9.
Note: Figures for fiscal year 1994 exclude both aliens legalized by provisions of the Immigration Reform and Control Act and legalization dependents.

> if they meet the income eligibility requirements. This credit reaches its maximum of $550 for persons earning $5,000 to $6,000 a year and declines to $0 for those earning more than $11,000 a year.

In general, immigrants cannot legally be excluded from these programs. Certainly, legal immigrants have such rights, but increasingly illegal immigrants have been extended these rights. As part of the general trend of expanding the rights of citizenship, courts have expanded the access of immigrants to public services. The Supreme Court's decision in *Plyer v. Doe* forced authorities in Texas to admit children of undocumented immigrants to public schools in Texas. In 1991, a lower court decision held that illegal aliens can sue for job discrimination. More recently, however, individual states have begun restricting access to welfare benefits for illegal immigrants and, in some cases, legal immigrants. California's Proposition 187 is the most dramatic example. It is unclear, however, whether these limits on benefits will withstand judicial scrutiny.

In the United States, it is particularly inaccurate to describe efforts to integrate immigrant groups by focusing only on government policies. The bulk of integrative programs in the United States are private and voluntary. In the early waves of immigration, settlement houses and other philanthropic organizations expended considerable efforts to assimilate immigrants. Gradually, as the pool of immigrants from particular countries and regions increased, these philanthropic efforts by the native population gave way to immigrant self-help groups. These groups provide a great deal of information, as well as emotional, logistical, and financial support to new arrivals. There is very little information on the extent and nature of these activities and they do not constitute a policy per se. Nonetheless, they are an aspect of society in the United States that facilitates the absorption of immigrant groups and that can make a difference in the impact of immigrants on major social institutions.

In summary, immigrant policy in the United States allows for a continuous flow of foreigners into the country. Criteria for admissions are driven more by family unification than by labor-force needs. Naturalization is relatively easy to attain and frequently bestowed. Controls on the legal immigrant population after admission are minimal. Aside from special programs for refugees, however, there are few governmental efforts to ease the transition of immigrants into the host society. The process of integration is left largely to private groups. The limited social welfare benefits available to U.S. citizens are currently available to legal immigrants, although there are efforts in some states to exclude this group from benefits. Illegal immigrants are subject to more substantial controls after entry and they are excluded from some public services and social welfare benefits. The actual level of control that can be exerted on illegal immigrants, however, is minimal given the enforcement resources available relative to the magnitude of illegal immigration.

Criminal Involvement

Empirical research generally does not support the allegations that immigrants are involved in criminal activity to a greater degree than the native population. This is the finding generally drawn from research that directly examines criminal involvement of immigrants. These studies, however, are sufficiently limited or flawed to leave the issue unresolved. In the case of direct studies, some involve only one local jurisdiction and, therefore, the generalizability of the results are questionable. In other studies, the data on criminal involvement is of questionable quality.

Indeed, most empirical work has been conducted at the regional level—typically at a county or municipal level. Some of this work is historical and some is more contemporary. The results are mixed. In his study of criminal activity among U.S. immigrants up to the first quarter of the twentieth century, Allen Steinberg is unable to substantiate the disproportionate involvement of immigrants in criminal activity.[28] Instead, he concludes that the rate of serious crime (e.g., property crime and/or crimes of personal violence) for native-born Americans exceeded the rate for immigrants, although the rate of petty crime (e.g., vagrancy, disorderly conduct, breach of the peace, and drunkenness) among immigrants periodically (e.g., 1820–1980 and 1890–1924) surpassed the rate for the native born. In addition, the overall rate of crime was significantly lower for immigrants than it was for native-born Americans when age and sex were controlled. (Most immigrants, especially illegal or undocumented entrants, are young men and the crime rate, across all populations, generally appears to be higher for young men than for others.)

Initiated in response to allegations that waves of immigration were responsible for the introduction of criminal elements into the country, the Dillingham Commission (established in 1907) attempted to link crime to a person's place of birth.[29] The study relied on records maintained by the New York City magistrate. However, the commission was unable to substantiate allegations that substantial numbers of immigrants from eastern and southern Europe (Jews and Italians) were engaged in criminal enterprises.

This pattern of results was corroborated by the work of John R. Commons.[30] Additionally, during the 1930s the rate of crime among immigrants and the children of immigrants was below the national average.[31] More recently, records maintained by Los Angeles city officials described comparatively few incidences of crime among its immigrants.[32]

In one of the few studies describing the rate of crime among contemporary illegal immigrants in Los Angeles, Thomas Muller and Thomas J. Espenshade note that the crime rates in the two most densely Hispanic populated districts were below the city average.[33] Texas crime statistics are highest for regions with comparatively low immigrant populations (e.g., Fort Worth, Amarillo, and Austin), while cities like San Antonio (which has the highest concentration of Mexicans in the country) and El Paso (predominantly Hispanic) have disproportionately low or average crime rates.[34] Ramiro Martinez and Matthew T. Lee cite multivariate regression analyses and find no relationship between immigration level and crime in Standard Metropolitan Statistical Areas.[35] However, in some California communities (e.g., San Diego and Los Angeles) there is evidence that the rate of crime is disproportionately high for immigrants, particularly illegals.[36] In San Diego, undocumented workers comprise 4 percent of the population, 26 percent of burglary arrests, and 12 percent of felony arrests.[37] In Los Angeles, the sheriff contends that 10 percent of the inmate population is composed of illegal immigrants. However, it is important to note that this statistic is actually somewhat low in light of the fact that an estimated 1.2 million of the 8.8 million in Los Angeles are illegal immigrants.[38] In addition, many of these illegals are arrested without cause on the basis of their physical appearance and limited English-speaking language skills.[39]

There are very few studies of the criminal involvement of immigrants that examine jurisdictions larger than a single city or town.[40] This is due largely to the fact that major national indicators of crime—the Uniform Crime Reports (UCR) and the National Crime Victimization Survey—do not or cannot provide information on the citizenship status of offenders.[41] The only nationally representative data on the criminal involvement of aliens come from the 1991 Survey of Inmates of State Correctional Facilities sponsored by the Bureau of Justice Statistics.[42] This is a self-report survey of a probability sample of inmates at state correctional facilities. Inmates were asked, among other things, about the crime for which they were sentenced and their citizenship status. Data from this survey suggest that approximately 4 percent of the state prison population are immigrants, while the 1990 census data suggest that 6 percent of the general population are immigrants.[43] When these data were used to compute an incarceration rate, the rates for the native-born population for violent and property crimes were substantially greater than those of the immigrant population (see table 1.16).

These estimates are contrary to the common wisdom that immigrants are disproportionately involved in crime relative to the native-born population. The only prevalent type of crime for which the incarceration rate of immigrants exceeds that of citizens is drug offenses. Here, the incarceration rate for immigrants is about 237 percent higher than it is for citizens.

Table 1.16 Estimated Incarceration Rates by Citizenship Status and Offense

Charge	*Citizenship Status*		*Alien-to-Citizen Ratio*
	Alien	*Citizen*[a]	
Violence	109.4	120.7	0.91
Homicide	38.7	29.7	1.30
Sexual Assaults	20.6	26.4	0.78
Robbery	26.6	41.6	0.64
Assault	23.5	23.0	1.02
Property	43.8	69.6	0.63
Burglary	26.9	34.8	0.77
Larceny	7.9	13.7	0.58
Drug Offenses	141.7	59.8	2.37
Other Offenses	22.2	20.5	1.08
Total	317.1	270.6	1.17

Source: Bureau of Justice Statistics, *Survey of Inmates of State Correctional Facilities, 1991* (Washington, D.C.: Bureau of Justice Statistics, 1991).

[a]Citizen = native born and naturalized.

But these incarceration rates are suspect as indicators of the criminal involvement of immigrants for two reasons. First, only a small proportion of offenders are ultimately incarcerated; therefore, incarceration rates are a particularly blunt instrument for assessing criminal involvement. Assuming, however, that the ratio of offenders who are ultimately incarcerated is the same for both native born and immigrants, this bluntness need not be fatal. If that assumption is correct, these rates may be an acceptable indicator of relative criminal involvement. The second problem with these data is that citizenship status is based on self-report. To the extent that immigrants, and particularly illegal immigrants, refuse to identify themselves as such, the immigrant incarceration rate will be in error. This may be the more fatal flaw in these data for the purposes of establishing the relative criminality of alien and native populations.[44]

Another source of data on the criminal involvement of immigrants in the United States is the Criminal Alien Report (CAR) compiled by the INS. This report is based on information provided by states as required by the 1990 Immigration Act. According to the act, states are required to report all immigrants (both legal and illegal) that come into contact with the criminal justice system. Since this is a very new statistical system, little is known about its error structure. The system may not cover all states or all states equally. Some states may report immigrants at the point of arrest, while others may report contact only after a person has been incarcerated. This would make a considerable difference in estimates of the level of criminal involvement of immigrants. Because this system is so new, we must treat these data with extreme caution.

These numbers are also questionable because data on criminal involvement of immigrants are only meaningful as a rate per unit of population. Consequently, some decisions must be made about the appropriate denominator to use in computing these rates. This decision is not problematic for the total population or for the legal immigrants since information on these populations is reasonably good. The total resident, noninstitutionalized population of the United States can be used as the denominator of the offending rate for the total population. Census estimates of the resident immigrant population can be used as the denominator of the offending rate for legal immigrants. It is more of a problem for illegal immigrants because estimates for this population are less reliable. For purpose of this comparison, we use estimates of the stock illegal immigrant population computed by Karen Woodrow and Jeffrey S. Passel.[45]

When CAR data are used to estimate the offending rate for legal and illegal immigrants and the UCR arrest data are used to estimate offending rates for the total population, the overall felony offending rate for immigrants (both legal and illegal) is substantially lower than the offending rate for the total population. This is the case for every class of felony except for homicide and drug offenses. In these areas, the overall rate of offending for immigrants is higher than that for the total population. These data also indicate a massive difference between legal and illegal immigrants. Legal immigrants have substantially lower offending rates than illegal immigrants in every category of offense including drugs and homicide. Table 1.17 details the differences among offenses.

Table 1.17 Estimated Offending Rates (per 100,000) by Citizenship Status and Type of Crime, 1992–1993

Charge	*Total Residents*	*Legal Immigrant*	*Illegal Immigrant*	*Total Immigrant*
Homicide	7.4	4.8	60.3	12.1
Robbery	55.2	5.4	134.8	22.5
Theft	481.9	5.6	226.1	34.8
Aggravated assault	146.1	3.4	61.8	11.1
Drug sale	103.5	55.1	788.9	152.4
All drugs	309.8	71.4	1,164.7	216.3
All felonies	1,488.1	108.6	2,092.7	371.6

Sources: Unpublished Criminal Alien Report data provided in tabular form by the Immigration and Naturalization Service; Karen A. Woodrow and Jeffery S. Passel, "Post-IRCA Undocumented Immigration to the United States: An Assessment Based upon the June 1988 CPS," in *Undocumented Immigration to the United States: IRCA and the Experience of the 1980s,* ed. Frank Bean, Barry Edmonston, and Jeffery S. Passel (Washington, D.C.: Urban Institute, 1992).

Legal immigrants have lower offending rates than the total population in every category of offense. These differences are quite large. The offending rate of legal immigrants for homicide is about one-half that of the total population, for robbery it is one-tenth that of the total population, and for aggravated assault one-seventieth that of the total population. Illegal immigrants, on the other hand, have higher offending rates than the total population overall. This is due in large measure to the very big differences for drug and homicide offenses.

In sum, the empirical evidence on the relative criminal involvement of immigrants and native-born citizens in the United States is reasonably consistent. In general, immigrants are involved in criminal activity at a much lower rate than citizens in the United States. This is the case for every type of serious crime except drug offenses. This seems to be the case even when attributes of immigrants that may account for differences in criminal involvement, such as race or educational attainment, are held constant.

Some data suggest that illegal immigrants have much higher rates of criminal involvement than legal immigrants. These same data indicate that rates of involvement in homicide and drug crimes are much higher for illegal immigrants than for citizens. But these data must be treated with some caution. The quality of the INS data on criminal aliens is unknown. It is extremely difficult to identify illegal immigrants even when they are imprisoned. Some of the high rates of criminal involvement for illegal immigrants may be due to misidentifying legal immigrants and naturalized citizens as illegal immigrants. More importantly, the nature of drug enforcement may result in illegals being targeted for enforcement at much higher rates than other groups. Hence, the high rates of drug arrests and incarcerations for illegals may be due to enforcement policy rather than their disproportionate involvement in drug crimes.

In addition, drug enforcement, unlike the policing of other crimes, is largely discretionary. There is no victim to call and demand a police response. Police choose their targets. A great deal of drug enforcement takes place at the border. Citizens are not searched or otherwise inspected at the border of the United States unless there is good reason to do so. Immigrants, however, are subjected to more extensive inspections at the border. These inspections increase the likelihood of finding drugs and charging immigrants with drug crimes. Even beyond border areas, the enforcement of immigration laws can serve as a targeting criteria and an excuse to frequent areas with high concentrations of illegals and thereby increase the prosecution of immigrants for drug crimes.

On the other hand, the high rates of incarceration for drug crimes among immigrants may simply be due to the fact that immigrants do indeed engage in these crimes to a greater extent than the native-born population. For some immigrant groups, their country of origin may provide the competitive advantage. In the case of drug offense statistics, it is difficult to differentiate the real from the artificial.

Public Opinion

The physical image that best describes the American public's attitude toward immigrants is that it sees them with rose-colored glasses turned backwards. In other words, those immigrants who came earlier, whenever "earlier" happens to be, are viewed as having made important and positive contributions to U.S. society in its economy and culture. But those who seek entry now, whenever "now" happens to be, are viewed, at best, with ambivalence, and more likely with distrust and hostility. There is some sign that public attitudes toward recent immigrants may be shifting in a more positive direction and they will be reported later in this section.

Tables 1.18 and 1.19 provide evidence for the traditional view of the rose-colored glasses turned backward.

In 1982, a national poll conducted by the Roper Center at the University of Connecticut asked the American public the following question: "Since the beginning of our country, people of many different religions, races, and nationalities have come here and settled. Here is a list of some different groups.

Table 1.18 Immigrants Who on Balance Have Been a Good Thing or Bad Thing for This Country, 1982

Nationality	*Good*	*Bad*	*Different in Percent*[a]
English	66	6	60
Irish	62	7	55
Jews	59	9	50
Germans	57	11	46
Italians	56	10	46
Poles	53	12	41
Japanese	47	18	29
Chinese	44	19	25
Mexicans	25	4	21
Koreans	24	30	−6
Vietnamese	20	38	−18
Haitians	10	39	−29
Cubans	9	59	−50

Source: American Institute of Public Opinion (Storrs: Roper Center, University of Connecticut, 1982).

[a]The two categories not shown are "mixed feelings" and "don't know."

Table 1.19 Public Opinion on Immigrants by Ethnicity, 1985–1993

	Benefit Country		*Create Problems*		*Difference (Benefits–Problems)*	
Nationality	*1985*	*1993*	*1985*	*1993*	*1985*	*1993*
Irish	78	76	5	11	73	65
Poles	72	65	7	15	65	50
Chinese	69	59	13	31	56	28
Koreans	52	53	23	33	29	20
Vietnamese	47	41	30	46	17	−5
Mexicans	44	29	37	59	7	−30
Haitians	31	19	35	65	−4	−46
Iranians	32	20	40	68	−12	−48
Cubans	29	24	55	64	−26	−40

Source: USA Today/CNN, 1993.

Would you read down the list and, thinking both of what they have contributed to this country and have gotten from this country, for each one tell me whether you think, on balance, they have been a good thing or a bad thing for this country?"

In 1982, the immigrants from southern and Eastern Europe (the Jews, Italians, and Poles) were viewed as having made positive contributions to U.S. society. The Chinese, against whom we passed special legislation (Chinese Exclusion Act, 1882) that barred all foreign-born Chinese from acquiring U.S. citizenship, were also viewed in a more positive than negative light. But the Mexicans, Koreans, Vietnamese, Haitians, and Cubans are perceived as very bad for the United States.

In 1985 and 1993, a *USA Today/CNN* poll asked the American public whether the following nationalities have "benefitted the country" or "created problems." Table 1.19 shows the result of that poll.

Like the 1982 poll, the earlier immigrant arrivals are viewed as having provided more benefits to the country than the later or "current" immigrant arrivals. Thus, Haitians and Cubans are currently perceived as particularly bad. So are the Iranians, but probably also because of the fear of terrorism that is associated with their country. Opinions about Koreans and Vietnamese have changed from a mainly negative to a generally positive view in the past decade.

As we mentioned in the beginning of this section, the post-1995 survey responses suggest that some changes are occurring on this issue of attitudes toward the current cohort of immigrants. Compare the public's response to the same item asked in a national survey in 1993 and then again in 1997.

Was immigration a good thing or a bad thing for this country in the past?

	1993	1997
	(in percent)	
Good	59	65
Bad	31	23

Is immigration a good thing or a bad thing in this country today?

Good	29	45
Bad	60	42

Source: Princeton Survey Research Associates, 1997.
Note: Respondents with no opinion are not included.

Between 1993 and 1997, there was more than a 50-percent increase in respondents (29 versus 45) who thought immigrants were a good thing for this country today.

Additional evidence of recent shifts in opinions in a more positive direction are shown by the responses to the following items.

Do you think immigrants mostly help the economy by providing low cost labor, or mostly hurt the economy by driving wages down for many Americans?

	Mostly help	*Mostly hurt*	*Neither*	*Both*	*No opinion*
1993	28	64	2	2	4
1997[a]	44	49	–	–	7
1999	42	48	3	1	6
2000	44	40	7	3	6

In the long run do immigrants become productive citizens and pay their fair share of taxes, or do they cost the taxpayers too much by using government services like public education and medical services?

	Pay their fair share of taxes	*Cost taxpayers too much*	*No opinion*
1993	37	56	7
1994	36	57	7
1995[a]	40	52	8
1999	47	45	8
2000	48	40	12

[a]The question was worded: "Does legal immigration have a positive or a negative effect on the national economy?"
Source: Princeton Survey Research Associates, 2000.

Responses to all of these items show that from the mid-1990s immigrants are perceived in a more positive light. They are seen as helping rather than hurting the economy, as paying their fair share of taxes, and as taking jobs most Americans do not want.

Table 1.20 Should U.S. Immigration Be Kept at Its Present Level, Increased, or Decreased?

	Response Categories			
Years	*More/Increase*	*Same/Present Level*	*Fewer/Decrease*	*No Opinion/ Don't Know*
1946[a]	5	32	37	12
1953	13	37	39	11
1965	8	39	33	20
1977	7	37	42	14
1981	5	22	65	8
1982	4	23	66	7
1986	7	35	49	9
1988	6	34	53	7
1990[b]	9	29	48	14
1992	4	29	54	13
1993	6	27	54	13
1995	7	24	65	4
1999	10	41	44	5
2000	13	41	38	8

Source: American Institute of Public Opinion (Storrs: Roper Center, University of Connecticut, 2000).

[a]In 1946, the question was phrased: "Should we permit more persons from Europe to come to this country each year than we did before the war, should we keep the number about the same, or should we reduce the number?" "None" was offered as a choice and 14 percent selected it. In the subsequent polls, the question was usually phrased: "Should immigration be kept at its present level, increased, or decreased?"

[b]In 1990, the question was phrased: "Is it your impression that the current immigration laws allow too many immigrants, too few immigrants, or about the right number of immigrants into this country every year?"

Table 1.20 compares responses to the following question that was asked of the American public on at least fourteen national polls from 1946 through 2000: "Should immigration be kept at its present level, should immigration be increased, or should immigration be decreased?"

Looking at the entire fifty-plus years time span, the responses show that during periods of economic expansion and growth, during periods of recession and high unemployment, during periods that included the Cold War, and during periods marked by a relaxation of tension among the major powers, the American public's willingness to increase the number of immigrants ranged from 4 to 13 percent. The percentage of Americans who favored decreasing the number of immigrants allowed to enter ranged from 33 to 66 percent. But now note the shift in responses in 1999 and 2000. On those two surveys, a majority of the respondents favored increasing immigration or maintaining it at its present level, which since the passage of the 1990 Immigration Act involves admitting over 700,000 immigrants a year.

Consistent with the shifts shown in the most recent period are responses to a question asked on a March 1999 national survey.

Suppose that on election day this year you could vote on key issues as well as candidates. Please tell me whether you would vote for or against a law that would stop almost all legal immigration into the United States for the next five years:

	Percent
Vote for	39
Vote against	58
No opinion	3

Source: Princeton Survey Research Associates, 2000.

Among respondents with opinions, nearly 60 percent were against closing off legal immigration to the United States over the next five years.

On a somewhat different theme, one that shows sympathy for the status of immigrants in American society, look at the responses to the following item:

I want to ask how much discrimination there is against groups in our society today. Would you say there is a great deal of discrimination, some discrimination, only a little discrimination or none at all against immigrants (January 2000):

	Percent
Great deal	26
Some	50
Only a little	13
None at all	5
Don't know/refused	7

Source: American Institute of Public Opinion (Storrs: Roper Center, University of Connecticut, 1999).
Note: This does not add up exactly to 100 percent due to rounding.

Among those who expressed their opinions, almost 80 percent believed immigrants were the target of some or a great deal of discrimination.

It is important that the shift in a more positive direction on the part of the American public not be exaggerated. The following, for example, are responses to recent polls that reflect the more traditional attitudes.

When it comes to immigration, which statement most closely represents your feelings? Statement A: Immigration strengthens the American character, as new arrivals increase our diversity and bring ambition and new approaches to the country. Statement B: Immigration weakens the American character, as new arrivals do not adopt our language and culture and put a strain on public services (March 2000).

	Percent
Immigration strengthens	36
Immigration weakens	50

Both	8
Neither	3
Not sure	3

Source: American Institute of Public Opinion (Storrs: Roper Center, University of Connecticut, 2000).

Among those who chose between statements A and B, 58 percent believed immigrants weaken the American character as opposed to 44 percent who believed immigration strengthens the American character.

And when asked to choose between "which is the greater threat to the United States remaining a major world power in the next century," Americans responded:

	Percent
Too much population growth within the United States	19
Too much immigration from foreign countries	69
Neither/other	10
Not sure	2

Source: American Institute of Public Opinion (Storrs: Roper Center, University of Connecticut, 2000).

Among those who made a choice, the ratio was almost four to one in perceiving immigration as the greatest threat to the United States remaining a major world power.

Also consistent with the traditional views favoring greater restriction are responses to the following item:

We should restrict and control people mostly coming into our country to live more than we do now (September 1999):

	Percent
Completely agree	38
Mostly agree	34
Mostly disagree	18
Completely disagree	6
Don't know	4

Source: American Institute of Public Opinion (Storrs: Roper Center, University of Connecticut, 1999).

By a ratio of at least three to one, most respondents favored greater restrictions and controls on immigrants coming into the United States.

In the last section, we report the highlights of a 1995 national survey of foreign-born adults in the United States. One of the items included focused on whether current immigration levels should be increased, decreased, or remain at their current level. It is the same question shown on table 1.20 that has been included on national surveys since 1946.

The responses of the foreign-born respondents in 1995 are:

	Percent
Want to see immigration increased	15
Prefer to keep immigration at present level	44
Want to see immigration decreased	15
No opinion	26

Source: Cable News Network/USA Today/Gallup Poll (May–June 1995).

Among those who expressed an opinion, 20 percent of immigrants wanted to see immigration levels decreased, compared to 67 percent of the general population. In 1995, other interesting findings that emerged from the immigration poll include: 93 percent believed that "people who work hard to better themselves can get ahead in this country," compared to 85 percent of all national adults; 70 percent of the immigrants believed their children "will have even better economic opportunities in this country" than they ever had; 75 percent of the immigrants said that the level of political freedom "is better than what they experienced in their homeland"; and 5 percent said their homeland was better.

Especially interesting, given all of the media and political attention to multiculturalism, is the finding that the so-called multiculturalism effort to preserve national identity is vigorously favored by only 27 percent of immigrants and 32 percent of native-born adults. In contrast, assimilation is favored by 59 percent of both native-born adults and immigrants. Not only do immigrants prefer the more traditional approach to immigration, but 75 percent believe the phrase "melting pot" accurately characterizes the United States today, although 20 percent disagree.

Finally, 69 percent of the immigrant respondents feel certain they would prefer to live out their lives in the United States, whereas 16 percent would prefer to live in the country in which they were born. The reason why the immigrant respondents came to the United States initially distinguished them as to their preferences for remaining. Among those who came because of job opportunities, 65 percent would prefer to remain, and only 45 percent of those who came for education believe they will remain permanently in the United States.

Summary

From 1820 until the mid 1990s, over sixty million immigrants have landed on American shores. Until the 1960s, most of them came from Europe (in the earlier period from northern and western Europe, and later from southern and eastern Europe). Beginning in the 1970s, the major sources of immigrants were from Asia, Mexico, and Latin American countries. Today, 10.4 percent of the American population are foreign born.

In 1875, Congress enacted the first federal statute to regulate immigration by preventing the entry of criminals and prostitutes. The major restrictions on immigration began with the Quota Acts of the 1920s and continued until 1990 when Congress passed the most liberal immigration bill since the Quota Act of 1921. The 1990 Immigration Act set the overall annual quota at 700,000 for the period from 1992 through 1994 and established a permanent annual level of 675,000 immigrants beginning in 1995. Most of the immigrants are admitted on the basis of family ties. As is true the world over, most immigrants come when they are young and eager to work. The median age of the foreign born who entered the United States between 1980 and 1990 was 28.0 years; that of the native populations was 32.5 years. Seventy-one percent of immigrants are working age compared to 56 percent of the natives. Although 37 percent of the immigrant population compared to 14 percent of the natives did not finish high school, 26 percent of both immigrants and natives hold at least a bachelor's degree and immigrants are twice as likely to hold a doctorate, as are natives. For those reporting occupations among the 1994 cohort, 44 percent work in managerial, professional, technical, and administrative support occupations.

Examination of the rate of illegal activities between immigrants and natives reveals that immigrants are less likely to be incarcerated than are natives for all categories of crime with one exception: drugs. But when immigrants are divided into those who entered legally and those who are here illegally, illegal immigrants have higher crime rates than natives for drugs, homicide, and robbery.

Finally, in examining the public opinion data, had we written this section before 1997 we would have reported that most of the American public, like most of the Canadian and Australian public, holds negative views toward those immigrants who are currently entering the country and wants to reduce their numbers. But, in the last three or four years of the 1990s there have been signs of a shift in a more positive direction toward recent immigrants. There are some signs—how stable they will prove to be has still to be tested—that the American public may appreciate the contributions that "even" a current cohort of immigrants can and do make to the economy and culture.

Notes

1. The Fifteenth Amendment to the U.S. Constitution, which was ratified five years after the end of the Civil War in 1870, states that the right of citizens of the United

States to vote shall not be denied or abridged by the United States or by any state on account of race, color, or previous condition of servitude.

2. Marcus Lee Hansen, *The Atlantic Migration, 1607–1860* (Cambridge, Mass.: Harvard University Press, 1940).

3. Rita J. Simon and Susan H. Alexander, *The Ambivalent Welcome: Print Media, Public Opinion and Immigration* (Westport, Conn.: Praeger, 1993), 13.

4. Simon and Alexander, *Ambivalent Welcome,* 13.

5. Simon and Alexander, *Ambivalent Welcome,* 14.

6. Simon and Alexander, *Ambivalent Welcome,* 14.

7. Simon and Alexander, *Ambivalent Welcome,* 14.

8. Simon and Alexander, *Ambivalent Welcome,* 15.

9. Simon and Alexander, *Ambivalent Welcome,* 15.

10. Simon and Alexander, *Ambivalent Welcome,* 15.

11. Simon and Alexander, *Ambivalent Welcome,* 15.

12. Simon and Alexander, *Ambivalent Welcome,* 15.

13. Simon and Alexander, *Ambivalent Welcome,* 15.

14. Simon and Alexander, *Ambivalent Welcome,* 15.

15. Simon and Alexander, *Ambivalent Welcome,* 15.

16. Simon and Alexander, *Ambivalent Welcome,* 16.

17. Simon and Alexander, *Ambivalent Welcome,* 16.

18. Simon and Alexander, *Ambivalent Welcome,* 16.

19. Simon and Alexander, *Ambivalent Welcome,* 16.

20. Simon and Alexander, *Ambivalent Welcome,* 17.

21. Simon and Alexander, *Ambivalent Welcome,* 17.

22. Simon and Alexander, *Ambivalent Welcome,* 17.

23. Peter H. Schuck, *Citizens, Strangers, and In-Betweens: Essays on Immigration and Citizenship* (Boulder, Colo.: Westview, 1998), 15.

24. Schuck, *Citizens,* 15.

25. Schuck, *Citizens,* 15.

26. Schuck, *Citizens,* 143–144.

27. John Miller, "The Naturalizers," *Policy Review,* no. 78 (July–August 1996).

28. Allen Steinberg, "The History of Immigration and Crime" (paper prepared for the Select Commission on Immigration and Refugee Policy, Columbia University, 1980).

29. Thomas Muller and Thomas J. Espenshade, *The Fourth Wave: California's Newest Immigrants* (Washington, D.C.: Urban Institute Press, 1985).

30. John R. Commons, *Races and Immigrants in America* (New York: Kelly, 1924), 1–7.

31. Donald Reed Taft, *Human Migration: A Study of International Movements* (New York: Ronald, 1936).

32. Thomas Muller, *Immigrants and the American City* (New York: New York University Press, 1993).

33. Muller and Espenshade, *Fourth Wave.*

34. Muller, *Immigrants.*

35. Ramiro Martinez and Matthew T. Lee, "On Migration and Crime," in *The Nature of Crime: Continuity and Change: Criminal Justice 2000,* vol. 1, ed. Gary Lafree et al. (Washington, D.C.: National Institute of Justice, 2000).

36. Muller, *Immigrants.*

37. Susan Pennell and Christine Curtis, "The Impact of Undocumented Aliens on the Criminal Justice System" (draft paper, San Diego Association of Governments, October 1986).

38. Muller, *Immigrants.*

39. Daniel Wolf, *Undocumented Aliens and Crime: The Case of San Diego County* (San Diego, Calif.: Center for U.S. Mexican Studies, University of California, 1988).

40. Muller, *Immigrants;* and Pennell and Curtis, "Impact of Undocumented Aliens."

41. A. D. Biderman and J. P. Lynch, *Understanding Crime Incidence Statistics: Why the UCR Diverges from the NCS* (New York: Springer-Verlag, 1991).

42. Bureau of Justice Statistics, *Survey of Inmates of State Correctional Facilities* (Washington, D.C.: Bureau of Justice Statistics, 1991).

43. A. J. Beck et al., *Survey of Inmates in State Prison, 1991* (Washington, D.C.: Bureau of Justice Statistics, 1993).

44. For a more complete discussion of the frailty of these data, see John Hagan and Alberto Palloni, "Immigration and Crime in the United States," in *The Immigration Debate,* ed. James P. Smith and Barry Edmonston (Washington, D.C.: National Academy Press, 1998). These authors arrive at a higher estimate of immigrant crime rates in part because they use the 1980 census estimate of the immigrant population rather than that from the 1990 census.

45. Karen Woodrow and Jeffrey S. Passe, "Post-IRCA Undocumented Immigration to the United States: An Assessment Based on the June 1988 CPS," in *Undocumented Migration to the United States: IRCA and the Experience of the 1980s,* ed. Frank Bean, Barry Edmonston, and Jeffery Passel (Washington, D.C.: Urban Institute, 1990).

2

Immigration in Canada

Canadian immigration policy is relatively open compared to other industrialized democracies. The ratio of annual legal admissions to total resident population is many times that of the United States. Admission policies are designed to serve both the economic needs of the nation as well as the demand for family unification. Canada's refugee and asylum policies are also generous. Naturalization requirements are even less stringent than those of other immigrant nations and a substantial proportion of all immigrants become citizens. There are extensive governmental programs to integrate immigrants into Canadian society and immigrants are subject to few restrictions while residing in Canada.

Historical Background and Major Legislation

The British North American Act of 1867 (section 95) assumed joint responsibility for immigration for the federal and provincial governments.[1] Previously, the land was governed by various French and English colonization schemes. Immigration to Canada was basically free until 1895 when restrictions were imposed on those who had physical or mental incapacities and were likely to become public charges, those who had moral character flaws, and those deemed "racially and culturally unassimilatable." For example, in 1885 the government instituted a basic tax of fifty dollars on all Chinese immigrants. In addition, the 1923 Immigration Act barred Chinese and most other Asians from immigrating to Canada. But even in the latter part of the nineteenth century, the promotion of immigrant activities from the United Kingdom ensured a relatively homogeneous group of immigrants. These immigrants were provided assisted passage and cheap land. Following the 1923 act, the next major piece of immigration legislation was the Canadian Act of March 1931 (P.C. 695), which admitted the following classes of immigrants to Canada:

1. British subjects as defined in a previous order-in-council (P.C. 183) as "British by reason of birth, or naturalization in Great Britain or Ireland, Newfoundland, or New Zealand, Australia, and the Union of South Africa"
2. U.S. citizens
3. the spouse, unmarried children under eighteen, and fiancé(e)s of legal residents of Canada
4. agriculturalists having sufficient means to farm in Canada
5. any Asian spouse and/or unmarried child under eighteen of any Canadian citizen who was in a position to receive dependents[2]

Under the revised Chinese Immigration Act of 1923, all persons of Chinese ethnic origin, except merchants, were prohibited from admission regardless of their nationality or religion.

In the first two decades of the twentieth century, Canada, like the United States, received a heavy influx of immigrants from southern and eastern Europe and, like the United States, sought ways to limit it. The 1931 act was one response to the "new immigrants." Major changes in Canadian immigration policy began to occur after World War II. For example, in 1946 the government formed a subcommittee to consider the question of postwar immigration to Canada.

The committee agreed on:

1. Emergency measures to bring refugees and displaced persons to Canada (5,000 to be admitted initially and the number would be increased)
2. Admitting three special movements of immigrants—Polish ex-servicemen in the United Kingdom and Italy, farmworkers from the Netherlands, and immigrants from Malta
3. Adding farmworkers, miners, and loggers to the admissible classes in view of the urgent need for labor in Canada's primary industries
4. Introducing a bill to repeal the Chinese Immigration Act of 1923
5. Placing citizens of France in the same category for admission to Canada as British subjects and U.S. citizens

In May 1946, Prime Minister Mackenzie King issued the following statement on Canadian immigration policy: "The policy of the government is to foster growth of the population of Canada by the encouragement of immigration. The government will seek legislation, regulation and vigorous administration, to ensure the careful selection and permanent settlement of such numbers of immigrants as can be advantageously absorbed in our national economy."[3]

The Canadian policy established six major premises:

1. Immigration is for population growth
2. Immigration is for economic development
3. Immigration must be selective
4. Immigration must be related to absorptive capacity
5. Immigration is a matter of domestic policy and its control is a national prerogative
6. Immigration must not distort the present character of the Canadian population

The policy therefore determined that immigration to Canada meant that the European immigration, and the restriction of Asiatic immigration, must continue. At that time, Asians referred to almost every one in the Eastern Hemisphere outside Europe. It included Turkey, Egypt, and Africa (except white South Africans). Blacks remained inadmissible unless they belonged to preferred classes, and preference for British, French, and American immigrants continued.

The Immigration Act of 1952 clarified and simplified immigration procedures and removed certain anomalies that had been brought to light during the continued movement of newcomers to Canada.

In 1962, new immigration regulations removed racial discrimination as the major feature of Canada's immigration policy.[4] But the privilege given to Europeans that allowed for the sponsoring of a wider range of relatives continued. On June 9, 1962, Canada granted amnesty to all Chinese who had entered Canada illegally before July 1, 1960.

The 1967 Manpower and Immigration Council Act established a council to advise the minister of manpower and immigration on all matters to which his "duties, powers, and functions" relate, including an advisory board on manpower and immigration research.

The Immigration Act of 1976 stated that Canada should continue to be a country of immigration for demographic, economic, family, and humanitarian reasons.[5] The act also stated that Canada should admit a minimum of 100,000 immigrants a year as long as present fertility rates prevailed. It established three classes of immigrants: (1) a family class defined as the immediate family and dependent children, and parents and grandparents; (2) refugees; and (3) other applicants selected on the basis of a point system that included independent applicants and "assisted relatives," that is, more distant relatives who are sponsored by a family member in Canada. Finally, the act made changes in the areas of exclusion by further identifying certain broad classes of persons whose entry to Canada might endanger public health, welfare, and security.

A point system first introduced in 1967, and revised in 1974, 1978, 1985, and 1996, was intended to support the federal government's intention to increase immigration levels to achieve a better balance among family reunion, humanitarian, and economic needs in the immigration movement. Finally, new immigration legislation passed in 1993 authorized the government to (1) place temporary limits on an immigrant's geographical mobility to employ his or her skills in areas where they are most needed; (2) provide tighter control over the entry of illegal immigrants through improved border controls; (3) set penalties for airlines that transport passengers without the required travel documents; and (4) introduce a one-step refugee determination system that processes claims within six months.[6]

Current Canadian immigration policy attempts to balance the demands of the economy with the demands of family reunification. It is clearly a policy that encourages permanent settlement. In balancing these demands, the Canadian government established preferences for family immigrants and economic immigrants.[7] The former are spouses, dependent children, and parents of permanent resident immigrants. There is some pressure, however, to restrict the admission of parents due to the anticipated effect that a large number of elderly immigrants would have on the public health care system. The latter, economic immigrants, are those who, because of the demand for their occupational skills, are admitted to Canada. This demand is determined by a point system. The Ministry of Citizenship and Immigration compiles the Designated and Open Occupations List that affixes points to each occupation class according to the need for persons in that class. Immigration applicants with more points are admitted before those with fewer points.

There is a second subclass of economic immigrants called "business immigrants." This group includes entrepreneurs, investors, and persons involved in family businesses. Entrepreneurs are persons who have expressed their intent to invest in Canadian business. In addition, a number of persons become immigrants by changing their status from a temporary to a permanent resident. This could occur, for example, when someone entering on a student visa or a temporary worker visa applies for permanent resident status. Table 2.1 summarizes the system.

In addition to economic and family preferences, Canadian admissions policies allow for humanitarian immigration. These include both refugees and asylum seekers. Refugees are persons who have been forced to leave their native country and are applying for entry into Canada. There are two subclasses of refugees: government sponsored and privately sponsored. The former are recruited from the refugee camps around the world. The latter are sponsored by groups of five or more Canadian citizens who take responsibility for the refugee for at least one year after admission. Asylum seekers are persons residing in Canada who seek to become residents because they have reason to believe that they will be persecuted if they return to their homeland.

Table 2.1 Selection Criteria for Independent Immigrants

	Units of Assessment	
Factors	*Previous*	*Revised (1996)*
Education	12 maximum	• 16 maximum • 0 points for less than high school diploma • 5 to 15 points for various types of high school and postsecondary training • 16 points for four-year university degree
Vocational skills	15 maximum	• 18 maximum • The score for this factor is based on whether the applicant has a designated occupation, and length of training, education, and/or apprenticeship for Canadian work (e.g., an aerospace engineer receives 18 points, a locksmith receives 11 points, and a janitor receives 0 points)
Work experience	8 maximum	• 8 maximum • The points are calculated based on the specific vocational experience (factor 3) and the years of experience; a maximum of 8 points is awarded to an applicant with the maximum specific vocational experience and 4 years or more experience in the occupation
Occupation	15 maximum "0" an automatic processing bar	• 10 maximum • 0 points if there are no listed occupations for which the candidate is qualified; if the applicant scores 0 on this factor, then he or she is automatically refused a visa • Intermediate points awarded on the basis of the candidate's qualified occupation (e.g., an aerospace engineer and a locksmith both receive 5 points) • 10 points if the candidate has arranged employment in Canada or has a designated occupation with high specific occupation preparation value

continued

Table 2.1 Selection Criteria for Independent Immigrants (continued)

	Units of Assessment	
Factors	*Previous*	*Revised (1996)*
Arranged employment	10; 10 penalty if none	• 10 maximum • 0 points if no arranged employment or a designated occupation • 10 points if the person has arranged employment or a designated occupation with a high specific vocational preparation • 10 points for a member of the clergy with a congregational position offering employment • 10 points for a full-time employment in a family business approved by the Canada Immigration Centre
Location	5 maximum; 5 penalty if designated no need	• Eliminated
Age	10 maximum; 10 if 18 to 35 years, 1 unit subtracted for each year up to 45	• 10 maximum • 0 points for 17 years • Increasing points for 18 to 20 years • 10 points for 21 to 44 years • Decreasing points for 45 to 48 years • 0 points for 49 years and over
Knowledge of French and English	10 maximum; 5 for fluency in one, 10 if fluent in both	• 15 maximum • 0 points if the person speaks English and French with difficulty • Intermediate points are awarded based on the reading, writing, and speaking of English and French • 15 points if the person is fluent in both French and English
Personal suitability	10 maximum	• 10 maximum • These points are awarded based on a personal assessment of a Canadian visa officer; the points are based on adaptability, motivation, initiative, and resourcefulness; the purpose is to predict whether the applicant and family will be able to settle successfully in Canada
Demographic factor	NA	• 8 maximum • These points are set by the federal government to adjust the volume of

Table 2.1 Selection Criteria for Independent Immigrants (continued)

	Units of Assessment	
Factors	*Previous*	*Revised (1996)*
		annual immigration; 8 points were awarded in 1996
Relative in Canada	5 units	• 5 maximum • 5 points are awarded if the applicant has a brother, sister, mother, father, grandparent, aunt, uncle, niece, or nephew as a permanent resident or Canadian citizen living in Canada
Total	100 units	• 100 units
Minimum needed	50 units	• 70 units
Bonus for "assisted relative" applicants	15 to 30	• 10 if accompanied by an undertaking of assistance

Source: Data from Employment and Immigration Canada, as cited in James Smith and Barry Edmonston, eds., *The New Americans* (Washington, D.C.: National Academy Press, 1997), 73–75.

The 1981 Task Force Report on Refugee Status Determination enlarged the definition of a refugee from Convention Refugees, as specified by the United Nations, to Designated Refugees.[8] The term "Designated Refugees" refers to persecuted minorities and to ad hoc situations that produce refugees, for example, events in Poland or El Salvador. "Convention Refugees" refers to persons who by reason of a well-founded fear of persecution based on race, religion, nationality, membership in a particular social group, or political opinion are outside the country of their nationality and are unable or unwilling to avail themselves of the protection of that country.

Throughout its history, then, Canadian immigration policy has attempted to balance the need for labor and population with the problems posed by incorporating diverse populations. Early on, this was done by encouraging immigration from Europe while discouraging immigrants from other parts of the world. After World War II, these exclusionary policies loosened somewhat, and in the 1960s these policies were abandoned entirely. They were replaced by a policy of family unification and a point system that screened new labor admissions for their ability to be integrated into Canadian society.

The Stock and Flow of Immigrants

As of 1996, immigrants made up 17.4 percent (4.9 million people) of the Canadian population.[9] Between 1821 and 1932, 5.2 million immigrants came to Canada.[10] Table 2.2 describes the flow of immigrants to Canada from 1946 through 2000. Immediately after World War II, the number of immigrants entering Canada annually was well under 100,000. This figure rose to about 200,000 by the end of the 1950s only to drop again in the early 1960s and to vacillate around 150,000 throughout the late 1960s to 1979. From 1980, when 143,000 immigrants arrived, a decline began that lasted through 1986, when 99,000 immigrants entered the country.[11] Beginning in 1987, admissions increased steadily from 152,000 to 254,000 in 1993. Since 1993, the number of admissions decreased to 174,000 in 1998 only to increase again to 227,000 in 2000. On average, admissions throughout the 1990s have been in excess of 200,000 persons annually.[12]

The ethnic composition of immigrants to Canada has also changed significantly over time. Table 2.3 describes the country of origin of immigrants to Canada from 1946 through 1987. And Table 2.4 reports the number of immigrants and their country of origin from 1981 through 1991. Table 2.5 presents similar information for the period 1995 through 2000.

In 1957, 95 percent of the 282,164 immigrants who came to Canada were Europeans and Americans. In 1987, of the 152,098 immigrants who entered Canada, almost 75 percent came from Asia, the West Indies, and other mainly

Table 2.2 Immigration to Canada, 1946–2000

Year	*Number*	*Year*	*Number*	*Year*	*Number*
1946	71,719	1965	146,758	1984	88,239
1947	64,127	1966	194,743	1985	84,302
1948	125,414	1967	22,876	1986	99,219
1949	95,217	1968	183,974	1987	152,098
1950	73,912	1969	164,531	1988	161,929
1951	NA	1970	147,713	1989	192,001
1952	164,498	1971	121,900	1990	214,230
1953	168,868	1972	122,006	1991	230,781
1954	154,227	1973	184,200	1992	252,842
1955	109,946	1974	218,465	1993	254,321
1956	164,857	1975	187,881	1994	224,373
1957	282,164	1976	NA	1995	212,869
1958	124,851	1977	114,914	1996	226,071
1959	196,928	1978	86,313	1997	216,039
1960	104,111	1979	112,093	1998	174,162
1961	71,698	1980	143,117	1999	189,911
1962	74,586	1981	128,618	2000	227,209
1963	93,151	1982	121,147		
1964	112,606	1983	89,157		

Source: Citizenship and Immigration Canada, *Facts and Figures: 2000 Immigration Overview* (Ottawa: Citizenship and Immigration Canada, 2001).

Table 2.3 Immigration to Canada by Country or Geographical Area of Last Permanent Residence, since 1946 (percent distribution)

Year	*UK*	*Other Europe*	*Africa*	*Asia/ Pacific*	*Australia/ Oceania*	*North America*	*Other N. America*	*South America*	*Total %*	*Number*[a]
1946–1967	22.5	55.9	1.0	3.9	1.8	1.1	6.6	3.2	96.0	132.8
1968–1976	16.0	29.3	4.0	20.0	2.7	4.6	13.2	10.3	100.1	164.1
1977	15.7	19.8	5.6	27.3	2.1	6.8	11.2	11.5	100.0	114.9
1978	13.7	21.2	4.9	27.8	2.2	7.9	11.5	10.8	100.0	86.3
1979	11.5	17.8	3.5	45.1	1.8	5.3	8.6	6.3	99.9	112.1
1980	12.8	16.0	3.0	50.0	1.8	3.8	6.9	5.7	100.0	143.1
1981	16.4	19.6	3.5	38.0	1.7	4.8	8.2	7.5	99.7	128.6
1982	13.6	24.5	3.7	34.4	1.8	5.6	7.7	8.5	99.8	121.1
1983	6.4	21.5	4.1	41.4	1.4	5.4	8.3	12.2	100.7	89.2
1984	5.8	17.9	4.0	47.5	1.3	4.6	7.8	11.0	99.9	88.2
1985	5.3	17.1	4.2	45.8	1.3	5.2	7.9	13.2	100.0	84.3
1986	5.1	17.6	4.8	41.9	1.0	6.6	7.2	14.9	99.1	97.5
1987	5.6	19.0	5.6	44.3	1.2	7.1	5.2	17.1	105.1	152.1

Sources: Department of Manpower and Immigration, *Annual Reports* (Ottawa: Department of Manpower and Immigration, 1967–1978); Employment and Immigration Canada, *Immigration Statistics* (Hull: Employment and Immigration, 1979–1987); annual reports to Parliament on immigration levels, since 1979.

Note: For 1946 through 1976, annual averages are used; for Asia and the Pacific, from 1979 to 1987 about 60,000 Vietnamese refugees are included; Other N. America includes Central America and the Caribbean; and Australia includes New Zealand, Papua, and Oceania, which includes other islands in the region. Rounding and inclusion of Not Stated in the final total explain the deviation of totals from 100.

[a]In thousands.

Table 2.4 Number and Country of Origin of Immigrants to Canada, 1981–1991

	1981		*1991*		*1981–1990 Total*	
	Number	*%*	*Number*	*%*	*Number*	*%*
Europe	**44,784**	**34.8**	**46,651**	**20.2**	**351,511**	**26.4**
Great Britain	18,912	14.7	6,383	2.8	81,460	6.1
Portugal	3,292	2.6	5,837	2.5	38,630	2.9
France	1,681	1.3	2,619	1.1	15,256	1.2
Greece	924	0.7	618	0.3	6,884	0.5
Italy	2,057	1.6	775	0.3	11,196	0.8
Poland	4,093	3.2	15,737	6.8	81,361	6.1
Other	13,825	10.7	14,682	6.4	116,724	8.8
Africa	**5,901**	**4.6**	**16,530**	**7.2**	**72,941**	**5.5**
Asia	**50,759**	**39.5**	**122,228**	**53.0**	**619,089**	**46.5**
Philippines	5,978	4.6	12,626	5.5	67,682	5.1
India	9,415	7.3	14,248	6.2	90,050	6.8
Hong Kong	4,039	3.1	16,425	7.1	96,982	7.3
China	9,798	7.6	20,621	8.9	74,235	5.6
The Middle East	5,409	4.2	24,497	10.6	90,965	6.8
Other	16,120	12.5	33,811	14.7	199,175	15.0
North and Central America	**10,183**	**7.9**	**18,899**	**8.2**	**114,073**	**8.6**
United States	8,695	6.8	5,270	2.3	63,106	4.7
Other	1,488	1.2	13,629	5.9	50,967	3.8
Caribbean and Bermuda	8,797	6.8	13,046	5.7	89,098	6.7
Australia	**1,020**	**0.8**	**735**	**0.3**	**5,877**	**0.4**
South America	**6,114**	**4.8**	**10,468**	**4.5**	**67,936**	**5.1**
Oceania	**1,024**	**0.8**	**2,213**	**1.0**	**10,040**	**0.8**
Other	36	—	11	—	375	—
Total	128,618	100.0	230,781	100.0	1,330,940	100.0

Source: Statistics Canada, *Canada Yearbook, 1991* (Ottawa: Statistics Canada, 1992), 116.

Third World countries. While Asian immigrants were excluded until 1946, Asian nations were the most prevalent sending nations in 1993. At least 49 percent of admissions in 1993 were from Asian nations. This substantial representation of Asians continued throughout the decade with 53 percent of admissions in 2000 coming from Asia. The proportion of admissions from Africa and the Middle East also increased during this period from 8.8 percent in 1981 to 17.9 percent in 2000.

The composition of the immigrants by admission class also changed as indicated in table 2.6. Between 1981 and 1985, admissions under the family preference class (234,000) were greater than admissions under economic preferences (184,000). In the period 1986 through 1990, admissions under

Table 2.5 Percent Distribution of Admissions by Region and Year of Admission

Region of Origin	*1995*	*1996*	*1997*	*1998*	*1999*	*2000*
Africa and Middle East	15.50	16.10	17.50	18.70	17.60	17.90
Asia and Pacific	53.00	55.20	54.20	48.30	50.80	53.00
South and Central America	9.60	8.40	8.10	8.10	8.00	7.50
United States	2.40	2.60	2.30	2.70	2.90	2.60
Europe and UK	19.40	17.70	17.90	22.10	20.50	18.90
Not stated	0.02	0.01	0.03	0.02	0.20	0.14
Total	100.00	100.00	100.00	100.00	100.00	100.00
Number	212,869	226,071	216,039	174,162	189,911	227,209

Sources: Citizenship and Immigration Canada, *Facts and Figures: 1997 Immigration Overview* (Ottawa: Citizenship and Immigration Canada, 1998); Citizenship and Immigration Canada, *Facts and Figures: 2000 Immigration Overview* (Ottawa: Citizenship and Immigration Canada, 2001), 8.
Note: Some of the columns do not add up exactly to 100 percent due to rounding.

Table 2.6 Admissions by Class and Year

	Class			
Years	*Family*	*Economic*	*Refugee*	*Other*
1981–1985	234,000	184,000	78,000	16,000
1986–1990	283,000	376,000	140,000	22,000
1991–1995	464,000	455,000	145,000	117,000[a]
1996–2000	294,944	578,317	129,555	29,696

Sources: Informetrica Limited, *Canada's Recent Immigrants: A Comparative Portrait Based on the 1996 Census* (Ottawa: Citizenship and Immigration Canada, 2000), 20; Citizenship and Immigration Canada, *Facts and Figures: 2000 Immigration Overview* (Ottawa: Citizenship and Immigration Canada, 2001), 5; Citizenship and Immigration Canada, *Facts and Figures: 1997 Immigration Overview* (Ottawa: Citizenship and Immigration Canada, 1998).

[a]The increase in the Other category is due to persons landed through the Backlog Clearance Program.

economic preferences (376,000) outstripped those for family unification (283,000). By the early 1990s, that is, 1991 to 1995, the number of admissions for economic (455,000) and family unification (464,000) were essentially equal. In the late 1990s, admissions under economic preferences (578,317) increased again substantially more than admissions for family unification (294,944).

Until about 1970, about 10 percent of all of Canada's postwar immigrants were refugees. The number of refugees admitted annually remained at about 15,000 until 1991 and 1992 when it increased to approximately 50,000. This was due mainly to increases in the Designated Refugees category[13] and specifically persons fleeing Hong Kong. Refugee admissions decreased dramatically in 1993 to 30,000, and again in 1994 to 20,000, due largely to reductions in these Designated Refugees. The total number of refugees admitted in a given year remained in the 20,000 to 30,000 range throughout the period 1994 to 2000.[14] Convention Refugees were about 2.5 times the Designated Refugees during this period. Table 2.7 describes the flow of refugees from 1980 through 2000.

Admissions policies and the flow of immigrants into Canada have changed dramatically since the end of World War II. At that time immigration policy was quite restrictive. Relatively few immigrants entered Canada and those who did were from Europe and North America. Currently, the number of immigrants entering Canada annually has increased severalfold since the immediate postwar period. Currently, very few of the immigrants entering the country are from Europe and North America and almost half of the persons entering are from Asia. Emphasis has shifted in a cyclical fashion throughout the period from family unification to economic immigration. Refugees and asylum seekers have become a larger but relatively stable component of annual admissions. Canada has reacted to these changes in the volume and di-

Table 2.7 Admission of Refugees by Category, since 1980

Year	*Convention*	*Designated*	*Total*
1980	952	39,396	40,348
1981	810	14,170	14,980
1982	1,719	15,136	16,855
1983	4,101	9,868	13,969
1984	5,625	9,717	15,342
1985	6,080	10,680	16,760
1986	6,490	12,657	19,147
1987	7,473	14,092	21,565
1990	11,398	28,291	39,689
1991	18,374	35,027	53,401
1992	28,699	23,176	51,875
1993	22,219	8,403	30,622
1994	19,264	1,120	20,384
1995	19,592	8,198	27,790
1996	20,487	7,872	28,359
1997	16,512	7,710	24,222
1998	15,303	7,397	22,700
1999	16,929	7,444	24,373
2000	19,106	10,661	29,767

Sources: Citizenship and Immigration Canada, *Facts and Figures: 1997 Immigration Overview* (Ottawa: Citizenship and Immigration Canada, 1998), 61; Citizenship and Immigration Canada, *Facts and Figures: 2000 Immigration Overview* (Ottawa: Citizenship and Immigration Canada, 2001), 5.

versity of immigrant groups by imposing selectivity criteria, such as the point system, that facilitate the absorption of these groups.

Internal Regulation of Immigrants

There are relatively few restrictions on permanent immigrant residents that are not shared by citizens. For example, immigrants cannot vote, run for office, or obtain a passport. Citizens are also given a preference for civil service jobs. Other than those restrictions, resident immigrants have all the rights of citizens. They have a right to medical care, social insurance benefits, and education, and there are no registration requirements.[15]

Naturalization Policy

Until 1977, the waiting period for citizenship was like that of the United States—five years. In 1977, the government shortened the period to three years.[16] Some of the impetus for the shortened time period was the realization that immigrants were making little use of their right to become citizens. A study found that most immigrants waited about ten years before applying for citizenship.[17] In 1973, about 100,000 immigrants sought citizenship. In 1978, the number increased to 223,214. Currently, almost all eligible immigrants living in Canada have become citizens. As of 1991, 81 percent of all those eligible to become citizens had done so.[18] Of the immigrants entering Canada before 1971, 88 percent had become citizens by 1991. This naturalization rate drops to 78 percent for persons entering between 1971 and 1980 and to 65 percent of those arriving between 1981 and 1987. A study conducted with the 1996 census data suggests that the lag between admission and naturalization may be decreasing. While 88 percent of the foreign born admitted before 1981 had become citizens by 1996, more than 80 percent of those admitted after 1981 had become citizens by 1996.[19] This is a very high naturalization rate relative to other nations.

Integration Policies

Unlike other immigrant nations, such as the United States, Canada takes an extensive and active role in facilitating the integration of its immigrants, as well as its refugees and asylum seekers. In 1998, more than 40 percent of the budget for Canada's federal immigration agency, Citizenship and Immigration Canada, was devoted to settlement activities.[20] The bulk of the government resettlement efforts, 80 percent, are devoted to language training. Some money is set aside for counseling services and other activities designed to ease the burden of integrating immigrants into Canadian society. Canada also provides a host family program in which an immigrant family is paired with a Canadian family that is responsible for guiding the immigrants into Canadian society. Refugees receive government-sponsored income support, which is not available to other classes of immigrants.

Prior to World War II, the settlement of immigrants was not the responsibility of government. It was left to voluntary associations, the immigrants, or those who brought the immigrant to Canada. In 1948, the Settlement Service was established. The service placed officers throughout the country to help families of Canadian soldiers and war refugees adjust to life in Canada.[21] The Settlement Service took a very active role in the assimilation process. In 1966, the service was disbanded and the settlement of immigrants was left to existing, mainstream services available to all Canadians. In 1974, the Canadian government resumed assistance to immigrant settlement through grants to nongovernmental organizations (NGOs) administered through the Immigration Settlement and Adaption

Program (ISAP). The ISAP is designed to facilitate the adaptation, settlement, and integration of immigrants through the funding of direct services provided by NGOs and through the provision of services that support and contribute to the delivery of these direct services.[22]

The Host Program was begun on a trial basis in 1984 and was made a permanent program in 1990. The program attempts to facilitate settlement in Canada by pairing immigrant families with volunteers who are familiar with the Canadian way of life. The hosts do not subsidize newcomers but help them become familiar with basic life skills including language facility, applying for school, dealing with banks and financial institutions, operating household appliances, and the like.[23]

Language Instruction for Newcomers to Canada (LINC) provides about $80 million annually for language instruction for immigrants.[24] Any adult immigrant who is a permanent resident or intends to become a permanent resident is eligible for up to three years of free language instruction through LINC. The language instruction is provided by service provider organizations (SPOs) that can be businesses, nonprofit organizations, or public organizations. LINC pays the SPOs for their services.

Income assistance to immigrants was provided to any eligible immigrant through the Adjustment Assistance Program established in 1948. In 1994, the rules governing eligibility for income support were revised to include only government-assisted refugees. This program was replaced in 1998 by the Resettlement Assistance Program, which is administered by the Refugee Branch of Citizenship and Immigration Canada.[25]

In addition to these special programs, immigrants are eligible for all social welfare benefits available to Canadian citizens. These policies are administered largely at the provincial or local level, but the funds are provided by the federal government. Additional funds are provided by provinces and local governments, in an effort to provide greater coordination of integration programs.

Illegal Immigrants

Canada, like most developed nations, has a problem with illegal immigration. But as of 1983, the number of illegals was estimated to be about 50,000, a much smaller number, proportionately, than estimates for the United States.[26] Canada's response to illegal entry has been twofold. First, like the United States, Canada has imposed sanctions against employers who hire foreigners without work authorizations. Second, Canada has made visas more difficult to obtain for visitors from countries who have a reputation for outstaying the time period for which they were legally admitted.

Demographic and Socioeconomic Characteristics of Immigrants

The demographic and socioeconomic characteristics of immigrants are constantly evolving as immigrants are absorbed into Canadian society and as new (and sometimes very different) waves of immigrants join those who have come before them. It is important to describe this complexity. To this end, the data on the sociodemographic characteristics of immigrants will use both the admissions in a given year as well as the stock population of immigrants at a given point in time. Whenever possible, distinctions will be made between those newly arrived and those immigrants who have been in Canada longer.

The Canadian immigrant population is younger than the native-born population. In 1991, the median age of Canada's immigrant population at the time of immigration was 23.6 years compared to 31.0 years for the Canadian born. Immigrant populations overrepresent persons in their most productive years and underrepresent older persons. The data in table 2.8 indicate that approximately one-half of the admissions in 2000 were between the ages of twenty-five and forty-four and the same is true for the recent immigrant population. Only 32 percent of the Canadian-born population are in this age bracket. In contrast, 29 percent of the Canadian born are over forty-four compared to 22 percent of recent immigrants and only 12 percent of admissions in 2000.

In both the immigrant and Canadian-born population, there are more women than men. Among the persons admitted in 2000, there were 97.7 men for every 100.0 women.[27] As of 1996, there were 92.4 men per 100 women among the immigrant population, and 97.6 men per 100 women among the Canadian born.[28] The increase in the overrepresentation of

Table 2.8 Age Structure of the Immigrant and Native Populations (percent distribution)

Age Intervals	*Admissions in 2000*	*Recent Immigrants*[a]	*Canadian Born 1996*
0–14	22.5	14.0	24.0
15–24	14.4	16.0	14.0
25–44	50.5	48.0	32.0
45–64	10.1	16.0	19.0
65 and over	2.4	6.0	10.0

Source: Informetrica Limited, *Canada's Recent Immigrants: A Comparative Portrait Based on the 1996 Census* (Ottawa: Citizenship and Immigration Canada, 2001).

[a]This includes foreign-born persons residing in Canada in 1996 who immigrated between 1981 and 1996.

women in the recent immigrant population could be due to a number of factors including the fact that more women are admitted to Canada for the purpose of family unification while more men may come as skilled workers. More of the former than the latter are likely to remain in Canada.

Of those aged fifteen or over, 68 percent of the immigrants admitted in 2000 were married, compared to 52 percent of the Canadian born.[29] In 1996, recent immigrants were more likely to be in legal marriages (as opposed to conjugal unions) than the native-born population. While 16 percent of Canadian couples live common law, just 6 percent of recent immigrant couples do.[30] Immigrant women, especially those from Central America, western Asia, and the Middle East, have higher birth rates (1,816 per 1,000) than do Canadian-born women (1,738 per 1,000).

About 18 percent of immigrants who were living as families in 1996 were married to native-born Canadians.[31] Not surprisingly, the rate of intermarriage between Canadians and immigrants increased with time in the country. Over 40 percent of immigrants who entered Canada before 1981 and who were in families in 1996 were married to native-born Canadians.[32]

Among the immigrants fifteen and older admitted to Canada in 2000, approximately 44 percent had a university degree compared to only 13 percent of the Canadian population in the 1996 census. The immigrant population in Canada seems to be increasingly better educated. Eighteen percent of those immigrating prior to 1981 had a university degree, 20 percent of those immigrating between 1981 and 1991 and another 24 percent entering Canada between 1991 and 1996.

But a larger proportion of immigrants entering Canada in 2000—15 percent—had less than a ninth-grade education.[33] Only 11 percent of the Canadian-born population had this level of educational attainment.[34] According to the 1996 census, however, fewer of the immigrants who stay in Canada tend to have low educational attainment.[35] Among women immigrants, 22 percent of those entering Canada before 1981 had less than nine years of education, while only 14 percent of those entering between 1991 and 1996 had this level of educational attainment. For male immigrants the comparable figures are 18 percent and 9 percent.

The differences between the admissions numbers in 2000 and the 1996 census data may be due to the speed with which new arrivals are acquiring education in Canada. The data in table 2.9 suggest recent immigrants to Canada are attending school at much higher rates than either the native-born population or immigrants who entered Canada previously. Ten percent of Canadian-born men between twenty-five and forty-four years of age were attending school compared to 23 percent of immigrants of the same age who entered between 1991 and 1996. The same differences are observed for women in these years of peak productivity. Thirteen percent of the Canadian born were attending school and 26 percent of very recent immigrants. The

Table 2.9 Persons Attending School As a Percentage of All Persons by Age Group and Gender, 1996

	Age Group		
Gender/Status	*15–24*	*25–44*	*45–64*
Women			
Canadian born	66.0	13.0	4.0
Entered before 1981	63.0	13.0	5.0
Entered 1981–1990	74.0	16.0	7.0
Entered 1991–1996	68.0	26.0	12.0
Men			
Canadian born	63.0	10.0	3.0
Entered before 1981	60.0	12.0	3.0
Entered 1981–1990	73.0	14.0	6.0
Entered 1991–1996	73.0	23.0	11.0

Source: Informetrica Limited, *Canada's Recent Immigrants: A Comparative Portrait Based on the 1996 Census* (Ottawa: Citizenship and Immigration Canada, 2001), 32

differences between the native population and earlier immigrants are less but in the same direction.

A substantial proportion of immigrants to Canada are able to speak one or both of the official languages. About 56 percent of the admissions in 2000 could speak French or English.[36] The 1996 census data in table 2.10 indicate that 89 percent of residents admitted between 1991 and 1996 can carry on a conversation in at least one of the official languages. The data in table 2.10 show that language ability among immigrants differs substantially by age and gender. Younger immigrants are more fluent than older immigrants and males generally claim greater ability than females. The differences across gender are nonexistent among younger immigrants but pronounced among those over forty-five.

As of 1996, 74.5 percent of all immigrants were in the labor force compared to 76.4 percent of all Canadian born.[37] The involvement of immigrants in the labor force is positively related to time in the country. Immigrants entering Canada before 1981 participate in the labor force at levels that equal or exceed that of the native-born population. Those immigrating between 1981 and 1990 have slightly lower participation than the Canadian born and the most recent arrivals have substantially lower rates of participation in the labor force. But a higher proportion of immigrants aged forty-five to sixty-four arriving before 1991 were in the labor force than were the Canadian born in the same age categories (81 percent compared to 78 percent).

Immigrants who are employed are overrepresented in the health and science industries and in the sales and service industries. More recent immigrants are distributed very differently across occupations than earlier immigrants who have distributions more similar to the native-born population.

Table 2.10 Proportion of Men and Women 15 and Older Who Immigrated between 1991 and 1996 and Are Able to Speak English or French, 1996

	Language (percent)			
Gender/Age	*English*	*French*	*Both*	*Total*
Women				
15–24	79	5	11	95
25–44	77	5	9	91
45–64	56	3	4	63
65 and over	34	4	2	39
Total	62	4	7	72
Men				
15–24	82	4	10	96
25–44	78	4	12	94
45–64	69	3	6	78
65 and over	46	3	3	52
Total	69	4	8	80

Source: Informetrica Limited, *Canada's Recent Immigrants: A Comparative Portrait Based on the 1996 Census* (Ottawa: Citizenship and Immigration Canada, 2001), 25.

The earlier immigrants tend to be overrepresented in higher-status occupations while more recent arrivals seem to be overrepresented in lower-status occupations.

The data in table 2.11 show that immigrants are more likely to work in the health and science industries than are native-born Canadians. Ten percent of Canadians work in these industries as opposed to 13 percent of immigrants, regardless of their arrival date. Immigrant men (and to a larger extent immigrant women) work in the sales and service industry. Seventeen percent of native Canadians are employed in this industry compared to 25 percent of immigrants arriving between 1991 and 1996. Immigrants arriving prior to 1981 participate in sales and service at the same rate as the native population. Earlier immigrants are more likely to be in management and social occupations than the native-born population, but more recent immigrants are less likely to be in these occupations than the native born. The opposite pattern is observed in processing and manufacturing industries. Early immigrants are underrepresented in these industries while more recent immigrants participate at higher levels than the native population.

The same general relationship between time since arrival and prestige of one's occupation can be seen in table 2.12. Here, occupations are rated in terms of skill levels. Level 1 includes jobs requiring short work experience and no formal education. Level 2 refers to jobs requiring secondary school plus a period of specific job training. Level 3 requires college-level education

Table 2.11 Occupations of Employed Persons 25 to 64 Years of Age by Gender, 1996

	Industry[a] *(percent)*						
Gender/Status	*1*	*2*	*3*	*4*	*5*	*6*	*Total*
Women							
Canadian born	26	6	34	21	2	12	4,058,700
Entered before 1981	26	9	31	20	2	12	643,300
Entered 1981–1990	30	15	26	14	2	13	232,500
Entered 1991–1996	40	15	20	13	2	10	154,800
Men							
Canadian born	17	16	10	21	26	10	4,727,400
Entered before 1981	17	13	10	24	23	13	787,500
Entered 1981–1990	20	17	10	18	21	14	279,800
Entered 1991–1996	25	18	10	17	16	13	192,500

Source: Informetrica Limited, *Canada's Recent Immigrants: A Comparative Portrait Based on the 1996 Census* (Ottawa: Citizenship and Immigration Canada, 2001), 58.
Note: Some of the rows do not add up exactly to 100 percent due to rounding.
[a]Industries: 1 = Sales and service; 2 = Processing; 3 = Administrative; 4 = Management and social; 5 = Trade and transport; and 6 = Health and science.

or trade apprenticeship. Level 4 jobs require university education. The table shows the distribution across skill levels of immigrants and the native born who have a university degree. Immigrants arriving in Canada before 1981 are distributed across the skill levels in a manner very similar to the Canadian-born population. Seventy-three percent of Canadian-born men with a university degree are working in jobs that require that degree. The same pro-

Table 2.12 Skill Levels of Jobs of University Graduates 25 to 64 Years of Age by Gender and Immigration Status, 1996

	Skill Levels (percent)			
Gender/Status	*Level 1*	*Level 2*	*Level 3*	*Level 4*
Women				
Canadian born	1	14	15	69
Entered before 1981	2	17	17	64
Entered 1981–1990	5	27	19	49
Entered 1991–1996	11	34	18	37
Men				
Canadian born	2	10	15	73
Entered before 1981	2	10	15	73
Entered 1981–1990	4	16	18	61
Entered 1991–1996	9	20	18	53

Source: Informetrica Limited, *Canada's Recent Immigrants: A Comparative Portrait Based on the 1996 Census* (Ottawa: Citizenship and Immigration Canada, 2001), 64.
Note: Some of the rows do not add up exactly to 100 percent due to rounding.

portion of immigrant men admitted before 1981 and possessing a university degree are working in these occupations. This proportion drops to 53 percent among immigrant men with a university degree arriving between 1991 and 1996. The pattern is roughly the same for females.

In terms of labor-force participation, then, immigrants overall participate at rates similar to the native born. Earlier immigrants participate at levels that exceed that of the Canadian-born population while more recent arrivals have lower levels of participation. Earlier arrivals also have more prestigious jobs that are more in keeping with their skills than do later arrivals. The labor-force performance of immigrants who have been in Canada for a longer time appears to equal or exceed that of the native population.

The income levels of immigrants and native-born Canadians in table 2.13 show the same patterns as labor-force participation. Immigrants who have resided in Canada for longer periods have incomes that equal or exceed those of the native population. More recent arrivals have lower incomes than native-born Canadians and the more recent the immigration the lower the income.

Immigration is often linked to the issue of dependency and government transfer payments. When immigrants do not participate in the labor force or do not earn sufficient income when they do work, then the government is forced to support them. In Canada, however, the proportion of income coming from government transfer payments is not radically different for the immigrant and native-born population. Eleven percent of the income of native-born men with income comes from government transfers and about 12 percent of the income of immigrant men comes from this source. For women, the comparable figures are 18 and 19 percent.[38]

Table 2.13 Level of Income by Gender and Immigration Status, 1996

Gender/Status	*Average Income ($)*
Women	
Canadian born	19,300
Entered before 1981	21,500
Entered 1981–1990	16,600
Entered 1991–1996	12,200
Men	
Canadian born	31,300
Entered before 1981	35,800
Entered 1981–1990	25,300
Entered 1991–1996	18,600

Source: Informetrica Limited, *Canada's Recent Immigrants: A Comparative Portrait Based on the 1996 Census* (Ottawa: Citizenship and Immigration Canada, 2001), 68.

While these simple descriptive statistics suggest that immigrants in Canada do not pose a dependency problem, much more complex treatment of this issue is required. For example, dependency among the elderly is not as worrisome as dependency among the working-age population. Similarly, outlays in the form of transfers must be weighed against the contributions that immigrant and native populations make to government revenues. In "The Impact of Immigration on Canada's Treasury, circa 1990," Ather H. Akbari examines this issue more complexly.[39] He compares the sources and average incomes of immigrant and nonimmigrant households in 1990.

Column 4 in table 2.14 shows that the labor-market earnings of all the 1946–1985 cohort of immigrant households exceeded those of native-born households. Table 2.15 shows that the total taxes paid by immigrants from 1946 exceeded those paid by nonimmigrants except for the 1981–1985 cohort of immigrants.

Finally, Akbari shows in table 2.16 that in 1990, all households, including those headed by postwar immigrants as well as those headed by native-born Canadians, paid more in taxes than they consumed in public services. He concludes "these results contradict the common belief that immigrants impose a cost on Canadian taxpayers."[40]

Criminal Involvement

Going back almost half a century, T. J. Samual and R. Taustino-Santos report that between 1951 and 1954 the native-born crime rate was twice as high as that of the foreign-born rate.[41] Specifically, for every 10,000 native-born males between fourteen and forty-nine years of age, an average of 86.6 native-born persons were convicted, compared to an average of 42.8 foreign born. Between 1966 and 1969, when immigrants represented between 3.1 and 4.3 percent of the population, they accounted for between 1.5 and 2.2 percent of the crimes committed. Samual and Taustino-Santos also report that incarceration and recidivism rates were lower for immigrants than for native born. As recently as 1986, they report that theft, assault, and vice "remained the most common types of offenses" for the foreign born.

In 1989 and again in 1991, random surveys were conducted of inmates in federal prisons who had been sentenced for two or more years. In the 1989 survey, 10.3 percent were foreign born and in 1991 11.9 percent were foreign born.[42] During both periods, the percentage of foreign born in the Canadian population was 18.9. In the 1991 survey, over 22 percent of the foreign born in the federal prisons were not naturalized Canadian citizens or landed immigrants. They were illegal immigrants, refugees, temporary visa

Table 2.14 Income by Sources, Average Immigrant, and Nonimmigrant Households, Canada, 1990

Immigrants' Year of Entry	*Wages and Salaries (1)*	*Self-Employment Income (2)*	*Military Pay and Allowances (3)*	*Total Household Earnings*[a] *(4)*	*Investment Income (5)*	*Retirement and Annuities (6)*	*Government Transfers (7)*	*Other Money Income (8)*	*Total Household Income*[b] *(9)*
Cohorts relevant to this analysis									
1946–1955	28,950	3,530	151	32,631	4,837	3,462	6,784	799	48,513
1956–1965	37,810	3,976	83	41,869	3,672	1,377	4,847	1,147	52,912
1966–1970	44,210	3,111	45	47,366	2,150	515	3,404	530	53,965
1971–1975	36,005	1,527	61	37,593	1,759	488	3,962	463	44,265
1976–1980	33,843	3,335	0	37,178	1,276	439	3,855	214	42,962
1981–1985	32,012	2,112	0	34,124	871	253	3,273	623	39,144
Cohorts not relevant to this analysis[c]									
Before 1946	7,340	1,229	5	8,574	7,441	3,740	10,716	593	31,064
1986–1991	22,265	1,014	54	23,333	3,657	483	2,934	348	30,755
Nonimmigrants	29,822	2,199	186	32,207	2,370	1,470	4,755	411	41,213

Source: Ather H. Akbari, "The Impact of Immigrants on Canada's Treasury, circa 1990," in *Diminishing Returns: The Economics of Canada's Recent Immigration Policy,* ed. D. J. DeVoretz (Toronto: C. D. Howe Institute, 1995), 120.

[a]The sum of columns 1 through 3.

[b]The sum of columns 4 through 8.

[c]Data not comparable to other rows in the table; the low income of the cohort before 1946 is due to their age; the year span 1986–1991 reflects a shorter stay in Canada.

Table 2.15 Taxes Paid, Average Immigrant and Nonimmigrant Households, Canada, 1990

	Taxes Other Than Income Taxes Based on Earnings				*Taxes Other Than Income Taxes Based on Income*			
Immigrants' Year of Entry	*Household Earnings (1)*	*Income Tax (2)*	*Other Taxes (3)*	*Total Taxes (4)*	*Household Earnings[a] (5)*	*Income Tax (6)*	*Other Taxes[b] (7)*	*Total Taxes (8)*
Cohorts relevant to this analysis								
1946–1955	32,632	9,220	12,299	21,519	48,513	9,220	14,263	23,483
1956–1965	41,870	10,793	15,781	26,574	52,910	10,793	15,555	26,348
1966–1970	47,366	11,421	17,852	29,273	53,966	11,421	15,866	27,287
1971–1975	37,593	8,187	14,169	22,356	44,265	8,187	13,014	21,201
1976–1980	37,178	7,922	14,012	21,934	42,962	7,922	12,631	20,553
1981–1985	34,125	7,674	12,862	20,536	39,144	7,674	11,508	19,182
Cohorts not relevant[c]								
Before 1946	8,575	4,899	3,232	8,131	31,065	4,899	9,133	14,032
1986–1991	23,333	5,545	8,794	14,339	30,755	5,545	9,042	14,587
Nonimmigrants	32,127	8,166	12,109	20,275	41,133	8,166	12,093	20,259

Source: Ather H. Akbari, "The Impact of Immigrants on Canada's Treasury, circa 1990," in *Diminishing Returns: The Economics of Canada's Recent Immigration Policy,* ed. D. J. DeVoretz (Toronto: C. D. Howe Institute, 1995), 122.

[a]37.7 percent of household earnings; discrepancies in dollar amounts result from rounding.

[b]29.4 percent of household income.

[c]Data not comparable to other rows in table.

Table 2.16 Net Public Treasury Effect of Immigration on Nonimmigrant Households, Canada, 1990

	Taxes Other Than Income Taxes Based on Earnings					*Taxes Other Than Income Taxes Based on Income*				
Immigrants' Year of Entry	*Taxes Paid (1)*	*Services Consumed (2)*	*Balance[a] (3)*	*Contributed for Public Goods[c] (4)*	*Net Effect (5)*	*Taxes Paid (6)*	*Services Consumed (7)*	*Balance[b] (8)*	*Contributed for Public Goods[c] (9)*	*Net Effect (10)*
Cohorts relevant to this analysis										
1946–1955	21,519	13,057	8,462	1,216	495	23,483	13,057	10,426	1,215	1,484
1956–1965	26,574	10,830	15,744	1,216	6,787	26,438	10,830	15,608	1,215	6,576
1966–1970	29,273	9,518	19,755	1,216	10,798	27,287	9,518	17,769	1,215	8,827
1971–1975	22,356	10,510	11,846	1,216	2,889	21,201	10,510	10,691	1,215	1,749
1976–1980	21,934	11,014	10,920	1,216	1,963	20,553	11,014	9,539	1,215	597
1981–1985	20,536	8,930	11,606	1,216	2,649	19,182	8,930	10,252	1,215	1,310
Nonimmigrants	20,275	10,102	10,173	—	—	20,259	10,102	10,157	—	—

Source: Ather H. Akbari, "The Impact of Immigrants on Canada's Treasury, circa 1990," in *Diminishing Returns: The Economics of Canada's Recent Immigration Policy,* ed. D. J. DeVoretz (Toronto: C. D. Howe Institute, 1995), 124.

[a]Column 1 minus column 2.

[b]Column 6 minus column 7.

[c]Computed as 6 percent of taxes paid by natives; nonimmigrants.

holders, and/or tourists. The largest group among them was from the United States, followed by Japan.

The most common types of major offenses for which the foreign born were incarcerated in 1991 were narcotics, robbery, murder, sex offenses, and conspiracy—in this order. For most Canadian born, on the other hand, the major offenses were robbery, murder, breaking and entering, sex offenses, and narcotics. About a third of those imprisoned for narcotics offenses were foreign born, as were approximately a quarter of those held for conspiracy. Both indicate an overrepresentation. But on the whole, for a period of some forty years, immigrants in Canada have had a lower rate of criminality than the native born.

Public Opinion

Given the positive position and role that the Canadian government has assumed vis-à-vis immigration, the results of national surveys on public attitudes toward immigration is somewhat puzzling. Table 2.17, for example, illustrates the responses to the following question that was asked in ten national polls from 1975 to 1993.

Over an almost twenty-year span, only 17 percent of the Canadian public at most favored increasing immigration and between 32 and 55 percent favored decreasing the number of immigrants permitted to enter. For the last three years of the survey, more respondents favored decreasing the number of immigrants admitted than maintaining the current levels.

In 1993, a poll asked Canadian citizens: "How do you view the increase in the number of immigrants arriving in Canada from Asia, the West Indies, and other mainly Third World countries?" Only 20 percent of respondents viewed immigration favorably. Others answered that immigration was very bad, bad, or simply a fact of life. Older respondents and less educated respondents were most likely to view it as bad or very bad.

But when asked in 1995 whether they agreed or disagreed with the statement "Immigrants increase crime rates," only 20 percent strongly agreed or agreed, compared to 53 percent who disagreed or strongly disagreed. Twenty-four percent said they neither agreed nor disagreed. The Canadian respondents were more likely to disagree with the observation about immigrants increasing crime than were respondents in the United States, Australia, Great Britain, and most especially Germany and Japan. Most respondents in these nations see a positive correlation between immigrants and crime.

When asked about granting "landed immigrant status without penalty" to persons who entered Canada illegally, public opinion shifted dramatically

Table 2.17 Should Canadian Immigration Be Kept at Its Present Level, Increased, or Decreased?

If it were your job to plan an immigration policy for Canada, at this time would you be inclined to increase immigration, decrease immigration, or to keep the number of immigrants at about the current level?

Response	Years										
Categories	*1975*	*1980*	*1982*	*1985*	*1987*	*1988*	*1989*	*1990*	*1991*	*1992*	*1993*
Increase	10	7	8	14	13	14	14	17	14	13	11
Decrease	39	42	55	42	41	41	34	32	45	46	45
Same level	43	44	35	38	42	42	47	46	38	37	40
Don't know	8	7	3	6	4	3	6	5	4	4	4

Source: American Institute of Public Opinion (Storrs: Roper Center, University of Connecticut, 1993).
Note: Some of the columns do not add up exactly to 100 percent due to rounding.

from an earlier, largely positive view to a largely negative one as demonstrated in three national polls conducted between 1983 and 1989:

	Approve	*Disapprove*	*Don't know*
1983	62	30	8
1988	31	62	7
1989	33	60	7

Source: American Institute of Public Opinion (Storrs: Roper Center, University of Connecticut, 1993).

On the matter of taking in refugees, most Canadians also believe that their country is doing *more* than its share, compared to other countries. When polled in 1986 and 1989, 72 and 74 percent, respectively, thought Canada was doing more than its share. Also during those years, most Canadians (58 and 59 percent, respectively) thought Canada should accept fewer refugees than its policies allowed (17 percent favored "no change" and 18 to 21 percent supported accepting "more" refugees). Thus, public opinion does not appear to be consistent with the government's proimmigration policy. Especially now, with the changing racial and ethnic characteristics of the "new immigrants," public support might decline further and ultimately result in more restrictive immigration policies by the Canadian government.

Summary

Like Australia and the United States, Canada is one of the major immigrant receiving nations of the world. As of 1991, immigrants made up 16 percent of the Canadian population. A point system initially introduced in 1967 and revised most recently in 1996 operationalizes the government's intent to increase immigration levels through economic and family preference and to provide refuge for persons who have been forced to flee their native country. In 1977, the waiting period for citizenship was shortened from five to three years.

The flow of immigrants to Canada has become increasingly diverse. In 1946, the vast majority of immigrants came from Europe and North America, but as of 1991 more than half, or 53 percent, of the immigrants arriving in Canada came from Asia. Nonetheless, immigrants appear to be highly integrated into Canadian society. Two-thirds of all immigrants were married. The immigrants' educational level demonstrated that more immigrants than native born held university degrees (14 percent versus 11 percent) and more immigrants than native born have less than a ninth-grade education. Sixty-five percent of the immigrants were in the labor force, mostly in a managerial level, technical category, or skilled trade. Immigrants who arrived in Canada between 1946 and 1985 reported higher earnings than did nonimmigrants and paid more in taxes.

Even on matters of lifestyle choices, immigrants seem to be very similar to native-born Canadians. The fertility rate of immigrants, for example, is very similar to that of Canadian women. Nearly all immigrants have facility in one of the two official languages of the host country.

Canada's pattern of criminal involvement by immigrants is similar to that of the United States and Australia. In all three countries, immigrant involvement in crime is lower than that of the native born. The Canadian government, however, takes a more active role than the U.S. government in facilitating the integration of immigrants and refugees through language training and classes, counseling services, a host family program, social welfare benefits, and, for refugees, an income support program. In almost every respect, then, Canada has been able and willing to absorb immigrants.

But while the Canadian government may take a proimmigrant stance, the Canadian public shares much the same opinion about the current cohort of immigrants as does the American public. It is wary of immigration's impact on Canadian society. Over the past eighteen years, by a ratio of four to one, more Canadians believe the number of immigrants admitted to their country should be decreased rather than increased. In 1993, only 20 percent thought that the increase in immigrants from Asia, the West Indies, and other mainly Third World countries was beneficial to their country. The Canadian public's view about immigrants is not only similar to that of the United States and Australia, but it is also similar to countries with little or no history of welcoming immigrants to their shores.

Notes

1. Freda Hawkins, *Canada and Immigration: Public Policy and Public Concern* (Kingston, Ontario: McGill-Queens University Press, 1988).
2. Hawkins, *Canada and Immigration*.
3. Citizenship and Immigration Canada, *Forging Our Legacy: Canadian Citizenship and Immigration, 1900–1977* (Ottawa: Citizenship and Immigration Canada, 2001).
4. Citizenship and Immigration Canada, *Forging Our Legacy*.
5. Manuel Gracia y Griego, "Canada: Flexibility and Control in Immigration and Refugee Policy," in *Controlling Immigration: A Global Perspective*, ed. Wayne Cornelius, Philip Martin, and James F. Hollifield (Stanford, Calif.: Stanford University Press, 1994).
6. Citizenship and Immigration Canada, *Highlights into the 21st Century: A Strategy for Immigration and Citizenship* (Ottawa: Citizenship and Immigration Canada, 1994).

7. Maurice Anderson et al., "Canada," in *International Immigration and Nationality Law: Immigration Supplement 2,* ed. Dennis Campbell and Joy Fisher (Boston: Nijhoff, 1993).

8. Freda Hawkins, *Critical Years in Immigration: Canada and Australia Compared* (Montreal: McGill-Queens University Press, 1989).

9. Informetrica Limited, *Canada's Recent Immigrants: A Comparative Portrait Based on the 1996 Census* (Ottawa: Citizenship and Immigration Canada, 2001).

10. Alexander M. Carr-Saunders, *World Population: Past Growth and Present Trends* (Oxford: Clarendon, 1936).

11. Citizenship and Immigration Canada, *Facts and Figures: 1997 Immigration Overview* (Ottawa: Citizenship and Immigration Canada, 1998).

12. Citizenship and Immigration Canada, *Facts and Figures: 2000 Immigration Overview* (Ottawa: Citizenship and Immigration Canada, 2001).

13. "Designated Refugees" refers to groups designated by the Canadian government on the basis of humanitarian considerations. These classes are designated by standing orders from the House of Commons. These classes do not need to establish that they fall within the definition of convention refugee. "Convention Refugees" refers to persons who are outside of their native country and cannot return because of a well-founded fear of persecution when returning to that country. This definition is adopted from the UN Convention regarding the Status of Refugees (1954).

14. Citizenship and Immigration Canada, *Facts and Figures: 2000 Immigration Overview.*

15. Anderson et al., "Canada."

16. Anderson et al., "Canada."

17. Citizenship and Immigration Canada, *Facts and Figures: 1997 Immigration Overview.*

18. Informetrica Limited, *Canada's Recent Immigrants.*

19. Informetrica Limited, *Canada's Recent Immigrants.*

20. Citizenship and Immigration Canada, *A Profile of Immigrants in Canada* (Ottawa: Citizenship and Immigration Canada, 1998).

21. Goss Gilroy, Inc., *Evaluation Framework of Immigrant Settlement and Adaption Program* (Ottawa: Citizenship and Immigration Canada, 2000).

22. Goss Gilroy, Inc., *Evaluation Framework of Immigrant Settlement.*

23. Goss Gilroy, Inc., *Evaluation Framework for Host Program* (Ottawa: Citizenship and Immigration Canada, 2000).

24. Goss Gilroy, Inc., *Performance Framework for the Language Instruction for Newcomers to Canada Program* (Ottawa: Citizenship and Immigration Canada, 2000).

25. Goss Gilroy, Inc., *Evaluation Framework for Immigrant Settlement.*

26. Citizenship and Immigration Canada, *Facts and Figures: 2000 Immigration Overview.*

27. Informetrica Limited, *Canada's Recent Immigrants.*

28. Informetrica Limited, *Canada's Recent Immigrants,* 24.

29. Informetrica Limited, *Canada's Recent Immigrants.*

30. Informetrica Limited, *Canada's Recent Immigrants.*

31. Informetrica Limited, *Canada's Recent Immigrants.*

32. Informetrica Limited, *Canada's Recent Immigrants,* 40.

33. Citizenship and Immigration Canada, *Facts and Figures: 2000 Immigration Overview.*

34. Informetrica Limited, *Canada's Recent Immigrants.*

35. Informetrica Limited, *Canada's Recent Immigrants.*

36. Citizenship and Immigration Canada, *Facts and Figures: 2000 Immigration Overview.*

37. Informetrica Limited, *Canada's Recent Immigrants.*

38. Informetrica Limited, *Canada's Recent Immigrants,* 68.

39. Ather H. Akbari, "The Impact of Immigration on Canada's Treasury, circa 1990," in *Diminishing Returns: The Economics of Canada's Recent Immigration Policy,* ed. D. J. DeVoretz (Toronto: C. D. Howe Institute, 1995), 30.

40. Akbari, "Impact of Immigration," 30.

41. T. J. Samual and R. Faustino-Santos, "Canadian Immigrants and Criminality," *International Migration* 29, no. 1 (1990): 53.

42. Samual and Faustino-Santos, "Canadian Immigrants and Criminality."

3

Immigration in Australia

With the exception of perhaps Israel, Australia is unique in the world in terms of its sheer volume of immigration per capita. Approximately one-quarter of Australia's population is foreign born. It is no accident, however, that Australia has encouraged immigration as a means of populating its vast continent. The country has accommodated the potential social disruption attendant to this influx in a number of ways. Initially, Australia restricted those who could enter the country based on race and country of origin. Later, Australia's immigration policy eliminated restrictions based on ascriptive characteristics and retained or extended restrictions based on language proficiency and other achieved characteristics. These policies resulted in an increase in the diversity of immigrants entering Australia, but at the same time increased the proportion of arrivals with the ability to integrate quickly into Australian society. These abilities included language facility, job skills, and family. This combination of homogeneity within diversity seems to have allowed Australia to absorb or integrate its massive and increasingly diverse immigrant population smoothly and relatively rapidly and with little of the negative social consequences observed in other countries. Nonetheless, there are signs that anti-immigrant sentiment is growing and that future immigration policies may be more restrictive than in the past.

Historical Background

When Australia was first settled by the British around 1787, the continent was inhabited by approximately 300,000 Aborigines and 1,000 settlers.[1] This population was spread over an area of three million square miles. The British were eager to increase the population and tried a number of policies to attract settlers including the infamous transportation policies (Australia was used as a penal colony) of the late eighteenth and early nineteenth centuries. Inducements for immigration also figured prominently in government policies after the colonial period. Consequently, immigration has been a major source of population increase for Australia throughout its history.

From 1788 to 2000, the population of Australia grew from some 300,000 to 18.9 million.[2] About 35 percent of that growth was from immigration and 65 percent from natural increase. Table 3.1 describes immigration growth up to 1921.

From 1920 to 1929, the net gain from immigration was 349,000. The worldwide depression, followed by World War II, brought immigration almost to a halt. But with the end of the war, immigration, as shown in table 3.2, increased sharply.

Between 1945 and 1990, about five million immigrants settled in Australia.[3] Some two million of them were assisted by the Australian government in the form of payments for the cost of their passage.[4] The practice of providing passage assistance to immigrants has been a staple of Australian immigration policy and about half of the 2.5 million settlers who came to Australia before 1939 were assisted by payment of their passage and other services. In the decade between 1982 and 1992, Australia had a net gain of 846,800 immigrants.

Table 3.1 Net Immigration and Population Growth, Australia, 1788–1920 (in thousands)

Years	*Population at End of Period*	*Increase during Period*	*New Immigration*
1788–1801	12	12	10
1812–1821	35	23	18
1822–1831	76	41	30
1832–1841	221	145	116
1842–1851	438	217	143
1852–1861	1,168	730	554
1788–1861	—	1,168	871
1862–1871	1,701	533	185
1872–1881	2,307	606	209
1882–1891	3,241	934	361
1892–1901	3,825	584	1
1902–1911	4,574	749	112
1912–1921	5,511	937	151
1862–1921	—	4,343	1,019

Source: Herbert London, *Non-White Immigration and the "White Australia" Policy* (New York: New York University Press, 1971).

Table 3.2 Net Immigration by Periods, Annual Averages

Annual Average	*1947–1950*	*1951–1960*	*1961–1970*	*1971–1980*	*1981–1990*	*1991–1999*
To Australia	95,104	117,408	133,964	95,676	99,163	85,900
From Australia	NA	NA	−22,773	−32,228	−19,980	−29,600
Net Total	110,361	78,234	111,191	63,448	79,183	56,300

Sources: Jing Shu et al., *Australia's Population Trends and Prospects, 1990* (Canberra: Australian Government Publishing Service, 1991), 28; Department of Immigration and Multi-cultural Affairs, *DIMA Fact Sheet 2* (Canberra: Department of Immigration and Multi-cultural Affairs, 2000).

As of June 1996, Australia's foreign-born population was approximately 23 percent of the total population. Among the foreign born, about 27 percent came from Britain and Ireland, 26 percent from other European countries, and 20 percent from Asia.

Major Legislation

Prior to 1901, Australia's regulation of immigration was quite minimal. During the transportation era (1788–1852), Australia had no problem regulating the flow of persons into the country.[5] As transportation declined, however, and the need for labor was filled by nonprisoners, other mechanisms for attracting immigrants were required. Distance and the cost of passage meant that the bulk of immigration was assisted in some form by the government. The exact form of assistance varied from paying for full or partial passage to providing free land to those who paid their own way. In essence, immigration could be controlled by focusing on assistance rather than changing laws and regulations governing admission and residence. Assisted immigration began in 1831 and was a prominent feature of Australian immigration policy until 1982. An estimated one million assisted immigrants were induced to Australia between 1931 and 1947 and an additional two million came between 1947 and 1982.[6] Prior to 1947, assistance was given only to British applicants (and to the Irish after 1921), but after 1947 assistance was also given to non-British, European applicants. Until the mid-1960s, Australia's assistance policy was a powerful tool for keeping its immigrant population mostly British and white.

Laws Governing Admissions

The extent and scope of immigration laws and regulations increased over time as the volume and nature of unassisted immigration changed. The first major nationwide legislation on immigration was passed in 1901.[7] The Immigration Restriction Act of 1901 prohibited the following persons from entering Australia:

1. Any person who, when asked to do so by an officer, fails to write out at dictation and sign in the presence of an officer a passage of fifty words in a European language directed by the officer
2. Any person in the opinion of the Minister or of an officer who is likely to become a charge upon the public or upon any public or charitable institution
3. Any idiot or insane person

4. Any person suffering from an infectious or contagious disease of a loathsome or dangerous character
5. Any person who has within three years been convicted of an offense, not being a mere political offense, and has been sentenced to imprisonment for one year or longer therefore, and has not received a pardon
6. Any prostitute or person living on the prostitution of others
7. Any person under contract or agreement to perform manual labor within the Commonwealth except for workmen exempted by the Minister[8]

This law was the legal foundation of Australian immigration policy from its passage in 1901 until 1949. Largely through the "dictation test" stipulated in section 1, the act afforded broad discretion to immigration authorities in determining who would be allowed to enter Australia and who would be allowed to remain. Immigration officers were free to select who would be required to take the dictation test, as well as the language in which they would be required to demonstrate proficiency. The 1903 instructions to officers regarding the test were as follows: "In administering the Immigration Restriction Act which is now in force, it will be necessary to use great care that no undesirable immigrants shall be permitted to enter the Commonwealth. . . . It must be understood that the law does not insist that every intending immigrant should be asked (to take the dictation test); and in the selection of those to whom the test is to be applied, tact and judgment will have to be exercised."[9]

These instructions stipulated further that: "The English language will be the one that will be most generally adopted for the purpose of the test, but if in the opinion of the officer, the immigrant is likely to pass a test in that language and at the same time would, for reasons that the officer would be prepared to state, be an undesirable immigrant, it may be better to adopt a passage from another language. The choice of the language will be left to your discretion."[10]

While there was some variation in the use of the substantial discretion accorded immigration authorities, it was used largely to exclude non-European immigrants and particularly nonwhites. Immigration officers were instructed that "all aboriginal inhabitants of Africa, Asia and Polynesia should be subjected to the test unless otherwise exempted. In the case of White races, the test will be applied only under special circumstances."[11]

The dictation test also served as a method of maintaining control of immigrant populations even after admission, due to changes in the period after admission during which immigrants could be required to take the test. Initially, immigrants were given the dictation test on arrival. This practice was altered in 1905 such that foreigners entering Australia could be required to take the test up to one year after entry. This limit was subsequently raised to three years and then to five years. But at any time during that five-year period, immigration officials could require the dictation test and, if the immigrant failed that test, he or she would be declared a prohibited immigrant. Once this occurred, he or she could be imprisoned for six months and then deported. Immigrants could be spared the dictation test, however, if they obtained a certificate of exemption that was granted and revoked at the discretion of immigration authorities.

In 1958, the vehicle that afforded control over immigrant populations changed from the dictation test to the entry permit. Immigrants could not enter Australia without an entry permit.[12] These permits were issued by the immigration authorities and were of two types: permanent and temporary. Permanent entry permits made the holder eligible for permanent residence status, while temporary permits did not. Also, temporary permits could be canceled by the minister of immigration at his or her discretion.

In 1979, Australia established a Numerical Assessment System as part of its immigration policy.[13] The system divided potential immigrants into four categories: family reunion, general eligibility, refugees, and special eligibility. In 1982, the Migrant Selection System was revised into five categories:

1. Family migration
   Applicants are nominated by close relatives who are residents in Australia. Family migration has three such categories:
   a. Spouses, fiancé(e)s, and dependent children
   b. Parents and aged, close relatives
   c. Nondependent children and brothers and sisters
2. Labor shortage and business
   This category includes people with occupations in demand, those with special business skills, and those with skills in short supply and who have been nominated by an employer.
3. Independent
   This category was introduced to ensure that the emphasis on family migration and labor demand migration did not prevent the entry of other people of obvious benefit to Australia. This includes people who have outstanding achievement in an occupation that is not necessarily in demand. In 1982–1983, this was the smallest of all eligibility categories.
4. Refugees
   Refugee policy has been a component of Australian immigration programs since 1947. Between 1947 and 1985, over 400,000 refugees and displaced persons were admitted.
5. Special Eligibility
   The government recognized that there are certain people who should for various reasons be admitted to Australia irrespective of whether they fit one of the categories already discussed. People with special

creative or sporting talents, self-supporting retirees, and children born overseas to Australian citizens are included.

Table 3.3 provides a description of the number of persons to be admitted under each category.

Australia revised its system again in 1991–1992. The current immigration program is divided into three main components: family, skill, and humanitarian migration.[14] The Family Migration component of the program has two categories. The Preferential Family category allows for the immigration of parents, spouses, fiancé(e)s, and dependent children of Australian residents. Intending immigrants in this category are not subject to points testing on English language or occupational skills. Other family members such as siblings, adult children, and nieces or nephews can apply to immigrate under the Concessional Family category. Selection in this category is based on a points test.

The Skill Migration component of the program includes the Employer Nomination Scheme, Business Skills, Distinguished Talent, and an Independent

Table 3.3 Eligibility Components and Categories of Settler Arrivals, 1990–1991 and 1991–1992

	1990–1991		*1991–1992*	
	No.	*Percent*	*No.*	*Percent*
Family Migration	53,934	44.4	48,621	45.3
Preferential				
Spouses/fiancé(e)s	17,148	14.1	16,269	15.1
Parent	10,667	8.8	7,422	6.9
Other	3,597	3.0	3,605	3.4
Concessional	22,522	18.5	21,325	19.9
Skill Migration	49,515	40.7	43,828	40.9
Employer nominees	6,651	5.5	3,663	3.4
Business migration	8,118	6.7	6,444	6.0
Distinguished talent	148	0.1	67	0.1
Independent	33,504	27.5	30,160	28.1
Humanitarian	7,745	6.4	7,157	6.7
Special Eligibility	11,588	9.4	11,279	10.5
Visaed	976	0.8	1,403	1.3
Nonvisaed	8,338	6.9	8,201	7.6
New Zealand citizens				
Other	2,274	1.9	1,675	1.6
Total	115,688	94.7	103,728	96.7
Total visaed	111,076	91.3	97,515	90.8
Total nonvisaed	3,961	3.4	6,213	5.9

Source: Jing Shu and Siew Ean Khoo, *Australia's Population Trends and Prospects, 1992* (Canberra: Australian Government Publishing Service, 1993).

category. Applicants in the Independent category have to meet a minimum number of points based on age, work skills, and English-language proficiency. Business Skills applicants are assessed on their business skills and experience as well as their potential interest in Australia.

The Humanitarian component of the program allows for resettlement in Australia of persons who meet the *UN Definition of Refugees*. It also has provisions for persons who do not qualify for refugee status to be granted permanent residence on broader humanitarian grounds. For example, a Special Assistance category was established in the 1991–1992 program to assist designated groups of people who are severely affected by violence and civil unrest within their own countries and/or who are seriously disadvantaged or suppressed minorities.

The major changes introduced into the 1991–1992 program are as follows (see table 3.4). First, Australia abolished its Business Migration Program (BMP) and replaced it with a new Independent Business Skills category. The new category differs from the BMP in that potential business immigrants will be tested for English-language proficiency and business skills. Points are awarded for age, English-language proficiency, the size of the business owned or managed, and the possession of capital available for transfer to Australia.

Table 3.4 Program Planning Levels, 1991–1992 and 1992–1993

Program Component	*1991–1992*[a]	*1992–1993*[a]	*Percentage of Change*
Family Migration			
Preferential Component	27.2	23.8	−12.5
Concessional	21.3	8.2	−61.5
Total Family	48.5	32.0	−34.0
Skill Migration			
Employer Nomination/ Labor Agreements	3.7	2.0	−45.9
Business Skills	6.4	3.6	−43.8
Distinguished Talent	0.07	0.08	14.3
Independent	30.2	16.5	−45.4
Total Skill	40.5	22.0	−45.7
Refugee, Humanitarian, and Special Assistance			
Refugee and Humanitarian	7.2	11.0	52.8
Special Assistance	1.4	1.1	−21.4
Total Refugee, Humanitarian, and Special Assistance	10.0	11.1	11.0
Total Program	97.5	66.3	−32.0

Source: Jing Shu et al., *Australia's Population Trends and Prospects, 1993* (Canberra: Australian Government Printing Service, 1994), 27; Department of Immigration, Local Government, and Ethnic Affairs.

[a]In thousands.

Next, in April 1992 the minister for immigration, local government, and ethnic affairs announced that there would be 80,000 places in the 1992–1993 immigration program, a reduction of 31,000 from the 110,000 places in 1991–1992. The program would provide 45,000 places for Family Migration, 23,800 for Skill Migration, 10,000 for those in the Refugee, Humanitarian, and Special Assistance component, and 1,200 in the Special Eligibility component. This represents a reduction of 19 percent in the Family Migration component, 44 percent in the Skill Migration component, and 17 percent in the Refugee, Humanitarian, and Special Assistance component (table 3.4). Within the Family Migration component, the cut was confined to the Concessional Family category, which was reduced by 68 percent. The Preferential Family category increased slightly by 5 percent.

The reduction in the number of places was related to the recession in the Australian economy. Also, changes occurring within the Australian economy and the associated industry restructuring were likely to make it increasingly difficult for low-skilled immigrants to find employment. Thus, the government also announced that there would be greater emphasis on more highly skilled immigrants, English-language proficiency, and matching of immigrant skills to labor-market requirements.[15]

Changes were also made in the point system for selecting Independent and Concessional Family immigrants, with greater emphasis on English-language skills.[16] The changes included an increase in the number of points needed to qualify for entry under both the categories, an increase in the number of points for occupations on the priority occupations list, and negative weighting for applicants who are medical practitioners. These changes favored potential immigrants with skills needed in the labor market. The negative weighting for applicants who are medical practitioners forms part of a national strategy to reduce the number of overseas-trained doctors immigrating to Australia.

Finally, the new program required prepayment of the cost of English-language training by principal applicants and adult dependents in the Concessional Family and Skills categories who do not have functional ability in English.[17] The number of points awarded to Independent category applicants who are proficient in English was increased. Applicants in both categories who have occupations where English is critical, such as in health and public safety, would have to be proficient in English. Principal applicants and adult dependents in the Independent, Concessional Family, and Skills Migration categories who do not have the required level of English-language skills would have to prepay the full or partial costs of language training in Australia prior to immigration.

Thus, the current Australian immigration policy is much more open than in the past. On average, since 1960 about 100,000 persons are admitted to Australia annually for the purpose of settlement. For a nation of eighteen million people, this is a considerable number of admissions. Groups are not excluded based on their ascriptive characteristics. Administrative discretion in the enforcement of restriction of admissions has also decreased. Preference categories have been established and admissions quotas or targets are set and announced. At the same time, Australia still screens immigrants in a manner that allows those with the skills to integrate more easily into Australian society. Specifically, the relative emphasis on job skills and productive capacity as opposed to family unification is consistent with the country's policy of maximizing the assimilation potential of immigrants. The same is true of language skills, another component of the point system that determines which of the applicants in each preference category will be admitted.

Naturalization

Historically, the opportunity to become a naturalized citizen of Australia was not uniformly available to immigrants. The 1901 act stipulated that naturalized citizens of the Australian states would automatically become citizens of the Australian Commonwealth. The Nationality and Citizenship Act of 1903 explicitly excluded the following from becoming naturalized citizens: "aboriginal native(s) of Asia, Africa or the Islands of the Pacific, excluding New Zealand."[18] This explicit reference to race was struck in the new Nationality Act of 1920 and replaced by language that gave immigration officials absolute discretion over the issuance of certificates of naturalization. British subjects, including citizens of Commonwealth nations, could become Australian citizens automatically. Other immigrants who were permanent residents could apply for naturalization after residing in Australia for at least two years. Prohibited immigrants—that is, anyone who could not pass the dictation test—could not become a permanent resident and therefore could not apply for naturalization. For those who did achieve permanent residence status and did apply for citizenship, the decision to grant citizenship was at the discretion of immigration authorities. This discretion was used to implement what the original statutory language dictated. In 1948, the Naturalization and Citizenship Act required that former British subjects (who would have been automatically eligible for citizenship) apply for registration to become citizens. This measure could be construed as an attempt to exert control over immigrants from the former British colonies who happen to be nonwhite.

After World War II, Australia's immigration laws and administrative policies became more accepting of non-European immigrants. For example, in 1956 the minister for immigration announced changes in policy that permitted groups of non-Europeans to enter the country and be naturalized.[19] Specifically, persons already permitted to remain in the country without obtaining periodic extensions of stay were allowed to apply for naturalization. Certain non-Europeans who were in Australia temporarily for humanitarian reasons were allowed to stay, and distinguished and highly qualified non-Europeans could be admitted for indefinite stays. The increasingly permissive policies for non-Europeans continued with the granting to non-European spouses of Australians the same qualifications for naturalization as European spouses of Australians. In 1957, Australia gave non-Europeans admitted for temporary residence the right to apply for naturalization after fifteen years of residence. These cracks in Australia's once restrictive immigration policy appeared largely as a result of the disruptions attendant to the war. Refugees and war brides were given the opportunity to enter Australia. Once they became part of the society, it became more difficult, both legally and politically, to exclude them from citizenship.

Australia's trend toward liberalizing its naturalization requirements continued. In 1966, the waiting period for non-European temporary residents before they could apply for naturalization was shortened from fifteen to five years.[20] Also, immigrants were permitted to bring their families with them at first arrival, rather than waiting to be granted permanent residence status.

The current naturalization process is also much more open than it has been in the past. There are no restrictions based on race or country of origin. Persons born in Australia before 1986 with at least one parent being an Australian citizen automatically acquire citizenship. Persons born in Australia after 1986 with at least one parent who is a citizen or a permanent resident are entitled to Australian citizenship. Persons born in Australia whose parents are not Australian citizens are not entitled to citizenship, but children who live in Australia continuously from birth for ten years can have citizenship conferred on them on their tenth birthday.

To be naturalized, applicants need only reside in Australia for two out of the previous five years, show a basic knowledge of English, and show an adequate knowledge of the responsibilities and privileges associated with Australian citizenship.[21] Basic knowledge of English is defined as enough English-language ability to be able to live in Australia and undertake activities associated with day-to-day living. This is a far cry from the earlier dictation test. The responsibilities of citizenship include voting, serving on juries, obeying the laws of the land, and defending Australia if the need arises. The letter of the law regarding naturalization suggests that becoming a citizen is quite simple.

Demographic and Socioeconomic Characteristics of Immigrants

The changes in the number and type of immigrants admitted and ultimately naturalized in Australia reflect the previously noted policy changes. As noted earlier, while levels of immigration have remained high in Australia overall, they decreased substantially in the early twentieth century from the levels observed in the mid-nineteenth century, only to rise again after World War I (see table 3.1). In the period 1852 to 1861, for example, the net increase in population due to immigration was 554,000, or an average of approximately 55,000 per year. In the period 1912 to 1921, the net increase had fallen to 151,000 or 15,000 per year. The average annual increase in population due to immigration remained below 15,000 until after World War II when the average net increase due to immigration climbed to 110,000 per year. This figure decreased to 78,000 in the 1950s but again increased to over 100,000 per annum in the late 1960s, settling at about 56,000 in the 1990s (see table 3.2). The effects of a tightened and then a loosened immigration policy are apparent.

The cumulative effect of these admissions policies has been a steady increase in the proportion of foreign born from World War II to the present. From just under 10 percent of the population in 1947, the percent of foreign born has increased to over 23 percent of the Australian population in 2000.[22]

Similarly, the effects of expanding the immigration policy to accept a more culturally diverse group of immigrants is also apparent. In the nineteenth century, the vast majority of immigrants came from Ireland and Great Britain. After World War II, the majority of immigrants (56.3 percent) came from countries in Europe other than Ireland and Great Britain. The proportion of immigrants coming from Europe increased to 64.4 percent in the period 1951–1961, only to decrease to 36.8 percent between 1961 and 1966 and 29.5 percent between 1966 and 1971 (see table 3.5). As shown in table 3.6, by 1992 only 25 percent of immigrant admissions were of European origin. The decrease in European immigration was offset by the increase in Asian immigration. In the period 1947 to 1951, only 1.6 percent of immigrants came from Asia. By the period 1966 to 1971, the figure had increased to 11.2 percent and, by 1992 50.7 percent of all immigrants came from Asia.

By the end of the 1990s, however, the composition of arriving immigrants changed again. The proportion of admissions coming from Europe stabilized at about 23 percent, the proportion from Asia decreased from about 50 percent to 32 percent and the proportion from Oceania (mostly New Zealand) increased dramatically from about 10 percent to 27 percent of arrivals. Arrivals from Africa (excluding North Africa) increased from approximately 3 percent in the early 1990s to approximately 9 percent in 1998–1999.[23]

The changes in preferences given to certain types of immigration, for example, family unification or skilled, are also reflected in the admissions data albeit imperfectly. While the distribution of admissions across categories has been volatile, the general trend has been toward lower admissions and an emphasis on skilled as opposed to family immigration. On average, throughout the period 1993 to 1998, 84,000 persons were admitted annually to Australia for settlement.[24] This is considerably less than the 110,000 and 120,000

Table 3.5 Net Immigration by Periods: Annual Averages and Percentage Distribution

	1947–1951	*1951–1961*	*1961–1966*	*1966–1971*	*1971–1973*	*Total*
British[a]	41.4	32.6	54.7	53.9	65.2	49.6
North Europe	7.5	26.3	0.8	4.9	–0.8	7.7
East Europe	37.3	5.0	6.6	13.3	7.6	14.0
South Europe	11.5	33.1	29.4	11.3	–3.5	16.4
Asia	1.6	2.3	5.2	11.2	21.2	8.3
Africa	0.1	0.2	1.5	1.5	2.8	1.2
America	0.5	0.4	1.8	3.8	7.5	2.8
Total Foreign	100.0	100.0	100.0	100.0	100.0	100.0

Source: Charles A. Price, *Australian Immigration: A Bibliography and a Digest* (Canberra: Australian National University, 1979), 8.
Note: Some of the columns do not add up to 100 percent due to rounding.
[a]Commonwealth countries in Africa and America are included with British.

Table 3.6 Birthplace of Settler Arrivals by Regions, 1989–1999

	1989–1990		*1990–1991*		*1991–1992*		*1998–1999*	
	No.	*Percent*	*No.*	*Percent*	*No.*	*Percent*	*No.*	*Percent*
Oceania	15,270	12.6	10,973	9.0	10,362	9.6	22,501	26.7
Europe and former USSR	38,386	31.7	32,333	26.6	26,870	25.0	19,608	23.3
Middle East and North Africa	5,754	4.7	7,154	5.9	7,021	6.5	5,195	6.2
Southeast Asia	28,201	23.3	29,417	24.2	22,325	20.8	10,934	12.9
Northeast Asia	16,395	13.5	22,100	18.2	21,473	20.0	10,869	13.2
Southern Asia	6,011	5.0	9,389	7.7	10,594	9.9	5,316	6.3
North America	3,015	2.5	2,811	2.3	2,570	2.4	1,624	1.9
South America	4,125	3.4	3,745	3.1	3,308	3.1	773	0.9
Africa excluding North Africa	4,061	3.3	3,734	3.1	2,823	2.6	7,246	8.6
Not Stated	9	0.0	32	0.0	45	0.0	NA	
Total	121,227		121,688		107,346		84,111	

Sources: Jing Shu et al., *Australia's Population Trends and Projections, 1992* (Canberra: Australian Government Publishing Service, 1993); Department of Immigration and Multi-cultural Affairs, *Key Facts* (Canberra: Department of Immigration and Multi-cultural Affairs, 2001).

entering in the 1980s and early 1990s. Of those admitted, 33,000 came in under the family unification category, which is less than the 45,000 targeted in 1992. Approximately 21,000 persons entered annually in the Skill Migration category, which is very close to the target of 23,000. The admissions under Humanitarian immigration was about at targeted levels, 10,000 when the target was 11,000. The largest increases occurred in the admission of New Zealanders. On average, approximately 17,000 New Zealanders were admitted annually over the period 1993 to 1998. Australia, then, has hit its targeted 84,000 admissions, a target considerably less than its historical highs of the 1980s. In hitting these targets, the expected level of admissions occurred for Skill Migration and for Humanitarian immigration. Family immigration was considerably lower than expected, presumably because of the need to offset very large increases in the admission of New Zealanders.[25]

What little data we have on the application of the naturalization law seems to suggest that the minimal naturalization requirements in Australia promote high rates of naturalization. After five years of residence, more than half of those born overseas had become Australian citizens; after twenty years, 70 percent had been granted citizenship. But the rate of naturalization varies across nationalities. Only 50 percent of the immigrants from English-speaking countries have taken up citizenship after twenty years of residence, compared to 80 to 90 percent for all other immigrant groups.[26]

Among the immigrants from non-English-speaking countries, the Lebanese have the highest estimated rate of naturalization with 87.2 percent of admissions ultimately applying for and being granted Australian citizenship.[27] They are followed by persons from the Philippines and Greece with naturalization rates of 81.6 percent and 81.3 percent, respectively, and the former Yugoslavia of 80.0 percent. Persons from Vietnam have a naturalization rate of 78 percent, followed by China (76.0 percent), Germany (58.6 percent), and the Netherlands (55.8 percent).[28] This pattern of naturalization across groups suggests that the prospect of returning and one's prospects on return to the country of origin have a great deal to do with the decision to naturalize. If it is easy or even possible to return to one's nation of origin, one is less likely to naturalize. Also, if the quality of life in the nation of origin is at least as high as it is in Australia, then one is less likely to naturalize. This pattern of naturalization is also consistent with an open naturalization policy where the choice to become a citizen is largely that of the immigrant and not the government of the host nation.

Both in policy and in practice, then, Australia has always been an immigrant nation. Its immigration policy and the composition of the immigrant population, however, have changed enormously over the last fifty years. From a policy that excluded non-British and then non-European immigrants, Australia has evolved into a nation that admits large numbers of immigrants from all over the world, immigrants that are quite different from the native population. Within this diversity, however, Australian immigration policy (to a greater extent than some other immigrant nations) includes features that give preference to applicants with the skills and resources necessary to integrate rapidly into Australian society.

Integration Policies

The Australian government plays an active, yet indirect, role in the integration of immigrants into Australian society. Persons arriving in Australia for permanent settlement are entitled to all of the social welfare benefits available to citizens.[29] In terms of special programs to assist immigrants, if we consider assisted passage a type of aid, then government assistance in integration has had a long history in Australia. If we consider assisted passage a means of regulating admissions and not assistance in integration, then active government involvement in the social integration of immigrants began during World War II. The Australian-Jewish Welfare Society was a voluntary organization that assisted the settlement of European Jewish refugees in Australia after World War II. While this group was privately financed, it did receive the official endorsement and support of the Australian government. This was the first official venture of the government into the business of immigrant settlement.[30] The absorption of European refugees after World War II led to a much more active involvement by the Australian government in the integration process. The acceptance of these refugees marked a major shift in Australian immigration policy because the majority of those coming were not from the United Kingdom and therefore had a different language and culture than previous waves of immigrants. These differences virtually demanded a more active role by the government in the settlement process.

The Australian government responded by making provision for the immediate lodging of these refugees and for massive English-language instruction. The government constructed camps to serve as areas of first settlement until the arriving refugees could find more permanent accommodations. The Australian Migrant Education Program provided English-language training. As the new arrivals left the camps to enter major cities, the responsibility for integration moved to good neighbor councils and to whatever public and private assistance was available. Good neighbor councils did not provide direct services but served as advocates for immigrants and catalysts in building services resources.

In the 1970s, the increase in unassisted immigration from southern Europe, coupled with dissatisfaction with mainstream charities organized through good neighbor councils and the rise of self-help groups, led to a broad-based dissatisfaction with existing immigration policies. This dissatisfaction resulted in a government inquiry directed by Frank Gallaby. This inquiry led to a radical restructuring of settlement policy. The new policy endorsed the principle of multiculturalism in terms of language and culture. The distribution of welfare relied on the ability of ethnic groups to provide assistance with government support and financing. Funding was withdrawn from the good neighbor councils and shifted to grant-in-aid workers and migrant resource centers. The government still funded hostels for new arrivals and adult language classes. These efforts were administered by community councils drawn from non-English-speaking immigrant organizations. In sum, the new program gave much more control of settlement to the organized entities within the immigrant communities themselves. Most of the major provisions of Gallaby's plan are still in place today.[31]

The Social Integration of Immigrants

The median age of immigrants who arrived in 1992–1993 was 27.6, compared to a median of 32.7 years for the total Australian population.[32] In 1993, 11 percent of the Australian population was sixty-five years and older as opposed to 3 percent for recent immigrants. More female than male immigrants (39,800 compared to 36,500) arrived in Australia in 1992–1993.[33]

The unemployment rate for the foreign-born Australians is not radically different from that of the native-born population (see table 3.7). In 1985, the former had an overall unemployment rate of 10 percent, while the latter had an unemployment rate of 8 percent. By 2000, the unemployment rate had declined overall and the gap between the unemployment rates of the foreign born and native born narrowed from 2 to 0.1 percent.[34] Those groups more culturally similar to Australians, for example, North Americans and Europeans, have lower unemployment rates than native-born Australians. Groups less similar culturally in terms of development, for example, Southeast Asians and Middle Easterners, to Australians have higher rates of unemployment than the natives. Immigrants from northern Asia, however, who are culturally dissimilar from Australians but similar in terms of economic development also have lower unemployment rates than native-born Australians.[35]

The rate of labor-force participation of immigrant groups does seem to be related to length of stay in the country. Foreign-born persons in the country for more than five years have an unemployment rate that is one-half that of persons in the country five years or less.[36] Time in the country substantially reduces the differences between native-born citizens and immigrants in terms of unemployment.

The types of occupations in which immigrants work do not differ drastically from those of the native-born population. About 13 percent of Australian-born males are in professional and technical occupations and about the same proportion of foreign-born males are in these occupations.

Table 3.7 Civilian Labor Force by Birthplace

	Employed		*Unemployed, Looking for Employment*			
Nation of Origin	*Full-Time*[a]	*Total*	*Full-Time*[a]	*Part-Time*[a]	*Percent Unemployed*	*Percent Employed*
Australia	3,914.0	4,810.0	360.0	61.0	8.0	60.6
Other than Australia	1400.3	1,651.9	164.0	19.7	10.0	61.9
Africa	46.0	54.0	—	—	7.1	66.7
Americas	44.0	55.0	5.4	0.7	9.9	66.2
Asia	185.0	216.0	40.2	2.5	16.5	61.7
Lebanon	20.0	22.0	8.8	0.3	29.4	56.6
Vietnam	22.0	24.0	12.0	0.3	33.9	68.2
Europe	1027.3	1213.6	8.8	14.2	8.8	60.7
Germany	56.3	67.0	4.7	0.8	7.6	62.6
Greece	69.0	76.0	4.8	1.1	7.1	61.4
Italy	128.0	148.0	10.4	0.4	6.8	58.0
Malta	31.6	34.5	—	—	—	64.3
Netherlands	45.2	55.0	4.1	0.4	7.6	60.4
Poland	22.0	24.3	—	—	—	47.6
UK/Erie	512.0	619.0	55.5	9.0	9.4	61.7
Yugoslavia	76.0	85.0	9.9	1.1	11.5	66.4
Oceania	98.0	113.0	11.8	1.7	10.6	73.5
New Zealand	81.0	94.0	9.2	0.8	9.6	74.5
Other						

Source: Ian Castles, "The Labour Force," *Australia: Historical Statistics, 1966 to 1984* (Canberra: Australian Bureau of Statistics, 1986).
Note: Excludes persons in institutions.
[a]In thousands.

The same parity exists in the categories of administrative, executive, and managerial jobs, transport and communications, service and recreation occupations, and mining and related industries. The large differences between immigrant and native-born males occur in the categories of farmers, fishermen, and timbering and in the class of laborers (see table 3.8). Almost 11 percent of Australian-born men work in farming, fishing, and timbering, compared to 4 percent of the foreign-born males. This may reflect the propensity of immigrants to settle in cities. Slightly over 38 percent of Australian-born males are laborers while 49 percent of foreign-born males are in these occupations. The large differences between Australian-born and foreign-born workers occur in manufacturing jobs, with the foreign born overrepresented in these occupations. This overrepresentation of immigrants in manufacturing occupations can be due to (among other things) differences in educational qualifications, absence of language proficiency, or discrimination.

When formal qualifications are held constant, the occupational distributions of immigrants and native-born Australians are remarkably similar (see table 3.9). Differences persist among those without formal qualifications. Here, the native born are overrepresented in the semiskilled and unskilled

Table 3.8 Occupational Distributions, Average for 1979–1983

	Males		*Females*		*Combined*	
	Native	*Foreign*	*Native*	*Foreign*	*Native*	*Foreign*
Professional/ Technical	12.75	12.82	19.59	15.22	15.31	13.64
Administrative/ Executive/ Managerial	8.83	8.83	2.47	2.47	6.45	6.64
Clerical	8.70	5.92	35.39	27.81	18.78	13.47
Sales	6.80	6.28	13.20	11.39	9.19	8.04
Farmers/ Fishermen/ Timbering	10.73	3.56	4.64	2.60	8.46	3.23
Miners/ Quarrymen	0.91	0.76	—	—	0.58	0.51
Transport/ Communication	7.63	6.02	2.21	1.67	5.60	4.52
Tradesmen/ Production/ Laborers	38.13	49.42	6.91	19.80	26.34	39.21
Service, Sport and Recreation	5.93	6.39	15.56	19.02	9.18	10.74

Source: Paul A. Inglis and Thorsten Stromback, *A Descriptive Analysis of Migrants' Labour Market Experience* (Canberra: Bureau of Labour Market Research, February 1984).
Note: Some of the columns do not add up exactly to 100 percent due to rounding.

Table 3.9 Australian and Migrant Occupational Distributions

	With Formal Qualifications		*Without Formal Qualifications*	
Occupation	*Australian Born*	*Overseas Born*	*Australian Born*	*Overseas Born*
Professional white collar	15.8	14.0	0.5	0.4
Skilled	19.8	16.9	4.3	4.4
Semiskilled and unskilled	13.6	11.9	22.3	17.3
Skilled blue collar: building	4.4	6.8	1.0	1.9
Skilled blue collar: other	14.6	17.2	3.6	4.7
Semiskilled and unskilled blue collar	9.0	10.7	17.0	23.9
Rural workers	2.7	1.0	5.5	2.2
Armed services	1.1	0.7	0.6	0.5
Other	2.4	3.3	3.4	5.4
Unemployed	2.1	3.1	4.8	5.1
Not in labor force	14.6	14.7	37.2	34.2
Total	100.0	100.0	100.0	100.0

Source: Paul A. Inglis and Thorsten Stromback, *A Descriptive Analysis of Migrants' Labour Market Experience* (Canberra: Bureau of Labour Market Research, February 1984).
Note: Some of the columns do not add up exactly to 100 percent due to rounding.

white-collar occupations (22.3 percent versus 17.3 percent) and immigrants are overrepresented in the semiskilled and unskilled blue-collar jobs (23.9 percent versus 17.0 percent). These data suggest that the differences in occupational distributions may be due to less language proficiency or discrimination. When the native born do not have the requisite educational skills, they obtain unskilled white-collar employment, while the foreign born without skills find employment in unskilled industrial work. It may well be that the newcomers do not have or are not perceived as having the social skills required to function in the service economy.

There is a substantial variance among the foreign born with regard to the occupational distribution. Specifically, refugees tend to be disproportionately employed as unskilled workers. In 1981–1982, 46.2 percent of the refugees claimed to be unskilled workers on admission as compared to 16.9 percent of those admitted under family unification and 7.6 percent of Special Eligibility immigrants.

Average weekly earnings is another indicator of the economic integration of immigrant groups. If the earnings of the foreign born approximate those of native-born Australians, then we can be reasonably sure that the foreign born are not relegated to a secondary or tertiary labor market. In 1983, the mean weekly earnings for native-born Australian males was $339 (see table 3.10). For males born in the main English-speaking countries, the average weekly salary was $373 and for males born in other countries it was $334. Taking only persons born in non-English-speaking countries then (the worst case from an integration perspective), weekly earnings for the foreign born are only 1.5 percent less than native-born workers. The pattern for females is similar by birthplace. A more recent study comparing the income of immigrants and the native born found similarly small differences between the two groups. Even these small differences disappear when the educational attainment and language fluency of immigrants is taken into account.[37] Thus, it appears that immigrants who are working for wages earn about as much as native-born workers and are not, therefore, trapped in secondary and tertiary labor markets.

The issue of entrepreneurship is often raised in debates about the economic impact of immigrants. Some allege that immigrants are more likely to be engaged in small businesses and entrepreneurship of various kinds than the native-born population is. Data from the Australian census on self-employment suggest that entrepreneurship is not substantially greater among immigrants than it is among native-born Australians. In June 1981, 10.6 percent of the Australian-born male labor force were self-employed and 9.9 percent of the foreign-born male labor force who were in the country more than five years were self-employed (see table 3.11). When comparisons are restricted to immigrants from non-English-speaking countries

Table 3.10 Mean Weekly Earnings of Full-Time Employees, by Birthplace (in dollars)

	Australia		*English-Speaking*		*Other*	
	Male	*Female*	*Male*	*Female*	*Male*	*Female*
1975	152	114	164	119	153	113
1976	173	131	188	140	174	136
1977	191	147	207	153	190	147
1978	209	162	228	173	206	163
1979	223	174	243	182	229	176
1980	249	193	269	204	246	193
1981	275	218	296	227	283	216
1982	318	244	354	258	320	251
1983	339	267	373	284	334	263

Source: Australian Bureau of Statistics, *Weekly Earnings of Employees (Distribution)* (Canberra: Bureau of Statistics, 1986).

Table 3.11 Self-Employment and Employer Status, by Sex, Birthplace, and Period of Residence, South Australia, June 1981 (percent of labor force)

	Period of Residence in Austrailia	Self-Employed		Employer	
		Males	Females	Males	Females
English-speaking countries	<1	3.2	3.0	1.1	0.3
	1 or 2	4.9	2.9	1.5	0.7
	3 or 4	5.6	2.7	3.1	1.7
	5+	6.9	4.7	3.1	2.5
Non-English-speaking countries	<1	1.3	2.6	0.2	0.6
	1 or 2	3.7	4.0	1.4	0.6
	3 or 4	4.8	5.8	4.9	4.6
	5+	13.4	0.6	6.6	4.9
Total overseas born	<1	2.4	2.9	0.7	0.7
	1 or 2	4.4	3.5	1.4	0.6
	3 or 4	5.3	4.0	3.9	2.9
	5+	9.9	7.1	4.7	3.5
Australian born		10.6	8.4	5.8	4.4

Source: Australian Bureau of Statistics, Census Table 27 (Canberra: Australian Bureau of Statistics, 1981) (microfiche).

and the native-born population, however, immigrants show greater levels of self-employment (13.4 percent of foreign-born males in the country five years or more) than the Australian-born population (10.6 percent of male labor force).

The same pattern is observed for employer status. A greater percentage of the Australian-born labor force employed others (5.8 percent) than did the foreign-born labor force (4.7 percent). These positions are reversed when comparisons are made between persons born in non-English-speaking countries and native-born Australians. The former have 6.6 percent of the male labor force as employers compared to 5.8 of the Australian-born labor force. That portion of the foreign-born labor force from non-English-speaking countries is more entrepreneurial than the native-born population, but immigrants from English-speaking countries are less so. It is important to note that the differences observed here are not substantial—only about 15 percent.

It is also interesting to note that the rates of self-employment and employer status increase according to length of time in the country. This is the case for immigrants from English-speaking and non-English-speaking countries. Immigrants from English-speaking countries have higher rates of self-employment (3.2 percent) and employer status (1.1 percent) than immigrants from non-English-speaking countries (1.3 and 0.2 percent, respectively) immediately after admission. In five years, the participation of immigrants from English-speaking countries in self-employment more than doubled, while that of immigrants from non-English-speaking countries increased thirteenfold. Lack of language facility seems to inhibit initial participation in entrepreneurship, but this is overcome relatively quickly.

Dependency

Typically, immigrants are often accused of being a drag on the host society by participating in welfare programs at higher rates than the native born. This is not the case in Australia. Overall, the overseas born have slightly lower welfare-recipient rates than do the Australian born. This parity between immigrant and the native born is often attributed to the fact that native-born populations are disproportionately pensioners, while the foreign born are disproportionately the unemployed or recipients of family assistance. This is not consistent with the fact that the foreign born have lower welfare-recipient rates than the native born across all age groups. For fifteen to twenty-four-year-olds, 16 percent of the native born receive some form of welfare payment while only 9 percent of the foreign born do so. Among the twenty-five to forty-four-year-olds, 16 percent of the native born received welfare compared to only 12 percent of the foreign born.[38]

Language

Proficiency in the language of the host country can be a problem both for the receiving nation and for the arriving immigrant. For Australia, the vast majority of residents born overseas were proficient in English. In 1991, approximately 53 percent of Australian residents born overseas spoke only English. Another 35 percent spoke English very well and about 11 percent could not speak English at all or not very well.[39]

The problem of language proficiency has not grown substantially with the increase in immigration from Asia. Although the proportion of the foreign-born population speaking only English declined between 1981 and 1991 (from 58 to 53 percent), the proportion of persons speaking English very well (but not exclusively) has increased from 30 to 35 percent.[40] These distributions remained essentially the same in 1996.[41]

The English-language proficiency of immigrants varies considerably by country of origin. In 1986, the percentage of persons arriving who spoke English well was lowest for persons born in Vietnam (33 percent), followed by China (50 percent), Taiwan (52 percent), Japan (55 percent), and Korea (58 percent). In contrast, over 90 percent of persons born in Malaysia, India, the Philippines, Fiji, and Sri Lanka were proficient in English. The picture was very much the same in the 1996 census.[42]

Intermarriage

The rate of intermarriage between the foreign born and the native born in Australia is quite high. In the period 1996 to 1998, about 16 percent of all marriages in Australia were between foreign-born persons and long-term Australian residents. Long-term Australian residents were defined as persons born in Australia from parents who were born in Australia.[43] This is a more restrictive definition of natives than simply being native born and so the intermarriage rate would be substantially higher if the more inclusive definition of Australian were used. Only 30 percent of the marriages involving foreign-born persons were unions between persons from the same nation of origin. An equal proportion of marriages of the foreign born involved marriage to a long-term Australia resident as defined earlier. Forty percent of the marriages of the foreign-born persons involved spouses who were either second-generation Australians or foreign-born persons from countries of origin different from their partner.

Criminal Involvement of Immigrants

The data from Australia show with reasonable consistency that immigrants participate in criminal activity at a lower rate than the native-born population. This is the case across states and over time. There is some variation in the criminal involvement of immigrants across ethnic groups and crime categories.

The earliest studies of the criminal involvement of immigrants were conducted for the Immigration Advisory Council by the Dovey Committee.[44] Three reports were prepared between 1951 and 1957 that compared conviction rates for the foreign born and the native born in the high courts. In all three reports the results were the same. The foreign born were convicted at rates substantially lower than those of the native born. In 1951, for example, native-born adults were convicted in the high court at a rate of 47 per 100,000 and the foreign born at 31 per 100,000. In the lower courts, the differences were even greater—520 per 100,000 to 286 per 100,000.[45]

The national census conducted by the Australian Bureau of Statistics in 1971 found that the stock incarceration rate for native-born Australians was 138.85 per 100,000 (see table 3.12). The comparable rate for the foreign born was 86.6. This is a difference of about 60 percent. The 1974 National Prisoners Survey provides information on jurisdictions other than New South

Table 3.12 Imprisonment Rates per 100,000 for Age 17 and Older by Birthplace, Australia, 1971

Australia	138.85
New Zealand	215.36
Eire	68.30
Malta	84.01
Austria	205.95
Hungary	182.28
Czechoslovakia	217.12
Yugoslavia	166.36
Poland	68.51
Soviet Union	256.52
France	113.37
Germany	172.52
Greece	46.88
Italy	45.95
Netherlands	74.24
Scandinavia	77.48
Iberia	33.98
Asia	47.68
Total average foreign born	86.6

Source: Ronald Francis, *Immigrant Crime in Australia* (St. Lucia: University of Queensland Press, 1981), 1887.

Wales. These data indicate that the incarceration rate for native-born Australians was about 46 percent higher than that of the foreign born.

The cumulative evidence from the early 1970s is that the foreign born had lower rates of criminal involvement than native-born Australians (table 3.12). The issue of the criminal involvement of the foreign born was reviewed again in 1987 by Kathleen Hazelhurst.[46] She found that on the basis of stock incarceration rates and annual conviction rates, native-born Australians engaged in criminal activity at a rate of about 50 percent higher than the foreign born (see table 3.13).

The stability of this relationship over a fifteen-year period is quite remarkable, especially in light of the massive change in the sources of immigration during the period. In 1971, 70 percent of the foreign born were of European origin, but by 1984 only 29 percent were from Europe.

The picture changes a bit in the 1990s. The foreign born still have lower overall incarceration rates than the native born but the differences between the groups have decreased. Native-born Australians have incarceration rates that are about 10 percent higher than the foreign born (table 3.14).

Furthermore, when immigrants and native-born Australians engage in crime, they pursue different types of activities (see table 3.15). Specifically, based on incarceration rates, a greater proportion of the crimes committed

Table 3.13 Prisoners by Birthplace, 1985

Birthplace	*No. of Prisoners*	*Population*	*Incarceration Rate*[a]	*Ratio to NB Rate*[b]
Australia	8,634	8,029,300	107.53	1.00
New Zealand	257	177,000	145.20	1.35
New Guinea	19			
Oceania	26			
Vietnam	25	41,000	60.98	0.57
Indo-China	7			
Asia	143	42,000		
United Kingdom	648	1,122,000	57.75	0.54
Greece	73	147,000	49.66	0.46
Italy	139	276,000	50.36	0.47
Yugoslavia	162	149,000	108.72	1.01
Other Western Europe	217	207,000	104.83	0.97
Eastern Europe	73	596,000	123.73	1.15
United States	40	50,000	98.00	0.91
Canada	9			
Other America	28	46,000	60.87	0.57
Africa	37	59,000	62.71	0.58
Lebanon	109	50,000	218.00	2.03
Turkey	51			
Other Middle East	29	57,000	50.88	0.47
Unknown/other	118	521,400	48.90	0.45
Total Immigrants	2,210	3,004,000	73.56	0.68

Source: Kathleen Hazelhurst, *Migration, Ethnicity and Crime in Australian Society* (Canberra: Australian Institute of Criminology, 1987).

Note: The Australian-born adult population is taken from Hazelhurst, *Migration, Ethnicity, and Crime,* 107, table 39. The immigrant population is taken from table 2. This is a slight overestimate of adult immigrant population. In table 39, the immigrant adult male population is listed as 2,928,700. This is a difference of 2 percent.

[a] per 100,000.

[b] NB = Native Born.

Table 3.14 Stock Incarceration Rates (per 1,000), All Offenses, by Country of Birth, 1992–1997

	Year		
Country of Birth	*1992*	*1995*	*1997*
Australia	0.88	0.98	1.05
Other	0.80	0.92	0.98

Source: Satyanshu Mukherjee, *Ethnicity and Crime* (Canberra: Australian Institute of Criminology, 1999).

Table 3.15 Prison Inmates by Country of Origin and Offense (in percent)

	Native Born	*Foreign Born*
Crimes against Persons	26.89	26.29
Robbery, Extortion	14.51	13.17
Crimes against Property	35.16	27.74
Crimes against Good Order	5.54	4.84
Drug Offenses	7.55	21.09
Traffic Offenses	9.86	5.79
Other	0.35	0.95
Unknown	0.14	0.14

Source: National Prison Census, June 30, 1985, as cited in Kathleen Hazelhurst, *Migration, Ethnicity and Crime in Australian Society* (Canberra: Australian Institute of Criminology, 1987), 63.
Note: The columns do not add up exactly to 100 percent due to rounding.

by native-born Australians involved burglary and theft. In contrast, a greater proportion of the crimes committed by the foreign born involved drug sale and possession. More than 35 percent of native-born prisoners in 1985 were incarcerated for property offenses as opposed to 28 percent of foreign-born prisoners. In contrast, 21 percent of immigrant prisoners were sentenced for drug offenses as opposed to 8 percent of native-born Australians. The proportion of persons in both groups incarcerated for other crimes against persons, such as robbery and extortion, crimes against public order, and other miscellaneous offenses were about the same. The proportion of Australian-born prisoners sentenced for traffic offenses was substantially higher than the percentage of immigrant prisoners imprisoned for the same offense.

The disproportionate involvement of the foreign born in drug crimes continued in the 1990s.

While the ratio of foreign-born and native-born incarceration rates were between 0.80 and 0.69, respectively, for violence and property crime from 1992 to 1997, they were in the range of 2.4 to 3.9 for drug crimes (see table 3.16).

Public Opinion

One area in which public opinion has clearly been consistent with behavioral indicators of support for immigration has been the transformation of the whites-only policy. Here, public support for the rejection of this policy tracked perfectly the legislative efforts that ultimately eliminated the ban on nonwhite immigration.

With the founding of the Commonwealth of Australia in 1901, Australia formally adopted an immigration policy that was directed at excluding all

Table 3.16 Offense-Specific Stock Incarceration Rates per 1,000 by Country of Birth, Australia, 1992, 1995, and 1997

	Type of Crime								
	Violence			*Property*			*Drugs*		
Country of Birth	*1992*	*1995*	*1997*	*1992*	*1995*	*1997*	*1992*	*1995*	*1997*
Australia	0.40	0.49	0.53	0.29	0.29	0.32	0.06	0.07	0.06
Other	0.32	0.41	0.43	0.21	0.20	0.22	0.15	0.21	0.23
Ratio of Other to Australian	0.81	0.84	0.80	0.75	0.71	0.69	2.42	3.28	3.92

Source: Satyanshu Mukherjee, *Ethnicity and Crime* (Canberra: Australian Institute of Criminology, 1999).

nonwhite people from the country. Before the onset of World War II, only minor modifications were made in the whites-only policy. During the war, Australia granted safe haven to some Asians who were escaping the Japanese invasions. But during and immediately following the end of the war, the Australian whites-only policy remained the law of the land.

In 1947, a UN Educational, Scientific, and Cultural Organization study reported the attitudes of the Australian public toward various racial and national groups see table 3.17.

In Herbert London's *Non-White Immigration and the "White Australia" Policy,* he interprets the responses as follows:

> Non-Europeans on the chart were perceived as a threat to Australia's development and unique cultural heritage. In most cases Australians argued that non-Europeans "do not fit in" or "are not like us." Many Australians regarded coloreds, because of their generally lower standard of living, as a threat to labor-employer relations. Oeser and Hammond claim this was partially explained by a working class "depression syndrome." Those whose social mobility was static or lower than their parents allowed a higher than average hostility to non-Europeans. In most cases hostility was a reflection of insecurity rather than a concern with the attributes of a migrant group. It was a function of self-interest operating as simple prejudice or as a "scapegoat reaction." Acceptance of migrants, according to the evidence, ultimately rests on their ability to serve the present interests of society without threatening entrenched labor positions.[47]

Table 3.17 Attitudes toward Ethnic Groups, 1947

Ethnicity	*Keep Out*	*Let a Few In*	*Allow Them to Come*	*Try to Get Them to Come*
British	0.9	1.8	25.0	72.0
American	3.0	12.0	48.0	37.0
Irish	6.0	22.0	45.0	26.0
Swedish	4.0	20.0	45.0	31.0
French	5.0	20.0	60.0	14.0
Baltic	12.0	37.0	39.0	12.0
German	23.0	32.0	28.0	17.0
Jew	39.0	31.0	26.0	4.0
Italian	38.0	35.0	23.0	4.0
Russian	57.0	25.0	16.0	2.0
Chinese	26.0	42.0	23.0	8.0
Indian	45.0	39.0	14.0	2.0
Negro	68.0	23.0	9.0	0.0

Source: American Institute of Public Opinion (Storrs: Roper Center, University of Connecticut, 1993).

Note: Some of the rows do not add up exactly to 100 percent due to rounding.

The major exception in this race-nation classification was the Chinese migrant who was clearly favored over the Italians, Russians, Indians, Negroes, and Jews. As shown by the data in table 3.18, public attitudes toward non-European immigrants also underwent a major change between 1943 and 1965.

In a February 1967 Gallup Poll, Australians indicated they were inclined to accept an increase of non-European migration. At least 60 percent approved the 1966–1967 increase of 1,000 non-European migrants a year.

In contrast to the close tracking of policy and public opinion with respect to the exclusion of nonwhite immigrants, opinion regarding increasing the level of immigration was not entirely consistent with the picture emerging from the behavioral indicators in the previous section. These indicators suggest that Australian society accepted, if not welcomed, immigrants. Public opinion, however, was not overwhelmingly in favor of expanding immigration.

In 1978 and again in 1986, the following questions were presented to the Australian public about how and whether to increase Australia's population: "Should any population increase be brought about mainly by a greater intake of immigrants or mainly through Australian families having more children?"

The responses show that by a ratio of three to one, 76 to 23 percent, Australians favored increasing their population through increased fertility as opposed to taking in more immigrants. In November 1986, the following ques-

Table 3.18 Attitudes toward Admitting Non-European Immigrants by Year (in percent)

Year	*No Non-Europeans*	*Limited*	*Unrestricted Entry*	*No Opinion*
1943	51	40	—	9
1944	53	35	—	12
1948	57	35	4	4
1950	54	39	3	4
1954	61	31	—	8
1956	51	42	—	7
1957	55	36	—	9
1958	45	44	—	11
1959	34	55	—	11
1960	33	59	—	8
1961	32	57	—	11
1962	30	64	—	6
1963	34	58	—	8
1964	22	73	5	—
1965	16	71	6	7

Source: American Institute of Public Opinion (Storrs: Roper Center, University of Connecticut, 1993).

tion appeared on a national poll: "Last year about 84,000 people were allowed to come into Australia to live permanently. It has been suggested that these people could help populate our northern regions. It also has been suggested that Australia should double the number of immigrants we take each year. Would you favor or oppose Australia doubling its migrant intakes next year?"

Of the responses, 64 percent opposed, 23 percent favored, 10 percent said it depends, and 3 percent had no answer. When the country of birth of the respondents was examined, the results showed that 52 percent of the respondents born in Asia favored such a policy, compared to 20 percent of native-born Australians and 28 percent of those born in the United Kingdom.

From 1988 through October 1991, the following basic question was asked of the Australian public: "Should Australia admit more, the same amount, fewer, or no immigrants this year?" The results are demonstrated in table 3.19.

Between 1988 and 1991, less than 10 percent of the respondents favored increasing immigration and 20 to 30 percent favored admitting no immigrants in the coming year. Most of the respondents favored admitting fewer than the government's targeted number. When asked in 1991 why they preferred fewer than the number targeted for the coming year, 76 percent of respondents cited unemployment as their most important consideration. Population pressures on natural resources and social tensions were the reasons given by the others. And on the same survey, Australians were asked: "Which of these statements comes closest to your view?: Australia is a country with rich resources and will benefit from immigration, or Immigration will lead to a growth in population which will put too much strain on Australia's land resources." Fifty-six percent responded that immigration will put too much of a strain on resources, and 39 percent thought Australia would benefit from immigration.

Table 3.19 Public Opinion Poll of Numbers of Immigrants Allowed to Enter Australia

Category	*1988 Target = 100,000*	*1989 Target = 150,000*	*1990 Target = 140,000*	*1991 Target = 111,000*
More	8.2	9.8	7.7	8.7
Same	22.4	21.4	23.8	16.2
Fewer	42.5	46.0	45.9	45.5
No immigrants this year	24.8	19.0	18.5	27.4
Don't know/no answer	2.1	3.8	4.0	2.2

Source: American Institute of Public Opinion (Storrs: Roper Center, University of Connecticut, 1993).

Note: Some of the columns do not add up exactly to 100 percent due to rounding.

Categories of immigrations and their countries of origin clearly influenced the choices expressed. In February 1988, respondents were asked whether they thought Australia should "encourage," "neither encourage nor prevent," or "prevent immigrants from coming" from the various regions listed in table 3.20.

Immigrants from Britain, Ireland, and western Europe are clearly preferred over the other parts of the world. Immigrants from the Middle East are the least "desired" followed by Asians, Africans, and eastern Europeans. Australians were also asked about types of immigrants: "If you were choosing immigrants, who would you favor most?" (The clear favorites are immigrants who bring skills useful to Australia).

	May 1988	*May 1990*	*October 1991*
Immigrants with money to invest	11.0	10.5	14.7
Immigrants with skills to invest	61.9	61.9	56.3
Immigrants with family in Australia	14.2	14.6	14.3
Refugees	6.8	7.6	10.0
Don't know/ no answer	6.1	5.5	4.5

Source: American Institute of Public Opinion (Storrs: Roper Center, University of Connecticut, 1993).
Note: The columns do not add up exactly to 100 percent due to rounding.

Table 3.20 Should Australia Encourage Immigrants from the Following Regions?

Region	*Encourage*	*Neither Encourage nor Prevent*	*Prevent*	*No Immigrants*	*Don't Know*
Britain and Ireland	41.3	29.1	3.4	24.5	1.8
Western Europe	40.9	29.1	3.2	24.7	2.0
Eastern Europe	29.9	33.6	9.2	24.9	2.4
Middle East	13.0	31.6	28.3	25.0	2.2
Asia	18.0	33.6	21.3	25.0	2.1
South Africa	20.3	33.8	17.9	25.2	2.8
Other parts of Africa	18.2	35.8	16.2	26.2	3.5

Source: American Institute of Public Opinion (Storrs: Roper Center, University of Connecticut, 1993).
Note: Some of the rows do not add up exactly to 100 percent due to rounding.

Australia, like other "traditional" immigrant receiving countries, is clearly ambivalent about welcoming new immigrants. Most of the respondents favor admitting fewer immigrants than the government's targeted number and most prefer immigrants with skills as opposed to the government's policy of favoring immigrants who have families in the country. Their concern about immigrants increasing the rate of unemployment among native born is the major stated objection to new immigrants. But there are also clear preferences about which immigrants are more or less welcome, with those from Britain, Ireland, and western Europe clearly favored over "more foreign" types from the Middle East, Africa, and Asia.

There is some indication that these anti-immigrant attitudes may be turning into political action. Recently, a political party has been formed with a platform that opposes immigration and aid to aboriginal people. The One Nation Party attracted 23 percent of the vote in the 1998 Queensland state elections, which translated into eleven seats in the state parliament.[48] In subsequent national elections, however, the party was able to win only one seat in the federal parliament, but it did get 8.4 percent of the vote.[49] This showing by the One Nation Party suggests that negative attitudes toward immigration will not result in a wave of anti-immigrant policy in the near future. Not many Australians feel comfortable actively advocating for a restrictive immigration policy. At the same time, it would not be surprising if more established national parties began to take a more restrictive stance on immigration to preempt the One Nation Party's appeal to certain portions of the electorate.

Summary

Australia is an immigrant nation. It is, with the exception of Israel, the nation with the highest proportion of the population born in other nations. While immigrants to Australia (by design and policy) have been relatively homogeneous culturally, a change has emerged since World War II. A large and growing proportion of the immigrant population now comes from Asia as well as non-English-speaking countries in Europe and the Middle East. Australia seems to have adjusted well to this change. The participation of the foreign born in major social institutions is on par with, or exceeds, that of the native-born population. Immigrants engage in undesirable behavior such as crime and dependency at lower levels overall than the native-born population. In addition, public opinion toward diversity in immigration has changed markedly over time. Public support for admitting more diverse immigrants has increased in step with the initiation of policies that encouraged diversity.

This picture of Australia as a nation in which immigrants are accepted and where immigrants are quick to assimilate is not without some problems.

Some groups, generally the most recent arrivals and those experiencing the disruption of refugee status, are not as well integrated as other foreign-born groups. Similarly, drug crimes stand out as the one area where immigrants participate at higher levels than the native-born population. It is not clear, however, whether these aberrations will pass with time or, indeed, whether some of these negative indications are not artifacts of the systems that we use to control and record criminal behavior. Finally, a large majority of Australians favor restricting immigration. This pattern of public opinion is similar to that found in other immigrant nations and, as in other nations, it is difficult to predict the policy implications of these opinions. Nonetheless, the negative public opinion is a noteworthy exception to the generally positive picture of immigration that emerges from the data examined here.

The overall impression from these data, then, is that at this point Australia lives up to its reputation of a nation where immigrants are accepted and where they can flourish.

Notes

1. Robert Hughes, *The Fatal Shore* (New York: Knopf, 1986).
2. Department of Immigration and Multi-cultural Affairs, *DIMA Fact Sheet 2: Key Facts on Immigration* (Canberra: Department of Immigration and Multi-cultural Affairs, 2000).
3. Gary P. Freeman and James Jupp, *Nations of Immigrants: Australia, the United States, and International Migration* (New York: Oxford University Press, 1992).
4. Freeman and Jupp, *Nations of Immigrants.*
5. "Transportation" refers to the practice of transporting convicted offenders from England and Ireland to Australia to serve their sentence in exile.
6. Freeman and Jupp, *Nations of Immigrants.*
7. Prior to 1901, a number of individual states passed laws restricting Chinese immigration and imposing head taxes on shippers bringing Chinese immigrants. See Herbert London, *Non-White Immigration and the "White Australia" Policy* (New York: New York University Press, 1971).
8. A. T. Yarwood, *Asian Migration to Australia: The Background to Exclusion, 1896–1923* (New York: Cambridge University Press, 1964), 157.
9. Yarwood, *Asian Migration to Australia,* 45.
10. Yarwood, *Asian Migration to Australia,* 46.
11. Yarwood, *Asian Migration to Australia,* 46.
12. Sev Ozdawski, "The Law, Immigration and Human Rights: Changing the Australian Immigration Control System," *International Migration Review* 6, no. 3 (1985): 565.
13. David G. Thomas and J. J. Flynn, "Australia," in *International Immigration and Nationality Law: Immigration Supplement 2,* ed. Dennis Campbell and Joy Fisher (Boston: Nijhoff, 1993).
14. Thomas and Flynn, "Australia."

15. Australian Bureau of Statistics, *Australia's Population Trends and Prospects, 1992* (Canberra: Australia Government Publishing Services, 1993), 32–35.

16. Australian Bureau of Statistics, *Australia's Population Trends and Prospects, 1992,* 32–35.

17. Australian Bureau of Statistics, *Australia's Population Trends and Prospect, 1992,* 32–35.

18. A. C. Palfreeman, *The Administration of the White Australia Policy* (London: Melbourne University Press, 1967), 104.

19. London, *Non-White Immigration,* 26.

20. London, *Non-White Immigration,* 26.

21. Thomas and Flynn, "Australia."

22. Australian Bureau of Statistics, *Population: Country of Birth* (Canberra: Australian Bureau of Statistics, 2001).

23. Australian Bureau of Statistics, *Population: Country of Birth.*

24. Australian Bureau of Statistics, *Population: International Migration* (Canberra: Australian Bureau of Statistics, 2001).

25. Australian Bureau of Statistics, *Population: International Migration.*

26. Australian Bureau of Statistics, *Population Composition: Australian Citizenship* (Canberra: Australian Bureau of Statistics, 2001), 2. In a more sophisticated analysis, M. D. R. Evans finds an even lower rate of naturalization for immigrants from English-speaking nations, 30 percent after twenty years. See M. D. R. Evans, "Choosing to Be a Citizen: The Time Path of Citizenship in Australia," *International Migration Review* 22, no. 2 (1988): 255.

27. Evans, "Choosing to Be a Citizen," 6.

28. Evans, "Choosing to Be a Citizen," 6.

29. Thomas and Flynn, "Australia."

30. James Jupp, "Immigrant Policy in Australia," in *Nations of Immigrants: Australia, the United States, and International Migration,* by Gary P. Freeman and James Jupp (New York: Oxford University Press, 1992), 131.

31. Department of Immigration and Multi-cultural Affairs, *Welfare Recipient Patterns among Migrants* (Canberra: Department of Immigration and Multi-cultural Affairs, 2001), 1.

32. Jing Shu et al., *Australia's Population Trends and Prospects, 1993* (Canberra: Australian Government Publishing Service, 1994).

33. Shu et al., *Australia's Population Trends.*

34. Australian Bureau of Statistics, *Australia Now: Characteristics of the Labour Force* (Canberra: Australian Bureau of Statistics, 2002).

35. Australian Bureau of Statistics, *Australia Now,* 3.

36. Stephen Castle et al., *Immigration and Australia: Myths and Reality* (St. Leonards, Australia: Allen and Unwin, 1998).

37. Heather Antecol, Deborah Cobb-Clark, and Stephen Trejo, "Immigration Policy and the Skills of Immigrants to Australia, Canada and the United States," in *Claremont College Working Papers in Economics* (Claremont, Calif.: Claremont Graduate University, 2000), 18.

38. Department of Immigration and Multi-cultural Affairs, *Welfare Recipient Patterns among Immigrants: Welfare Recipient Rate Findings* (Canberra: Department of Immigration and Multi-cultural Affairs, 2001), 1.

39. Shu et al., *Australia's Population Trends,* 66–68.

40. Shu et al., *Australia's Population Trends,* 66–68.

41. Department of Immigration and Multi-cultural Affairs, *English Proficiency: 1996 Census* (Canberra: Commonwealth of Australia, 2001).

42. Department of Immigration and Multi-cultural Affairs, *English Proficiency,* 31.

43. Australian Bureau of Statistics, *Australian Trends 2000: Family: Cultural Diversity in Marriage* (Canberra: Australian Bureau of Statistics, 2001), 4.

44. Kathleen Hazelhurst, *Migration, Ethnicity and Crime in Australian Society* (Canberra: Australian Institute of Criminology, 1987).

45. Hazelhurst, *Migration, Ethnicity and Crime.*

46. Hazelhurst, *Migration, Ethnicity and Crime.*

47. London, *Non-White Immigration.*

48. James O'Conner, "One Nation—A Qualified Victory," *Spearhead* (November 1998).

49. "Hansons' Dreams in Tatters," *Reuters News Service*, 4 October 1998.

4

Immigration in Great Britain

For most of its history, Great Britain has been an exporter of immigrants and not a receiving country. The founding and maintenance of the British Empire and later the Commonwealth required sending many British citizens to far flung parts of the world. The colonies also reduced the pressure that led other countries to begin admitting, even recruiting, immigrants. Britain benefited from the cheap labor and raw materials available in the colonies. Rather than recruiting immigrants to fill its marginal labor needs at home, Britain could use the labor available in the colonies without ever bringing those laborers to its shores. While there was free movement within the Commonwealth, the long distances and the expense of travel from distant colonies to the motherland ensured that the flow of people was generally from Great Britain rather than to it. The Irish, however, were an exception because they filled much of the need for marginal labor and were free to come and go from Great Britain in the same manner as British citizens.

Historical Background and Major Legislation

Immigration laws in Great Britain have been consistent with the nation's status as an "exporter" rather than an "importer" of immigrants. Until 1905, Great Britain had a policy of free immigration. In 1905, the Aliens Act gave the home secretary powers to control the entry of undesirable and destitute immigrants. Aliens were defined as only those foreigners who came as steerage passengers.[1]

In 1914, tougher legislation was introduced primarily for security reasons. The home secretary was given the power to refuse foreigners entrance to the country and to deport those who had already entered.[2] For the first time, all immigrants had to register with the police. But the right to political asylum was reaffirmed. The act did not apply to British subjects and hence was not applicable to the overseas dominions and colonies of the British Empire. The 1914 act was renewed after World War I in the form of the Aliens Restrictions Act of 1919, the main provisions of which were that immigrants could be refused entry at the discretion of an immigration officer. Immigrants without a visible means of support would be permitted only a short stay unless they secured a work permit from the Ministry of Labour, and immigrants could be deported by the court or by the home secretary if that official deemed such a measure "conducive to the public good."[3]

Prior to the end of World War II, British immigration policy was ad hoc and reactive rather than centrally planned and managed. Before 1939, Great Britain viewed immigration policy as being concerned with facilitating emigrants from its shores to the colonies. However, the demands of World War II and the subsequent independence of the colonies radically changed the immigration situation in Great Britain. The extreme demand for labor during the war and thereafter prompted the recruitment of laborers from the Commonwealth and European nations to work in the war industries in Great Britain and to contribute to rebuilding the nation.[4] Between 1945 and 1948, immigration became more centrally planned to the extent that European volunteer workers were specially recruited on purely economic grounds and under stringent conditions to meet the needs of labor-strained industries. In 1950, other European workers, mainly Germans, Italians, and Spaniards, came under the same work permit scheme as volunteer workers, but they were allowed to bring their families.

In the period between 1948 and 1962, there was also substantial and uncontrolled immigration of West Indians and Asians because they were British colonial and Commonwealth citizens. Since these recruits had the full rights of British citizenship, it was easy for them to stay in Great Britain after the war. These small ethnic enclaves grew throughout the postwar period as a result of the natural process of family unification and the flow of information about jobs and opportunities.[5] By the early 1960s, the presence of a large number of nonwhite members of the Commonwealth in Great Britain had become noticeable and a source of strain. Race riots ensued.[6]

In response to these strains, the British government abruptly and radically changed its immigration policy. Citizens of Commonwealth nations no longer had uniformly free access to Britain. The Commonwealth was divided into the New Commonwealth and the Old Commonwealth. The latter included Australia, Canada, and New Zealand, while the former included India, Pakistan, Hong Kong, and the British West Indies. Citizens of the Old Commonwealth nations were still free to enter and to leave Britain without restriction. People from the New Commonwealth, however, were denied admission unless they had an employment voucher. The British government only issued these vouchers for very restricted classes of workers that were in critically short supply.

This transformation of British immigration policy began with the restrictions imposed by the Commonwealth Immigration Act of 1962.[7] This policy has only become more restrictive since its enactment in 1962.

The 1914 British Nationality and the Status of Aliens Act and the 1948 British Nationality Act did not have a definition of citizenship that only applied to persons residing in Britain or with some "close historical connection to the United Kingdom." Prior to 1962, citizenship was defined not only as persons who would normally have been citizens of the United Kingdom (UK), but also as those who were citizens of the remaining colonies. Beyond citizens of the UK and colonies was the broader category of Commonwealth citizens, or British "subjects." All citizens of the dominions and former colonies retained their citizenship after independence, as long as their countries remained within the Commonwealth. Commonwealth citizenship provided free entry to Great Britain until the passage of the 1962 Immigration Act.

The First Commonwealth Immigration Act adopted in 1962 provided for three categories of employment vouchers: (1) for Commonwealth citizens with a specific job waiting; (2) those issued by British high commissions overseas to those with such recognized skills or qualifications as were in short supply; and (3) anybody at all on a first come, first served basis with priority given to those with war service.[8] Between 1962 and 1965, the government issued vouchers liberally in accordance with previous rates of immigration.

Immigration was a big issue in the 1964 elections. As a result, the Labour government decided to stem the flow of New Commonwealth immigrants in an attempt to end the immigration of nonwhite immigrants. In August 1965, the government restricted the number of employment vouchers to 8,500 (of which 1,000 were reserved for Malta).[9] With a waiting list of over 400,000, the third category of vouchers was abolished.

In 1968, the government introduced additional controls to reduce the entry of British passport holders of Asian descent from East Africa. The Commonwealth Immigration Act of 1968 required that all citizens of Great Britain and colonies who had no substantial connection to Great Britain (e.g., by birth or descent) obtain an entry voucher before arriving. This was the first time such a distinction was made. The clear intention of the act was to control nonwhite immigration from the Commonwealth while allowing most white Commonwealth citizens of British descent unrestricted access.

At first, 150 vouchers were made available per year for heads of households from East Africa. The Immigration Act of 1971 raised the quota to 3,000 with an additional 1,500 vouchers for people in special difficulty issued on a one-time-only basis. In 1975, the government raised the quota to 5,000.

The 1971 act replaced all previous legislation with one statute that made provisions for controlling the administration and stay of Commonwealth citizens and foreign nationals.[10] The act also recognized a "right to abode" for citizens of Great Britain and colonies and certain Commonwealth citizens because of a "close connection with the U.K. by birth, descent, or marriage." People who have this right are known as "patrials" and are entirely free from immigration control and may live and work in Great Britain without restriction. The 1971 act defines patrials as:

1. Citizens of the UK and colonies who have citizenship by birth, adoption, registration, or naturalization in the UK or that have a parent or grandparent who was born in the UK and who has acquired citizenship by adoption, registration, or naturalization
2. Citizens of the UK and colonies who have come from overseas, have been accepted for permanent residence, and have resided in the UK for five years
3. Commonwealth citizens who have a parent born in the UK
4. Women who are Commonwealth citizens (including citizens of the UK and colonies) and are, or have been, married to a man in any of these categories

The government required work permits for all foreign nationals seeking employment except patrials, nationals of the European Economic Community (EEC), immigrants of independent means seeking to establish themselves as self-employed businessmen, and young Commonwealth citizens on working holidays.

The British Nationality Act of 1981 limited the right of admission further by defining citizenship more narrowly than the 1971 act.[11] The 1981 act defined three classes of citizens. The first, British citizens, are defined as persons born in the UK or whose parents or grandparents were born or naturalized in the UK. These citizens have the right to enter and abide in the UK. Second, citizens of dependent territories are people whose parents were born in dependent or associated states. These citizens have no right to enter or abide in the UK. Third, British overseas citizens are children of British citizens born outside of the UK. These citizens have the right to enter and abide but cannot pass on to their children the status of citizenship and the attendant right to enter and abide.

The only avenues for admission open to noncitizens (who are not refugees) is through family unification, work permits, and admission as a student. Relatives (e.g., wives, children, husbands, and elderly dependents) of men and women settled in the UK may be admitted, but it is not automatic. Family members must obtain an entry certificate before entering the UK and they must show proof of relationship. Both of these requirements make possible the administrative regulation of admissions. Making these determinations can take considerable time for applicants from specific countries. In India, for example, the expected time to the first interview with immigration officials is one year.[12]

Work permits are only available for overseas workers holding recognized professional qualifications of a high degree of skill or experience. Employers, not workers, must apply for permits. For most occupations, they are only issued to workers aged twenty-three to fifty-four with a good command of the English language. Work permits are issued for a particular job with a specified employer when there is no suitable worker in the UK or other EEC country. The permits are usually issued for twelve months and extensions are granted by the Home Office for up to five years. After four years, permit holders can apply for the removal of the time limit and, if granted, they are regarded as settled and are free to take any employment with approval. Relatively few permit holders apply for settlement. In 1998, for example, only 3,160 permit holders settled in the UK, while some 70,000 permits were granted in that year. Dependents of work permit holders are entitled to remain in the UK during the period in which the permit is valid, as long as they do not become dependent on public funds. Dependents are free to work, even at jobs that do not satisfy the work permit conditions. In 1998, 20,000 dependents of work permit holders were admitted to the UK.

There are a number of smaller work-related and business categories of admissions including:

- Working holiday exceptions—admissions of Commonwealth immigrants between seventeen and twenty-seven years of age who are allowed to work up to two years as long as the employment is part of a vacation
- Seasonal agricultural workers—approximately 15,000 workers admitted until November 30 of the year in which they entered
- Innovators and entrepreneurs—a few hundred persons are admitted annually to start companies or for investing large sums of money in UK businesses[13]

Persons can enter the UK as students if they are accepted for admission at a university or some other recognized institution. Students may stay for the term of their study, but usually not longer. Extensions can be obtained, however. Applicants can be denied entry if immigration authorities believe that applicants will stay in the country beyond their term of study. About 12 percent of applicants are rejected on these grounds. The rejection rates get as high as 25 percent for applicants from some Asian and African nations. In 1998, 266,000 students were admitted into the UK.[14]

Between 1931 and 1939, most of the 60,000 immigrants who arrived annually were refugees escaping Nazi Germany.[15] Immediately following the end of World War II, the British government admitted some 70,000 Poles who had fought on the side of the Allies but were anti-Russian and unwilling to return to Poland. The government also admitted displaced persons and former prisoners of war from Lithuania, Latvia, the Ukraine, and Yugoslavia.

Great Britain was one of the first countries to sign on to the UN Convention that defined the treatment of refugees and the special admissions policies applicable to them. Refugees are a special category and may be admitted if the only country that they could be sent to is one where they are unwilling to go for fear of prosecution (e.g., Ugandan Asians in 1972, Vietnamese in 1979, and Hungarians in 1956).

Stock and Flow of Immigrants

The changes in immigration laws and policies described earlier are consistent with the changes in the flow of immigrants into Great Britain and the changes in the composition of that flow over time. In the early 1950s, very few legal immigrants were entering Great Britain and almost all of these admissions were from the West Indies. In 1953, for example, only 2,000 immigrants entered Great Britain and all of these were from the West Indies. By 1956, admissions had increased to 46,800, with approximately 64 percent coming from the West Indies. In 1961, the flow had increased to 132,400, with only 50 percent coming from the West Indies. As shown in table 4.1, this

Table 4.1 Estimated Net Immigration from the New Commonwealth, 1953–1962

Year	*West Indies*	*India*	*Pakistan*	*Others*	*Total*
1953	2,000	—	—	—	2,000
1954	11,000	—	—	—	11,000
1955	27,500	5,800	1,850	7,500	42,650
1956	29,800	5,600	2,050	9,350	46,800
1957	23,000	6,600	5,200	7,600	42,400
1958	15,000	6,200	4,700	3,950	29,850
1959	16,400	2,950	850	1,400	21,600
1960	49,650	5,900	2,500	−350	57,700
1961	66,300	23,750	21,100	21,250	132,400
1962[a]	31,800	19,050	25,080	18,970	94,900

Source: Zig Layton-Henry, "Britain: The Would-Be Zero-Immigrant Country," in *Controlling Immigration: A Global Perspective,* ed. Wayne A. Cornelius, Philip Martin, and James Hollifield (Stanford, Calif.: Stanford University Press, 1994).

[a]The number of immigrants for 1962 are for the first half of the year only.

was a massive increase in immigration in less than a decade. Moreover, the national origin of immigrants had changed drastically—from exclusively West Indian to increasingly Asian. This change resulted from the restrictions contained in the Commonwealth Immigration Act of 1962.

The effects of the 1962 act and subsequent restrictions are also apparent in the numbers shown in table 4.2. The flow of immigrants dropped from 132,400 in 1961 to 56,071 in 1963. Admissions remained at these levels from 1963 through 1968, when additional restrictions were imposed by the 1968 act. Between 1968 and 1971, the average number of admissions was 47,591. After the enactment of the Immigration Act of 1971, the flow of immigrants dropped again. Between 1972 and 1980, the average number of annual admissions was 44,500. This number fell to 30,650 after the enactment of the British Nationality Act in 1981. In 1970, 37,893 newcomers from the New Commonwealth were accepted for settlement compared to 24,800 in 1984. The number of West Indian immigrants dropped from 15,000 in 1969 to 3,000 in 1982.

In 1996, the government gave 61,700 persons the right of indefinite residence in Great Britain. The overwhelming majority of these persons entered the country for family unification purposes and were granted the right to permanent settlement after the requisite waiting period. In that same year, 29,000 short-term labor migrants and 11,000 long-term work permit holders migrants entered Great Britain in 1996 along with 17,000 dependents under the work permit scheme. In addition, approximately 23,000 immediate family members were admitted.[16]

Table 4.2 Immigration to the United Kingdom from the New Commonwealth, 1962–1991

Year	*Number of Immigrants*	*Year*	*Number of Immigrants*	*Year*	*Number of Immigrants*
1962[a]	16,143	1972	68,519	1982	30,300
1963	56,071	1973	32,247	1983	27,500
1964	52,840	1974	42,531	1984	24,800
1965	53,887	1975	55,103	1985	27,100
1966	48,104	1976	55,103	1986	22,500
1967	60,633	1977	44,155	1987	20,900
1968	60,620	1978	34,364	1988	22,800
1969	44,503	1979	36,597	1989	22,900
1970	37,893	1980	33,700	1990	25,700
1971	44,261	1981	31,000	1991	28,000

Source: Zig Layton-Henry, "Britain: The Would-Be Zero-Immigrant Country," in *Controlling Immigration: A Global Perspective,* ed. Wayne A. Cornelius, Philip Martin, and James Hollifield (Stanford, Calif.: Stanford University Press, 1994), 108.

[a]The number of immigrants for 1962 are for the second half of the year only.

Asylum

Historically, the number of persons applying for asylum has been small due primarily to the anti-immigrant stance of the British government, but more recently the number of asylum seekers has increased sporadically and in some cases dramatically. The data in table 4.3 show that in 1979 there were only 1,600 applications for asylum. This figure rose to 30,000 in 1990 and 44,000 in 1991. Applications dropped in the early 1990s and increased dramatically in the late 1990s to 71,000 in 1999. The source of this volatility in asylum applications and particularly the very recent sharp increases is not clear. Since a large portion of the increase is due to Kosovars, it is understandable that upheavals in Europe and elsewhere contribute to increases in

Table 4.3 Asylum Applications, 1979–1999

Year	*Number*[a]
1979	1.6
1980	9.9
1981	2.9
1982	4.2
1983	4.3
1984	3.9
1985	5.4
1986	4.8
1987	5.2
1988	5.7
1989	16.5
1990	30.0
1991	44.8
1992	24.6
1993	22.4
1994	32.8
1995	43.9
1996	29.6
1997	32.5
1998	46.0
1999	71.1

Sources: Organization for Economic Cooperation and Development, *Trends in International Migration (SOPEMI), 1979–1990* (Paris: Organization for Economic Cooperation and Development, 1992); Jo Woodbridge, Di Burgum, and Tina Heath, *Asylum Statistics United Kingdom, 1999* (London: Home Office, 2000).

[a]In thousands.

applications for asylum. The large drops in applications in other European nations known for their liberal asylum policies may also contribute to the increase in asylum applications in Great Britain. Both Germany and the Netherlands experienced sharp decreases in asylum applications in 1999.[17]

The very recent large increases in applications for asylum can cause inordinate strain in the systems that control immigration. Unlike other immigrant populations, asylum seekers are often not screened before entry and they are often in the host nation and must be dealt with by that nation. This was particularly the case in 1999 when 41,700 of the 71,100 applicants for asylum applied while in Great Britain. Dealing with this population involves some form of adjudication to determine the asylum seekers' legal status and their right to stay in Great Britain. The sheer size of the increase slows this adjudication process down. The number of outstanding applications at the end of 1999 was 57 percent greater than that for the previous year and 96 percent more than at the end of 1998.[18] The longer the process takes, the more asylum seekers must be accommodated. While the determination of asylum status is being made, asylum seekers (unlike many other classes of immigrant) cannot work. Consequently, they must be supported by the state at some level. This raises the question of whether these applicants will become a drain on the nation and other familiar issues about the costs and benefits of immigration generally. Small increases in asylum seekers can cause big political and social headaches.

In the face of these recent increases in applications, immigration authorities seem to be more rather than less willing to grant some form of relief. In 1996, 77 percent of the decisions made regarding applications denied the applicant both refugee status and leave to stay in Great Britain until a suitable third country could be found. By 1998, the refusal rate was down to 66 percent and it fell to 48 percent in 1999. Most of the increase in relief came in the form of grants of refugee status and asylum. Only 7 percent of decisions made in 1996 granted refugee status and asylum. This increased steadily to 13 percent in 1997, 19 percent in 1998, and 36 percent in 1999.[19] These statistics do not include approximately 15,000 decisions handled under special provisions designed to reduce the backlog of asylum applications. About 90 percent of the cases processed under these provisions were granted leave to stay. If these cases were included, the proportion of decisions awarding some form of relief would be higher still.

In the 1980s, the asylum seekers were mainly from Sri Lanka, India, Pakistan, and Bangladesh. In later years, persons seeking asylum came from Turkey, Haiti, and Uganda. In 1996, about 40 percent of the applications were made by Africans, 35 percent by Asians, and 25 percent by Europeans. Almost half the grants of asylum in 1996 were granted to nationals from the Federal Republic of Yugoslavia (FYR). The main nationalities granted exceptional leave to remain were Somalis (70 percent), Afghans (10 percent), and Yugoslavs (5 percent).[20] By 1999, the proportion of asylum seekers from Europe increased to about 40 percent of the total applicant pool and Africans decreased to about 25 percent of the applicant pool. Much of the increase in applications from Europe came from the FYR, which accounted for 400 applicants in 1996 (or 6 percent of the applicants from Europe) and 11,465 in 1999 (or 40 percent of applicants from Europe). Applicants from the FYR also accounted for the vast bulk of persons granted refugee status and asylum. Over 80 percent of grants made in 1999 were for applicants from the FYR.[21]

The recent influx of asylum seekers and the government's response has become a controversial issue. In an effort to minimize the disruption caused by asylum seekers awaiting the adjudication of their claim, immigration authorities disperse the claimants throughout the country. This often means that remote towns are exposed to foreign populations, something to which they are unaccustomed. Some of these towns are experiencing economic contractions and the presence of foreigners being supported by the government is a sore spot. This tension has led to a number of attacks on asylum seekers and opposition to the dispersal policy. The Home Office is under pressure to curtail the influx of immigrants, to accelerate the adjudication of their claims, and to find alternatives to the dispersal policy.[22]

It is clear that immigration law in Great Britain has become immigration policy. The law has increasingly restricted the eligibility of persons from the New Commonwealth for admission to Great Britain. The restrictive laws imposed in the early 1960s, which have been progressively tightened, have led to a 300 percent decrease in the flow of immigrants into Great Britain.

The effect of changes in the immigration laws can be seen in the stock population as well. In 1990, 3.8 percent of the population of Great Britain comprised immigrants.[23] If we broaden the concept of immigrant to coincide with ethnic minority, then 2.6 million persons residing in Great Britain, or 5 percent of the population, were in that status. The major increases in the stock population of immigrants between 1984 and 1990 occurred among persons from the EEC, Ireland, and Portugal. These groups increased during that period by 27, 30, and 110 percent, respectively. At the same time, as shown in table 4.4, the stock population of immigrants from the New Commonwealth decreased by 11 percent.

Admissions, differential fertility, repatriation, and naturalization rates drive these differences between the various immigrant groups. It is not clear which of these factors is most important in producing the changes observed.

Naturalization

British citizenship may be acquired by a Commonwealth citizen through registration and by a foreign national through naturalization.[24] The requirements

Table 4.4 Change in Stock of Foreign Population in Great Britain, 1984–1990

Nationality	*1984*[a]	*1984*[b]	*1990*[a]	*1990*[b]	*Percent of Change*
Italy	83	5.2	75	4.0	−9.6
Ireland	491	30.7	638	34.0	29.9
Spain	25	1.6	24	1.3	−4.0
Portugal	10	0.6	21	1.1	110.0
New Commonwealth	442	27.6	394	21.0	−10.9
Other countries	550	34.4	723	38.6	31.5
Total	1,601		1,875		17.1
EEC[c]	701		889		26.8
Total less EEC	900		986		9.6

Source: Sarah Collinson, *European and International Migration* (London: Pinter, 1993), 83.
[a]In thousands.
[b]In percent.
[c]EEC = European Economic Commission.

include five-year residence, good moral character, sufficient knowledge of English, and the intention to reside in Great Britain. Foreign nationals are also required to take an oath of allegiance. The only exceptions to this general process are Irish nationals who have resided in Great Britain since 1971 and patrials with five years of residence. These groups can become citizens automatically.

In 1996, 43,000 persons were granted citizenship status in the UK and 5,000 of those who applied were refused citizenship.[25] The number of naturalizations remained relatively constant at about 45,000 since 1992. This constituted about 46 percent of the number of persons admitted in 1996 or about 2.3 percent of the stock population of foreigners in England in 1990. By 2000, the number of persons granted citizenship increased to 82,000, up from 55,000 and 54,000 in 1999 and 1998, respectively.[26] It remains to be seen if these high levels of naturalization will continue. A Home Office study of a random sample of immigrants eligible to apply for citizenship and still residing in the UK found that 35 percent had applied for naturalization. In interviews with this random sample, 58 percent claimed to have applied for citizenship with the vast majority being successful.[27]

Policies for Control of Immigrants

British immigration policy does not allow for elaborate controls on immigrants once they are admitted.[28] Only persons admitted on work permits have significant reporting obligations or limitations on their behavior. As noted earlier, persons admitted on work permits must apply for renewal of that permit every twelve months for a period of five years. During that period, the immigrant must remain at the same job. After four years, the person can apply for settlement. When settlement status is granted, the person may seek employment in jobs other than the one for which he or she was initially admitted. He or she is also free to apply for admission of dependents as defined in the 1981 act. These dependents must obtain an entry certificate and produce proof of relationship to the settled worker.

Illegal Immigrants

In 1995, 10,240 persons were dealt with as illegal entrants, which was 38 percent more than in 1994.[29] By 1999, the number of persons dealt with as illegals increased to 21,650 and in 2000 the number was 47,325. This large increase in persons dealt with as illegal entrants is due more to changes in enforcement policy and resources rather than increases in illegal entrants per se. The Home Office does not publish official estimates of the number of illegal immigrants living in Great Britain.[30]

Social and Policy Integration

The British approach to assimilating immigrants has emphasized guaranteeing equal opportunity rather than supplemental programs, for example, language classes, subsidies, and the like. The strategy gives immigrants many of the social welfare benefits and other entitlements of citizenship and establishes mechanisms to see that these rights are respected.

Immigrants, with some exceptions, have the right to work, to education, to health care, and to other benefits. Emergency health care is available to immigrants on arrival and nonemergency health care after one year of residence. Children of immigrants can attend school. All immigrants have the right to work except asylum seekers during the period that their refugee status is being determined. Housing assistance and public assistance is generally available except for persons admitted under family unification. Spouses and dependents do not have access to this support until they have been in the UK for a year. Grandparents must wait five years to be eligible.[31] These exclusions are designed to ensure that family members will not become public charges.

There are no special programs to facilitate the integration of immigrants into society. Approximately £1.5 million was budgeted in 2000 for language education. This money was given to local authorities who could match these funds in providing language instruction. The result has been "spotty" provision of language education for immigrants. There are no programs to facilitate finding employment and the like.[32]

Asylum seekers receive more assistance largely because they are denied the right to work while their case is being decided. The Home Office's National Asylum Support Service provides housing and financial support.[33]

While the British government does not provide services to integrate immigrants into the society, it has enacted laws to ensure that immigrants (and native-born minorities) receive the rights to which they are entitled. The immigrants believed to be at greatest risk of discrimination are those from the New Commonwealth who differ from the native British population not only in nationality, but also by race. Hence, the legislation designed to guarantee equal opportunity was a series of race relations acts.

The first of these laws was enacted in 1965. The Race Relations Act of 1965 prohibited discrimination on the basis of race in public accommodations such as hotels, restaurants, and bars.[34] This was followed by the Race Relations Act of 1968, which prohibited discrimination in employment, training, promotion, and dismissal.[35] These early efforts to guarantee equal opportunity were criticized for not taking account of the discriminatory impact of universally applied standards. In addition, there were no governmental bodies specifically designated to monitor and adjudicate complaints of discrimination. The Race Relations Act of 1976 attempted to address these criticisms by explicitly prohibiting discrimination resulting from the application of universal standards.[36] Moreover, it created the Commission on Racial Equality to handle discrimination complaints.

British immigration policy, then, is a mixture of inclusion and exclusion. Severe restrictions were placed on admissions in the early 1970s. These restrictions were particularly severe for immigrants from the New Commonwealth who were racially and culturally most dissimilar from the British. Moreover, the government took no special steps to integrate immigrants into the society. At the same time, naturalization rates for immigrants admitted to the country are quite high and legislation and administrative remedies for the discrimination against immigrants and ethnic minorities have been created to ensure equal treatment. The British have chosen to essentially stop the flow of immigrants and work on the assimilation of those who have come in a manner that minimizes friction with the native population.

In general, immigrants tend to participate in major social and economic institutions at rates equal to or higher than the native born. This parity, however, is not universal across all institutions and it varies considerably across immigrant groups.

The average income of the foreign born in the UK is about 12 percent greater than that for the native born.[37] Much of this high-average income is due to the overrepresentation of immigrants among very high-income workers. There are still a considerable number of the foreign born in the lower-income groups. In contrast, the foreign born have lower rates of employment and higher rates of inactivity than the native born. About 66 percent of the native born are employed compared to approximately 54 percent of the foreign born. Thirty percent of the foreign born are inactive compared to 20 percent of the native born.

The distribution of immigrants across occupations is quite similar to that of the native born. Examination of the distribution of immigrant workers by major industry division reveals that they are not overrepresented in any category. As shown in table 4.5, except for "other services," their distribution is similar to that of British nationals. The modal categories are "other services" and distributive trades.

There is also mixed evidence with respect to the "assimilation hypothesis" that assumes that immigrants have lower rates of employment and other economic activity than natives at the time of admission, but higher

Table 4.5 Distribution of National, Foreign, and Total Employment between the Eleven Major Industry Divisions in Great Britain, 1991

Divisions[a]	*Nationals*	*Foreigners*	*Total*
00	2.4	0.5	2.3
10	2.2	1.0	2.2
20	3.2	2.6	3.1
30	9.8	8.3	9.7
40	8.7	7.8	8.7
50	7.5	7.3	7.5
60	20.3	21.4	20.4
70	6.3	5.6	6.2
80	11.4	10.7	11.4
90/1	6.6	4.4	6.5
90/2	21.6	30.2	22.0
Total	100.0	100.0	100.0

Sources: Organization for Economic Development and Cooperation, *Trends in International Migration, Annual Report 1991* (Paris: Organization for Economic Development and Cooperation, 1992); Eurostat, *Labour Force Survey* (Paris: Organization for Economic Development and Cooperation, 1991).

Note: Some of the columns do not add up exactly to 100 percent due to rounding.

[a]00 = agriculture, hunting, forestry and fishing; 10 = energy and water; 20 = extraction and processing of nonenergy-producing minerals and derived products, chemical industry; 30 = metal manufacture, mechanical, electrical, and instrument engineering; 40 = other manufacturing industries; 50 = building and civil engineering; 60 = distributive trades, hotels, catering, and repairs; 70 = transport and communications; 80 = banking and finance, insurance, business services, and renting; 90/1 = public administration, national defense, and compulsory social security, diplomatic representation; 90/2 = other services.

rates after a number of years in residence. This is not the case for employment but it is for income. Throughout their time in the host nation, immigrants have lower levels of employment than natives, but after six or seven years of residence immigrants have the same income as the native born. Thereafter, immigrant income is higher than that of the native born.[38]

Refugees and asylum seekers fare worse than other immigrant groups in economic activity. More than 42 percent of refugees and 68 percent of asylum seekers are unemployed.[39] This is undoubtedly due to the greater disruption of being forced to flee one's home as opposed to planning to leave. There are also restrictions in immigration laws and policies that preclude the employment of asylum seekers, which also contribute to their high unemployment rates.

Finally, immigrants do not seem to be a net drain on British society. Immigrants pay more taxes to the government than they receive in services. Stephen Glover et al. estimate that immigrants contribute "around 10 percent more to Government revenues than they receive in Government expenditure."[40]

Immigrants have both more and less education than the native population in the UK. The proportion of foreign born with a higher degree is slightly greater than the proportion among the native born. At the same time, the proportion of persons with minimal education in the immigrant population is substantially greater than that in the UK-born population.[41]

Approximately 69 percent of ethnic immigrants speak English fluently or fairly well. This varies considerably across ethnic groups with virtually 100 percent of Caribbean immigrants speaking English, as compared to 49 percent of those from Bangladesh.[42] Afro-Asian immigrants had high levels of fluency with 84 percent speaking fluently or fairly well followed by the Chinese (69 percent), the Indians (64 percent), and the Pakistani (51 percent). Fertility patterns among foreigners and native born in Great Britain followed the same pattern observed in the other countries. Foreign women have higher fertility rates than native-born women, although the fertility rate for both groups is decreasing. Between 1970 and 1983, the fertility rate for British women dropped from 2.4 to 1.7 and for immigrant women from 4.0 to 2.8.[43]

Criminal Involvement

As in some of the other nations examined in this book, the only available national data on the criminal involvement of immigrants in Great Britain comes from the correctional system. But in 1988, a national crime survey was conducted (the British Crime Survey) that collected data on victimizations by ethnic groups. The results showed that the rates of victimization were higher among both Afro-Caribbean and South Asians than among white people. Table 4.6 provides a detailed breakdown of the types of victimization by ethnic group.

In 1992, about 7 percent of convicted prisoners serving sentences in Great Britain were foreign nationals,[44] and by 1997 that proportion had increased slightly to 7.6 percent.[45] This is a substantial increase over 1988 when only 1 percent of the prison population was immigrant.[46] The proportion of the prison population that comprised foreign nationals is greater than their representation in the general population. According to the 1991 census, 3.3 percent of the population in Great Britain are foreigners.

The vast majority of immigrants serving sentences in British prisons have been convicted of drug offenses. Martin Richards et al. estimate that 98 percent of the immigrants in prison have been convicted of offenses related to drug importation.[47] One can infer this from the fact that foreign nationals have a higher incarceration rate than native-born citizens for

Table 4.6 Victimization Reporting Rates by Ethnic Group

	White	*Afro-Caribbean*	*Asian*
Household Victimization			
Household vandalism	4.7	3.6[a]	7.5[b]
Burglary with loss	2.7	6.4[b]	3.5
Vehicle crime (owners)			
Vandalism	9.4	8.7	13.7[b]
All theft	17.9	26.3[b]	19.5
Bicycle theft (owners)	4.2	8.4[a]	3.9
Other household theft	7.9	6.9	9.3[a]
All household	29.8	32.7[a]	35.5[b]
Personal Victimization			
Assault	3.4	7.4[b]	4.4
Threats	2.5	3.9	5.3[b]
Assaults or threats	5.5	9.4[b]	10.8[b]
Robbery/theft from person	1.1	3.3[b]	30.0[b]
Other personal thefts	4.0	5.5	3.1
All personal	9.6	16.1[b]	14.8[b]

Source: Pat Mayhew, David Elliot, and Lizanne Dowds, *The 1988 British Crime Survey* (London: Her Majesty's Stationery Office, 1989), table 11.

[a]Statistically significant at the 10 percent level (two-tailed test, taking account of the sample design factor). For further explanatory details, see original table.

[b]Statistically significant at the 5 percent level (two-tailed test, taking account of the sample design factor). For further explanatory details, see original table.

drug crimes, but have a much lower involvement than native-born citizens in other types of crime.

Public Opinion

The data provided in this section report public attitudes toward the various race relations acts and the work of the commission that handles complaints. On four national polls beginning in 1983, the British public was asked:

There is a law in Britain against racial discrimination; that is, against giving unfair preference to a particular race in housing, jobs, and so on. Do you generally support or oppose the idea of a law for this purpose?

	1983		*1984*		*1986*		*1989*	
	Percent	*Number*	*Percent*	*Number*	*Percent*	*Number*	*Percent*	*Number*
Support	69.0	1,186	69.6	1,145	64.6	1,000	68.4	1,000
Oppose	28.3	487	25.5	419	31.8	492	27.7	405
Don't know	2.0	35	3.2	53	3.1	48	2.9	43
No answer	0.7	11	1.7	28	0.6	9	1.0	14
Total	100.0	1,719	100.0	1,645	100.0	1,548	100.0	1,461

Source: British Social Attitudes Cumulative Sourcebook, Social and Community Planning Research (London: Gower, 1992).

Some two-thirds of the respondents demonstrated consistent support for laws against discrimination. However, British citizens were then asked to respond to the following: "Britain controls the number of people that are allowed to settle in this country. Please say, for each of the groups below, whether you think Britain should allow more settlement, less settlement, or about the same amount as now."

As shown in table 4.7, the British public exhibited a clear preference for "white" immigrants from Australia and New Zealand and from European common-market countries, as opposed to Indians, Pakistani, and West Indians (see also table 4.8). For all groups, the preferences were expressed mainly by the extent to which the public preferred less settlement. Thus, for people from Australia and New Zealand and common-market countries, in 1989, 32 and 41 percent, respectively, preferred "less" settlement, as opposed to 67 and 62 percent, respectively, who preferred less settlement of Indians and Pakistani and West Indians.

Part II of this book compares public opinion data across countries, demonstrating that the British public has been more welcoming toward immigrants from the mid-1980s on than have the respondents in the other

Table 4.7 Should Britain Allow More, Less, or the Same Amount of Settlement? (in percent)

Settler's Home Country and Choice	*1983*	*1984*	*1986*	*1989*
Australia/New Zealand				
More	15.7	11.5	8.6	9.0
Less	27.7	35.0	33.9	31.8
About the same	55.1	51.2	55.8	56.7
Don't know/no answer	1.5	1.8	1.5	2.3
Indians/Pakistani				
More	1.9	2.0	2.0	1.2
Less	71.2	73.5	67.6	66.9
About the same	25.6	22.4	29.1	29.5
Don't know/no answer	1.3	2.2	1.3	2.4
People from Common-Market Countries				
More	6.9	5.4	5.7	8.0
Less	44.4	49.2	45.8	40.5
About the same	46.8	42.6	47.0	48.8
Don't know/no answer	1.9	2.7	1.5	2.7
West Indians				
More	1.9	2.2	2.2	1.7
Less	66.7	68.9	64.3	61.5
About the same	28.4	26.0	32.0	34.1
Don't know/no answer	3.0	3.0	1.4	2.7

Source: American Institute of Public Opinion (Storrs: Roper Center, University of Connecticut, 1989).

Note: In 1991, the British public was again asked about its attitude toward particular groups of immigrants. As shown in table 4.8, most respondents did not express "dislike" for any group, but they did show preferences for groups that they "liked," with north Europeans receiving support from 57.6 percent of the respondents. The North Africans, Turks, black Africans, and Asians were liked by less than 40 percent of the respondents. Also note that some of the columns do not add up exactly to 100 percent due to rounding.

countries included in this volume. Of course, fewer immigrants have come to Great Britain than to all of the other countries, except for Japan.

The British have not only been more welcoming to immigrants, they have also expressed support for them receiving treatment equal to native-born citizens. For example, look at the responses to the following 1984 national poll:

I am going to read out a list of policies that the government could adopt towards immigrants living in Britain. I would like you to tell me whether you agree or disagree with each one.

	Agree	*Disagree*	*Don't know*
Make sure that all immigrants who are here have treatment equal to other Britains	81	13	6

Table 4.8 British Attitudes toward Particular Groups, 1991

Group	*Opinion*	*Percent*
South Europeans	dislike	4.3
	indifferent	45.7
	like	50.0
North Africans	dislike	12.4
	indifferent	51.2
	like	36.4
Turks	dislike	12.2
	indifferent	52.8
	like	35.0
Black Africans	dislike	12.2
	indifferent	48.9
	like	38.7
Asians	dislike	12.6
	indifferent	48.9
	like	38.4
Southeast Asians	dislike	12.8
	indifferent	49.6
	like	37.6
West Indians	dislike	12.8
	indifferent	47.1
	like	40.3
Jews	dislike	5.5
	indifferent	54.2
	like	40.3
North Europeans	dislike	3.0
	indifferent	39.4
	like	57.6

Source: American Institute of Public Opinion (Storrs: Roper Center, University of Connecticut, 1993).
Note: Some of the columns do not add up exactly to 100 percent due to rounding.

Introduce tougher penalties against racial discrimination	48	39	13
Abolish the race relations legislation because too much is done to help immigrants at present	47	39	14
Allow some discrimination in favor of immigrants applying for jobs	19	72	9

Source: American Institute of Public Opinion (Storrs: Roper Center, University of Connecticut, 1984).
Note: The rows do not add up exactly to 100 percent due to rounding.

Eighty-one percent of British citizens wanted immigrants to receive equal treatment, and only 19 percent wanted immigrants to receive especially favorable treatment.

Most citizens in Great Britain believe that the British government is providing the "right amount of help" to Asian and West Indian immigrants. But almost four times as many believe the government is providing "too much" help than those who believe the government is providing "too little" help. Look, for example, at the responses to the following question:

Do you think, on the whole, that Britain gives too little or too much help to Asians and West Indians who have settled in this country, or are present arrangements about right?

	1983		*1986*		*1989*	
	Percent	*Number*	*Percent*	*Number*	*Percent*	*Number*
Too little	7.4	128	10.2	158	10.1	147
Too much	32.4	557	32.6	505	36.6	534
Right amount	55.0	946	50.1	785	46.5	679
Don't know	4.1	71	6.1	95	6.1	89
No answer	1.0	17	0.3	5	0.8	12
Total	100.0	1,719	100.0	1,548	100.0	1,461

Source: American Institute of Public Opinion (Storrs: Roper Center, University of Connecticut, 1984).
Note: The columns do not add up exactly to 100 percent due to rounding.

Like the publics in the other countries, when the British were asked to choose between more or less immigrants, most opted for the latter. For example, examine the responses when British citizens were asked the following in 1984:

Which of these statements best describes the policy that you would like to see the government adopt towards immigration control?

Statement	*Percentage*[a]
Encourage as many immigrants as possible to go back home	29
Stop all further immigrants from the New Commonwealth	32
Only allow in the wives and dependents of those immigrants who have been here 3 years or more	24
Encourage immigrants with specific skills that the country needs to settle here	23
There should be no immigrant controls	6
Don't know	5

Source: American Institute of Public Opinion (Storrs: Roper Center, University of Connecticut, 1993).
[a]The responses add up to more than 100 percent because respondents were allowed to check more than one category.

Sixty-one percent of respondents favored stopping all immigrants from the New Commonwealth (i.e., nonwhite) and encouraging immigrants already in their country to go home.

In 1989 and 1992, British citizens were asked: "Would you say that the number of immigrants presently accepted by Britain as permanent residents each year is too high, too low, or about right?" In 1993, they were similarly asked: "Do you think that the controls on the number of immigrants are too strict, not strict enough, or about right?" The results looked like this:

		Years (in percent)	
Category	*1989*	*1992*	*1993*
Too high (or "not strict enough")	58	53	63
Too low (or "too strict")	6	6	6
About right	23	28	23
Don't know	13	13	8

Source: American Institute of Public Opinion (Storrs: Roper Center, University of Connecticut, 1993).

In 1989 and 1992, only 6 percent thought the numbers of immigrants admitted were too low and in 1993 ten times as many believed the numbers were too high. But when the same question was asked about refugees, 11 and 14 percent of the British public believed that the number they were accepting each year was "too low."

In a 1993 poll, British citizens were asked more specifically: "Is the presence of foreigners disturbing, do the children of foreigners in schools lower the level of education and do foreigners increase unemployment?" Thirty-three percent answered "yes, foreigners increase unemployment," and 24 percent said, "yes, the children of foreigners lower educational levels." Only 9 percent said they found immigrants disturbing. Again in 1993, a poll asked: "Are foreigners from non EEC countries good or bad for your country?" The results show 50 percent saying "a little good" or "good," compared to 31 percent saying "bad" or "a little bad."

The British public, like that of most other nations examined here, is opposed to increasing immigration. This opposition is greater for groups of immigrants who are culturally dissimilar than for immigrants who are more similar to the British public. While the British public opposes immigration, it does not support negative statements about immigrant groups and shows strong support for equal treatment for immigrants living in the country. It is equally adamant that immigrants should not receive preferential treatment relative to citizens. The British public seems to have struck a balance between the desire to maintain cultural homogeneity and equitable treatment of persons living in the country.

Summary

Following the end of World War II, Great Britain experienced a change of status from that of an exporter to an importer of immigrants as a solution to severe labor shortages, along with the independence of many of its colonies and the desire of colonial and Commonwealth citizens to "return to the mother country." By the early 1960s, however, the entrance into the country of many nonwhite colonials resulted in strong racial tensions and riots. Great Britain then changed its immigration laws and made it much more difficult for immigrants to enter from the New Commonwealth nations, that is, Pakistan, India, Hong Kong, and the British West Indies.

The British Nationality Act of 1981 and the operative statute as of 1997 limited admissions even further than the laws passed in the 1960s and 1970s. As of 1981, the only avenues open to persons who are not declared refugees are family unification or work permits. Under family unification, relatives are defined as wives, husbands, children, and elderly dependents of men and women settled in Great Britain. Work permits are only available for oversees workers who hold recognized professional qualifications. Unlike Germany, and like the United States, Australia, and Canada, immigrants may be granted citizenship after five years of residence and "good" character.

After the race riots of the early 1960s, Great Britain passed laws that were designed to guarantee equal opportunity and prohibit discrimination on the basis of race in employment, public accommodation, and education. Between 1983 and 1989, when the public was asked how it felt about these antidiscrimination laws, between 65 and 70 percent indicated its support of them. But like the respondents in the other countries studied, when asked during the same time periods whether it favored more, less, or the same number of immigrants from various parts of the world, less than 10 percent of the British public favored accepting more immigrants. The large majority said it favored fewer immigrants especially from India, Pakistan, and the West Indies. And more recently, in 1989, 1992, and 1993, between 53 and 63 percent thought that the controls on the number of immigrants admitted were not strict enough. The picture that emerges from these data is that the British public prefers fewer immigrants, and especially fewer nonwhite immigrants, but when admitted, wants all immigrants treated fairly.

British immigration policy has severely restricted the admission of groups that are culturally and racially dissimilar to the native population. It has also set in place procedures that would facilitate the incorporation of immigrants into British society through liberal naturalization policies and antidiscrimination measures. At the same time, the British government has not established supplementary programs to facilitate integration of immigrants, perhaps because this would antagonize the native population. The British public seems to have embraced this policy in that while it is opposed to immigration and especially the entry of culturally dissimilar groups, it also shows strong support for equal treatment of residents. The extent to which immigrants have been integrated into major social institutions in British society suggests that this policy is achieving the desired results.

Notes

1. Zig Layton-Henry, *The Politics of Immigration: Immigration, "Race," and Race Relations in Post-war Britain* (Oxford: Blackwell, 1992), 7.
2. Layton-Henry, *Politics of Immigration,* 7.
3. Layton-Henry, *Politics of Immigration,* 7.
4. Zig Layton-Henry, "Britain: The Would-Be Zero-Immigrant Country," in *Controlling Immigration: A Global Perspective,* ed. Wayne A. Cornelius, Philip Martin, and James Hollifield (Stanford, Calif.: Stanford University Press, 1994), 91.
5. Catherine Jones, *Immigration and Social Policy in Britain* (London: Tavistock, 1977), 134.
6. Elliot J. B. Rose, *Colour and Citizenship: A Report on British Race Relations* (London: Oxford University Press, 1969); and Layton-Henry, *Politics of Immigration,* 38.
7. Layton-Henry, "Britain," 103.
8. Layton-Henry, "Britain," 103.
9. Layton-Henry, "Britain," 104.
10. Layton-Henry, "Britain," 104.
11. Layton-Henry, "Britain," 105.
12. Stephen Glover et al., *Migration: An Economic and Social Analysis* (London: Home Office, 2001), 22.
13. Glover et al., *Migration,* 22.
14. Glover et al., *Migration,* 22.
15. Layton-Henry, *Politics of Immigration,* 8.
16. Keith Jackson and Barry Birdwell-Snow, *Control of Immigration Statistics United Kingdom: Second Half and Year, 1996* (London: Home Office, 1997), 1.
17. Jo Woodbridge, Di Burgum, and Tina Heath, *Asylum Statistics United Kingdom, 1999* (London: Home Office, 2000).
18. Woodbridge, Burgum, and Heath, *Asylum Statistics,* 1.
19. Woodbridge, Burgum, and Heath, *Asylum Statistics,* table 1.2.
20. Woodbridge, Burgum, and Heath, *Asylum Statistics,* 3.
21. Woodbridge, Burgum, and Heath, *Asylum Statistics,* 6.
22. Tom Baldwin, "Migrants May Have to Learn English," *The Times,* 18 August 2001, 12.
23. Sarah Collinson, *Europe and International Migration* (London: Pinter, 1993), 83.
24. Home Office, *Information on the Right of Abode in the United Kingdom* (London: Home Office, 2000), 1.
25. Keith Jackson and Peter Kilsby, *Persons Granted British Citizenship, 1996* (London: Home Office, 1997).

26. Jill Dudley and Paul Harvey, *Persons Granted British Citizenship, 2000* (London: Home Office, 2001).

27. Glover et al., *Migration,* 47.

28. Glover et al., *Migration,* 24–27.

29. Jackson and Birdwell-Snow, *Control of Immigration Statistics,* table 5.2.

30. Dudley and Harvey, *Persons Granted British Citizenship, 2000,* 24.

31. Dudley and Harvey, *Persons Granted British Citizenship, 2000,* 25.

32. Dudley and Harvey, *Persons Granted British Citizenship, 2000,* 26.

33. Dudley and Harvey, *Persons Granted British Citizenship, 2000,* 25.

34. Timothy Hatton and Stephen Wheatly-Price, "Migration, Migrants and Policy in the United Kingdom," Discussion Paper no. 81 (Bonn: Institute for the Study of Labor, 1999), 1.

35. Hatton and Wheatly-Price, "Migration," 1.

36. Hatton and Wheatly-Price, "Migration," 1.

37. Glover et al., *Migration,* 33.

38. Glover et al., *Migration,* 34.

39. Glover et al., *Migration,* 35.

40. Glover et al., *Migration,* 44.

41. Glover et al., *Migration,* 31.

42. Christian Dustmann and Francesca Fabbri, "Language Proficiency and Labour Market Performance of Immigrants in the UK," Discussion Paper no. 156 (Bonn: Institute for the Study of Behavior, May 2000).

43. Glover et al., *Migration.*

44. Martin Richards et al., "Foreign Nationals in English Prisons: Some Policy Issues," *The Howard Journal* 34 (1995): 195–208.

45. Philip White and Jo Woodbridge, *The Prison Population in 1997* (London: Home Office, 1998).

46. Katrina Tomasevski, *Foreigners in Prison* (Helsinki, Finland: European Institute for Crime Prevention and Control, 1994).

47. Richards et al., "Foreign Nationals in English Prisons."

5

Immigration in France

France has had a long history of receiving, and even encouraging, immigration. But throughout this history there has always been some ambivalence about the goal of immigration. In some periods, the goal appears to have been labor-force needs, while in others it seems to have been population replacement. In recent years, a significant social movement has emerged under the leadership of Jean-Marie Le Pen that has sought to close French borders and return foreign workers to their homelands. Former president Valey Giscard d'Estaing has lent vocal support to this movement. Both Le Pen and d'Estaing have warned of "invading Muslim hordes."

Historical Background and Major Legislation

Between 1850 and 1913, the number of immigrants entering France increased from 380,000 to 1.6 million.[1] In this period, immigration was encouraged as industrialization accelerated and peasants left the rural areas for work in the cities. Following World War I, the need for immigrants increased again as a function of the labor shortage, which was due both to military casualties and expanding construction in housing and industry. Between 1921 and 1931, the number of immigrants increased from 1.5 million to 2.7 million, with large numbers arriving from China, Vietnam, and other parts of Asia and Africa.[2] During the 1930s, France, like other industrial countries, experienced an acute economic depression that resulted in virtually no immigration and the adoption of policies for encouraging foreigners to leave the country. Thus, for the first time France began the controlled recruitment of immigrants.

The end of World War II, however, marked the beginning of an active and centrally controlled French policy favoring immigration.[3] The demand for foreign labor was driven by the need to repair damage from the war. During this postwar period, demand for labor outstripped the bureaucracy's ability to process applications. As a result, the proportion of illegal immigrants began to rise and only 10 to 30 percent of the immigrants entering France during this time were believed to be legal. This trend increased throughout the 1960s as the French economy began to expand rapidly.

When the French and most other European economies slowed after 1973, severe restrictions were again placed on legal immigration.[4] Immigration policy changed to favor family unification rather than the recruitment of workers. This policy continued into the 1980s, when the goal of French immigration policy was the stabilization of the immigrant population and its assimilation. Table 5.1 demonstrates the evolution of the immigrant population in France from 1921 to 1990.

The Office of National del' Immigration (ONI) was established in November 1945 and it is the major source of French immigration policy.[5] Whatever the legal basis for this agency's action, it also has substantial discretion over the country's admission policy and its administrative regulations have the force of law.[6]

Soon after its creation, the ONI issued a directive that regulated the residence and employment of foreigners. The directive stated that anyone who wished to engage in a steady occupation in France must obtain both a residence and a work permit that could be valid for one, three, or ten years. However, citizens of the European Economic Community (EEC), Algerians, and citizens of certain West African countries did not need either of those permits. In addition, work permits were denied to spouses.

In 1974, the government tightened this policy considerably.[7] Preferences were no longer given on the basis of labor needs, that is, work permits; and the active recruitment of guest workers stopped. Rather, the government now gave preference to relatives of immigrants and citizens. Exceptions to this rule were made for certain industries, notably mining, construction, and agriculture.

Under the policy of family unification, the immediate family of foreign workers can gain entry. Nonetheless, these persons are required to show proof of employment and access to adequate housing. Episodically, there have been efforts to discourage family unification by restricting access to work permits or by employing stricter standards for proving that adequate housing is available.

From 1977 to May 1981, the government tried to reduce the size of the immigration population with several measures including: (1) an allowance of 10,000 francs to certain categories of immigrants if they and their families would return to their country of origin and never come back (the policy was

Table 5.1 Evolution of the Foreign Population in France, 1921–1990 (census data)

	1921	*1931*	*1954*	*1975*	*1982*	*1990*
Total population	38,797,540	41,228,466	42,781,370	52,599,430	54,273,200	56,625,000
Total foreign population	1,566,333	2,815,979	1,983,022	4,672,658	5,356,560	5,392,544
% of foreigners in total population	4.0	6.8	4.6	8.9	9.9	9.5
European nationalities (including the Soviet Union)	1,435,976	2,457,649	1,431,219	2,102,685	1,760,000	1,453,360
African nationalities	37,666	105,059	229,505	1,192,300	1,573,820	1,652,870
Algerians	—	—	211,675[a]	710,690	795,920	619,923
Moroccans	36,277	82,568	10,734	260,025	431,120	584,708
Tunisians	—	—	4,800[b]	139,753	189,400	207,496
French West Africans	—	16,401	—	70,320	138,080	178,133
American nationalities	22,402	32,120	49,129	41,560	50,900	77,554
Asian nationalities (not including the Soviet Union)	28,972	86,063	40,687	104,465	293,780	417,020
Turks	5,040	36,119	5,273	50,860	123,540	201,480

Source: James F. Hollifield, "Immigration and Republicanism in France: The Hidden Concensus," in *Controlling Immigration,* ed. Wayne Cornelius, Philip Martin, and James Hollifield (Stanford, Calif.: Stanford University Press, 1994), 151.

[a]French Muslim Algerians.

[b]Individuals from within the French empire (l'Union française) are counted as French, except French Muslim Algerians, who were counted as foreign during this period.

directed mostly at Algerians to induce the return of 35,000 Algerians per year); and (2) a 1932 law granting power to establish a ceiling on the number of foreigners employed in certain professions in industrial sectors.[8] These measures appeared to have little effect on the immigrant population.[9]

In principle, immigration is now open de jure only to aliens who have special links with France, to some relatives in the process of family reunification, to refugees, and to European Community (EC) citizens.

Aliens must apply for a long-term visa from the French consular post of their foreign domicile. Within two months of arrival in France, the alien must apply either for a resident's card, if entitled to one, or for a temporary sojourn card (*carte de sejour temporaire* [CST]).

A resident's card is the permanent immigration entitlement. Valid ten years and renewable with no conditions, it allows the holder to undertake any professional activity. A resident's card is available to aliens who prove that they have had uninterrupted residence in France, in compliance with applicable laws and regulations, for at least three years (*Ordonnance* no. 45-2658 of November 5, 1945, article 14). The delivery of the card will be subject to proof of living conditions, including the conditions of the person's professional activity, and, eventually, the circumstances that can be used to assess his or her intention to settle steadily in France.

The resident's card can be refused to anyone whose presence in French territory causes a threat to public order.

A resident's card is also issued with no conditions to the following categories of aliens:

1. The spouse of a French citizen
2. The child of a French citizen, if the child is under twenty-one or dependent on his or her parents, and dependent ancestors of the French citizen and of his or her spouse
3. The father or mother of a child who is a French citizen residing in France, if the parent has legal authority over the child or supports the child financially (*Ordonnance* no. 45-2658 of November 2, 1945, article 15)

The CST is valid for a period of time that depends on information contained in the documents on the basis of which the alien has entered France, as well as those pursuant to which the CST has been delivered, but not exceeding one year. After expiration of the card, the alien must leave the territory unless the card is renewed or a resident's card is issued. The procedure for renewal of the card is the same as the initial issuance procedure.

Citizens of EC member states have the right to reside in France provided that they have a general health insurance covering all risks in the member state and sufficient financial means not to become dependent on the host state's social security services. Financial means are deemed to be sufficient when they exceed the level of financial resources under which the host state's citizens are granted social assistance, or when the applicant's financial means are higher than the minimum welfare pension. This right is extended to the spouse of the EC citizen, his or her dependent descendents, and dependent ancestors. Denial of these rights is possible only for reasons of public order, health, and security. EC citizens receive an EC citizen's card valid for five years.

Algerian citizens also have special status. Algerian citizens immigrating to France are provided initially with a one-year residence certificate; this document is delivered on presentation of documents comparable to those required for a CST and that vary with the intended activity. After three years of continuous residence in France, Algerian citizens are delivered a ten-year residence certificate if they prove they have a sufficient and stable income and if their presence does not cause a threat to public order. The Algerian spouse or relative of a French national as well as Algerians living in France for ten years or more are automatically given a ten-year residence certificate.

The principle is that an alien regularly residing in France has a right to bring his or her spouse and children under eighteen (or under twenty-one if dependent) if the alien is a citizen of a country that is a member of the European Social Charter. These relatives may not be denied the right to work by a general regulation (such a denial would be an obstacle to family reunification).

Administrative provisions require that the alien, whom the family is joining, must have been regularly residing in France for at least one year (except for Algerian citizens), that financial resources be stable and sufficient, and that the accommodations be appropriate.

The situation of EC citizens (including French citizens) who want their families (EC or non-EC citizens) to immigrate is regulated by the *Decret* no. 81-405 of April 28, 1981. Their spouse and children benefit from the unconditional right to immigrate as long as the person's own situation with regard to immigration law is not objectionable.

The right to asylum has constitutional value in French law as it was recognized in the preamble of the 1946 constitution to which the 1958 constitution, actually applicable, refers. France has a restrictive definition of political asylum and does not open its territory to economic refugees. Individuals denied refugee status are not allowed to remain in the territory after the admission procedure is terminated. The length of time required for completing this procedure has been reduced from several years to six months at most, in order to minimize the human consequences of a refugee status denial.

Individuals who claim to be refugees and wish to enter France are not required to provide the documents generally mandatory for all aliens (passport and visa, proof of purpose, conditions and means of stay, and repatriation guarantees). Following their entry into France, they are provided by the local government representative (prefet) with a temporary sojourn authorization that is valid for one month, which entitles them to remain in France while their application for refugee status is filed.

Along with the temporary sojourn authorization, they are provided with an application form for refugee status. The application for refugee status must be filed with the Office for the Protection of Refugees and Stateless Persons (OFPRA) without delay. These documents do not give the applicants the right to work; applicants receive monthly "integration" allowances until the OFPRA decides on their status. However, refugees from Southeast Asia who have entered France through organized procedures receive a six-month renewable sojourn document that entitles them to work.

The decision of the OFPRA conferring or refusing the refugee status is notified to the applicant. If the applicant is granted refugee status, he or she will be issued a resident's card valid for ten years and automatically renewable (see the earlier discussion on the general requirements for immigrants). The refugee may also ask for a circulation permit in accordance with the Geneva Convention. If the alien is definitively denied refugee status (i.e., after failure on review), the prefecture notifies the applicant of his or her obligation to leave the territory within one month.

Between 1975 and 1980, France admitted about 160,000 refugees, mostly from Chile, Lebanon, and Southeast Asia. In December 1984, there were 169,863 refugees registered in France, 57 percent from Asia, 32 percent from Europe, 6 percent from the Americas, and 5 percent from Africa. The following chart describes the requests for asylum from 1981 through 1995.

Year	*Number of Requests (rounded off)*
1981	20,000
1982	22,000
1983	29,000
1984	29,000
1985	26,000
1986	28,000
1987	28,000
1988	34,000
1989	61,000
1990	55,000
1991	47,000
1992	29,000
1993	28,000
1994	26,000
1995	20,000

Source: U.S. Committee for Refugees, *Worldwide Refugee Information: Country Report: France* (Washington, D.C.: U.S. Committee on Refugees, September 6, 2001).

In 1984, France rejected one-third of the asylum seekers. From 1990 on, it rejected between 71 and 84 percent of the asylum seekers, with Africans representing the largest proportion of the persons rejected. In 1995, 84 percent were rejected.

Stock and Flow of Immigrants

It is not clear that the flow of admissions has strictly followed changes in policy. Admissions were quite high in the postwar years but dropped in the 1960s and 1970s and have not been reduced much since despite the obvious restrictiveness in policies. In 1945, 1.6 million immigrants entered the country and 1.5 million entered in 1954. Between 1963 and 1973, an average of 130,000 immigrants entered France annually. In the 1980s, annual admissions averaged about 175,000. These estimates, however, exclude illegal immigrants. If we assume that the ratio of stock to flow is the same for legal and illegal immigrants, then we would estimate that about 11,000 illegals entered the country annually. Under this assumption, the flow of immigrants into France annually is approximately equal to 0.3 percent of the stock population.

The stock population of immigrants in France was approximately 4 million in the 1980s and 3.6 million in 1990.[10] This constitutes 6 percent of the population. When estimates of foreigners (3.6 million) and naturalized citizens (1.2 million) are combined, the estimate of foreign born is 4.8 million or about 8.8 percent of the population. The number of illegal immigrants in the stock population in 1990 was estimated at 313,046. When this estimate is added to the number of foreigners and naturalized citizens, about 9.4 percent of the French population is foreign born.

Naturalization

There are three ways in which an immigrant can become a citizen of France.[11] The first is automatic on reaching the age of eighteen. This pertains only to children born in France to foreign parents, and to children born in France and who resided in France since the age of thirteen. The second method is by declaration, that is, simply by registering. This option is available to foreigners married to French citizens and to residents from former French colonies. The latter group includes Algerians who entered France before 1962. The government may veto the acquisition of nationality within one year following the declaration on the grounds of lack of dignity or lack of integration. The declaration is not open to the alien or stateless person who is undergoing a procedure of expulsion. The third method is by decree. In this instance, application must be made after residing in France for five or more years. This method is available for legal as well as illegal immigrants. More recent legislation permits the denial of citizenship to applicants convicted of serious crimes. Naturalization can only be granted to individuals who are over eighteen, who have good moral qualifications (individuals who have been convicted of crimes are generally excluded), and who prove their integration into the French community, especially by their knowledge of the French language.

French nationality can be lost at the request of the individual or of the French government or tribunals. Dual or multiple nationality is not a cause of automatic loss of French nationality. However, a French national who becomes a citizen of another country and has his or her usual residence abroad may relinquish French nationality within one year following the acquisition of the new nationality. Loss of French nationality may be imposed by the court if a French national by birth has no reputation of being a French national, has never resided in France, and if the ancestors from whom the person acquired French nationality have not had the reputation of being French nationals and have not had their usual residence in France for more than half a century.

Loss of French nationality may also be imposed by the government against an individual who has not resigned from his work or services for a foreign country, public service, or international organization of which France is not a member, after the government has ordered the individual to do so. Individuals who have become French nationals may lose their nationality if they are convicted of a crime against the security of the state (*crime contre la surete de l'Etat*) or against civil liberties (articles 109 to 131 of the Penal Code); if they have eluded their duties with regard to military service; if they have acted toward a foreign government in a way contrary to the quality of a French national and to the interest of France; or if it they have been convicted, in France or abroad, of a deed that would be a crime under French law and for which they have spent at least five years in prison.

Philip E. Ogden estimates that 38 percent of foreigners entering France became naturalized citizens.[12] Other estimates have 27.5 percent of all foreigners in the stock population as naturalized citizens.[13] The latest year for which naturalization rates are available for France is 1991, and in that year 2.75 out of every 100 aliens became citizens. The French government grants approximately 80 percent of all applications for citizenship.

Policies for Control of Immigrants

French immigration policy affords ample opportunity to control the behavior of foreigners. As noted earlier, work and residence permits are requirements for entry. These permits are for limited periods of time and for specific industries or companies. Consequently, immigrants must reapply for permits when they expire or when any of the specific conditions on which the permits are predicated change. This gives the Ministry of Justice an opportunity to expel persons whom it considers undesirable.

Residence permits must be obtained from the Ministry of Justice. These permits allow immigrants to reside in France and are of three types: temporary, ordinary, and privileged.[14] Temporary permits are valid for one year, ordinary for three years, and privileged for ten years. Granting of these permits is entirely at the discretion of the immigration authorities. Immigrants must also demonstrate that they have adequate housing.

There are a number of exceptions to the requirement of residence permits. For example, EEC citizens can come and look for work without obtaining residence permits; Algerians have automatic one-year residence permits that can also serve as work permits; and former West African colonies have specific bilateral agreements allocating a certain number of permits for specific durations.

Work permits are issued by the Ministry of Labor and there are two types. One type permits foreigners to work in a specified job in a specified area. If the job changes or the area in which the person works changes, then a new permit must be obtained. The second type of permit is not limited to a specific job or a specific area. Work permits can be denied at administrative discretion. Applicants for permits or the potential employers must demonstrate that the occupation does not include unemployed French citizens.

Immigrants can be expelled from France on several grounds. Persons without the requisite permits and foreigners with all of the required permits who are considered a threat to public order (i.e., persons convicted of a crime and sentenced to prison for one year or more) can be expelled. But foreigners who were born in France, who arrived before the age of eleven, who lived in France for more than twenty years, or who have immediate relatives in France cannot be expelled. The expulsion procedure is no longer an administrative procedure entirely at the discretion of immigration officials. Rather, the power is held by a commission, presided over by a judge, with no immigration officials present.[15] Persons expelled can return after ten years.

Illegal Immigrants

The issue of illegal immigrants is much more salient in France than in Great Britain or Germany, and perhaps more severe than in the United States. The "illegals problem" was fostered in part by the government's willingness to wink at the legal immigration process during the period of economic boom between 1963 and 1973,[16] when only 10 percent of immigration was estimated to be legal. In addition, a policy of ad hoc legalization of persons wrongfully residing in France contributed to the flow of illegal immigrants. In the decade of the 1990s, the number of people who were caught trying to enter the country illegally increased from 8,700 in 1993, to 10,100 in 1995, to over 12,000 in 1996.[17]

In the mid-1980s, the French government imposed a number of sanctions to reduce illegal immigration.[18] First, tighter controls were imposed at the border by expanding the power of the border patrol to send "phony" tourists home. Second, after 1982 the government imposed sanctions on those employing illegal immigrants. Third, a one-time amnesty was offered to illegal immigrants in 1981, coupled with severe sanctions on illegal immigrants effective in 1982. These sanctions included imprisonment for one year followed by deportation.

Demographic and Socioeconomic Characteristics of Immigrants

The policies described earlier have had some effect on the nature of the immigrant population in France. They influence the size of that population as well as the cultural and social structural similarity between the immigrants and the native population.

As of 1992, immigrants comprised 9.4 percent of the population of France. This is a relatively large proportion of the resident population comparable to that found in immigrant nations such as the United States.

There are some indications that cultural barriers between the immigrant and native population are breaking down. In 1980, 6.2 percent of the marriages were between a foreigner and a native; in 1985, they were at 7.9 percent; and in 1990, 10.6 percent. In two out of three of those marriages, the husband was the foreigner and the wife was the native. The level of intermarriage and the increase in the rate of intermarriage suggest the integration of immigrant populations.

In contrast, as shown in table 5.2, the fertility rate of foreign women from Turkey and North Africa are consistently higher than those for French women or other European foreigners. While the fertility rates of natives and immigrants have both declined over time, the fertility rates for Algerians, Tunisians, Turks, and Moroccans have remained multiples of the rate for natives. The trend in fertility rates for immigrants from Portugal, Spain, and Italy have declined over time to the point that they are similar to that of the native population. Since the decision to have children is so central to cultural beliefs, this is a powerful indicator of the cultural similarity of the native and immigrant groups. The European immigrants are becoming more similar to the French while the Turks and North Africans remain quite distinct.

Table 5.2 Total Fertility Rates (per 1,000), 1982–1985

Year	*Total*	*Nationals*	*Foreigners (born in France or abroad)*	*Algeria*	*Morocco*	*Portugal*	*Tunisia*	*Turkey*	*Spain*	*Italy*
1968	2.57	2.50	4.01	8.92	3.32	4.90	NA	NA	3.20	3.32
1975	1.93	1.84	3.33	5.28	4.68	3.30	5.27	NA	2.60	2.12
1982	1.91	1.84	3.20	4.29	5.23	2.17	5.20	5.05	1.77	1.74
1983	1.79	NA	3.13							
1984	1.81	NA	3.10							
1985	1.82	1.75	3.05							
			Foreigners (born abroad)	*Algeria*	*Morocco*	*Portugal*	*Tunisia*	*Turkey*	*Spain*	*Italy*
1982			3.30	4.98	5.18	2.10	5.37	4.91	1.74	1.72
1983			3.26	4.69	4.90	1.93	5.11	5.08	1.74	1.59
1984			3.24	4.51	4.76	1.81	4.78	4.95	1.73	1.68
1985			3.19	4.24	4.47	1.73	4.67	4.55	1.84	1.88

Source: Michele Trabalat, *Cent ans d'immigration, étrangers d'hier Français d'aujourd'hui: Apport démographique, dynamique familiale et économique de l'immigration étrangère* (Paris: Presses Universitaires de France, 1991).

The participation of immigrants in major social institutions suggests that their integration into these institutions is not complete. Between 1981 and 1992, the percentage of foreign students in the French school system remained relatively stable between 8 and 9 percent. This is close to the representation of immigrants in the population, but since immigrants are younger than the native population, they must be somewhat underrepresented in educational institutions. Moreover, the participation has remained relatively stable over time rather than increasing. Also, the representation of immigrants in secondary education is less than their representation in the population and less than their participation in primary education.[19] The rate of participation in secondary education is increasing over time. Table 5.3 illustrates the breakdown by education level.

The participation of immigrants in the labor force lags behind the native population. Foreign workers made up 6.3 percent of the labor force in 1993, but 11.3 percent of the unemployed.[20] In 1975, slightly less than 5 percent of the immigrant labor force was unemployed compared to 3.8 percent of the French labor force. In 1982, the difference was 14 percent versus 7 percent.

Immigrants from the non-EU nations made up a larger percentage of the foreign labor force than did the EU immigrants, and the differences are greater among the male than the female workers. The forty-year-old and older women are more likely to come from the EU.

In terms of occupational prestige, immigrants in France rank lower than the native population. In 1991, building and civil engineering were the occupational categories in which most of the immigrants worked (21.7 percent of foreigners compared to 6.8 percent of nationals), along with other service industries (19.1 percent of foreigners compared to 22.2 percent of nationals) and distributive trades, such as hotels, catering, and repairs (17.5 percent of foreigners compared to 17.2 percent of nationals). France has a number of

Table 5.3 Percentage of Pupils Who Are Foreign Born

Year	*Preschool*	*Primary*	*Secondary*	*Total (average)*
1981	NA	14.4	6.2	6.9
1982	9.8	10.1	6.4	8.8
1983	9.8	10.7	6.7	9.1
1984	9.8	11.0	6.8	9.2
1985	9.6	10.9	7.0	9.2
1986	9.7	10.9	7.1	9.2
1987	9.4	10.7	7.2	9.1
1988	9.1	10.5	7.3	9.0
1992	8.1	10.1	7.3	8.5

Source: Ministère de l'Education Nationale, *Direction de l'Evaluation et de la Prospective* (Paris: Ministère de l'Education Nationale, 1993).

policies and programs designed to accommodate foreigners into French society. There are educational and vocational training programs as well as special housing for immigrants. In addition, immigrants are eligible for most of the social benefits available to French citizens after a short period of residence. It is not clear, however, whether these policies contribute to the integration or the segregation of immigrants.

In sum, immigrants in France remain quite distinct culturally from the native population and participate in major institutions to a lesser degree than French citizens. This is more the case for immigrants from North Africa and Turkey than it is for immigrants from Europe.

Criminal Involvement

As in the case of the United States, the sources of data on the criminal involvement of immigrants in France are of two types: detailed studies of immigrant groups in specific localities and national statistics. Unlike the United States, however, the French routinely record citizenship status as part of their statistical systems pertaining to crime and criminal justice. The police record this information as do correctional officials. These data are also reported by type of offense. The picture that emerges from these data is that criminal involvement of immigrants is higher than that of the native-born population in France.

In 1991, the offending rate (based on police-recorded serious crimes) for foreigners in France was approximately three times that of French citizens. Table 5.4 breaks the numbers down by types of crime. The difference between immigrants and the native born were smallest for burglary (2 to 1) and

Table 5.4 Estimated Offenses by Citizenship and Types of Crime, France, 1991

Offense	*Number of Foreigners*	*Per 100,000*	*Number of Citizens*	*Per 100,000*
Homicide	198	5.48	1,191	2.09
Attempted homicide	149	4.13	826	1.45
Assaults	6,813	188.78	4,275	60.24
Drug offenses	12,090	335.00	47,612	83.69
Trafficking	3,530	97.81	6,551	11.51
Robbery	2,966	82.18	12,899	22.67
Burglary	5,097	141.23	44,219	77.72
Theft	34,096	944.75	181,496	319.01

Sources: Aspects de la criminalité et de la délinquance constates en France en 1991 (Paris: La Documentation Français, 1992). Estimation of foreign population from Sarah Collinson, *Europe and International Migration* (London: Pinter, 1993).

greatest for drug trafficking (9 to 1). In every category except homicide, the offending rate for immigrants exceeded that for native-born citizens.

Table 5.5 compares the types of offenses for which foreigners and French citizens were sentenced in 1991. The biggest difference occurred in the drug offenses, for which immigrants accounted for 74.1 percent of the persons sentenced compared to 50.3 percent of native-born citizens.

As of 1993, immigrants comprised 33 percent of the prison population and were six times more likely to be imprisoned than were native-born citizens.[21] As the data in table 5.6 show, the imprisonment rate of immigrants may be higher than the suspect rate because some may have been incarcerated for immigration offenses and not violations of criminal law.

Table 5.7 lists the 1995 prison population by nationality. Among immigrants, Algerians comprise the largest single category.

Some of the differences in the involvement of immigrants in the criminal justice system may be due to the enforcement of immigration laws. Since only foreigners are subject to processing for these immigration infractions, including them in our indicators of criminal involvement will inflate the numbers for immigrants relevant to native-born citizens. When these infractions are removed from the data, the differences in the criminal involvement of immigrants and native-born citizens decrease, but they are still substantial. For example, when immigration violations are included, the police processing rate for immigrants is 3.6 times greater than that for native-born citizens and the stock incarceration rate is 7.2 times greater. These ratios are much smaller when immigration violations are excluded: 2.5 and 3.0, respectively. The large decline in the incarcerated population ratios when immigration violations are taken into account is not surprising, since the police consider immigrants a high risk for absconding and therefore believe detention is required. This theory is consistent with the fact that the ratio of immigrants to native-born prisoners in the stock population (6.0) is lower than the same ratio for the admissions to secure custody (7.2) when immigration law violations are included (see table 5.8). This is due to the fact that persons incarcerated for immigration violations are kept for shorter periods of time relative to sentenced populations. At the same time, however, the difference in the ratios of immigrants and native-born citizens in the stock population (4.9) is substantially larger than that based on admission (3.0) when immigration infractions are excluded. Such data suggest that the disproportionate inclusion of immigrants in the incarcerated population is because they receive longer sentences than native-born citizens.

The involvement of immigrants in the criminal justice system increases substantially over time, but the bulk of this increase is due to increases in the enforcement of immigration laws as shown in table 5.9.

In addition, the proportion of police matters involving immigrants has increased from 10.9 percent in 1973 to 19.8 percent in 1993. When violations of the immigration laws are excluded, the change is from 10.2 percent to

Table 5.5 Sentencing Following Trial, Percentage of Unsuspended Prison Sentences (with or without Partial Suspension) for At Least One Year, According to Immigrant Status, 1991[a]

	Total		*Native Born*		*Foreigners*	
	Number	*Percentage*	*Number*	*Percentage*	*Number*	*Percentage*
Possession and purchasing of narcotics	2,901	60.6	1,615	50.3	1,198	74.1
Theft with violence	3,408	39.9	2,502	39.8	747	42.8
Illegal use of narcotics	1,347	23.5	858	23.8	444	23.9
House-breaking	5,875	21.3	4,787	21.7	864	20.4
Simple receiving and concealing	3,023	20.2	1,842	19.1	1,069	22.0
Intentional assault and battery with TWI, less than one week with aggravating circumstances[b]	1,410	14.4	1,073	13.2	285	19.6
Simple larceny	15,033	11.2	10,525	11.3	3,864	11.2

Source: Pierre Tournier, "La délinquance des étrangers en France: Analyse des statistiques pénales," in *Immigrant Delinquency: Social Construction of Deviant Behaviour and Criminality of Immigrants in Europe,* ed. Salvatore Palidda (Luxembourg: European Commission, 1997), 156.

Note: The total column includes persons whose citizenship was not known or not recorded. The columns for citizens and for foreigners exclude these cases.

[a]Crimes for which at least 20 percent of sentences involved unsuspended imprisonment (with or without partial suspension).

[b]TWI = temporary work incapacitation.

Table 5.6 Percentage of Admissions by Pretrial Detention and Breakdown of Summary Trials by Offense, 1993

Offense	*Total*	*Immigrants*
Immigration laws	90.3	90.5
Simple larceny	69.7	79.5
Drunken driving	83.2	88.7
Theft involving violence and other aggravated thefts	49.9	56.8
Intentional assault and battery	47.6	53.6
Receiving and concealing	39.4	46.0
Trafficking in narcotics	22.2	27.3
Morals offenses	22.0	25.9
Embezzlement, swindling, and breech of trust	20.8	26.1

Source: Pierre Tournier, "La délinquance des étrangers en France: Analyse des statistiques pénales," in *Immigrant Delinquency: Social Construction of Deviant Behaviour and Criminality of Immigrants in Europe,* ed. Salvatore Palidda (Luxembourg: European Commission,

14.4 percent over that same period. The changes in the incarceration of immigrants demonstrates a similar pattern in the period 1984 to 1995. The number of immigrants in custody increased by 48 percent overall, while the increase for native-born citizens was 29 percent. When immigration offenses are excluded, the change in the number of immigrants in custody was 28 percent. Since the size of the foreign population in France has re-

Table 5.7 Foreign Prison Populations by Nationality, January 1, 1995

Nationality	*Number*	*Percent*
French	36,644	71.0
European Community	2,295	4.4
Other Europe	731	1.4
Algeria	4,076	7.9
Morocco	2,712	5.3
Tunisia	1,096	2.1
Other Africa	2,388	4.6
Americas	443	0.9
Asia and Oceania	1,192	2.3
Stateless or unknown	46	0.1
Total prisoners	51,623	100

Source: Pierre Tournier, "La délinquance des étrangers en France: Analyse des statistiques pénales," in *Immigrant Delinquency: Social Construction of Deviant Behaviour and Criminality of Immigrants in Europe,* ed. Salvatore Palidda (Luxembourg: European Commission, 1997), 137–138.

Table 5.8 Ratios of Processing Rates for Foreigners and Citizens by Stage of Processing and Whether Violations of Immigration Laws Are Included or Excluded

Charges Included	*Police Charges*	*Incarcerations*
Immigration violations included	3.6	7.2
Immigration violations excluded	2.5	3.0

Source: Pierre Tournier, "La délinquance des étrangers en France: Analyses des statistiques pénales," in *Immigrant Delinquency: Social Construction of Deviant Behaviour and Criminality of Immigrants in Europe,* ed. Salvatore Palidda (Luxembourg: European Commission, 1997), 135–162.

Table 5.9 Proportion of Police Matters Involving Foreigners by Whether Immigration Offenses Are Included or Excluded by Year

Year	*Immigration Offenses In*	*Immigration Offenses Out*
1973	10.9	10.2
1974	12.5	11.7
1975	13.5	12.6
1976	15.5	14.4
1977	15.3	14.2
1978	15.3	14.0
1979	15.5	14.2
1980	15.1	13.7
1981	14.6	13.2
1982	15.0	14.0
1983	15.0	13.1
1984	15.2	12.9
1985	15.4	13.0
1986	16.1	13.0
1987	16.8	12.9
1988	16.2	12.5
1989	17.1	13.1
1990	17.0	13.2
1991	18.0	13.6
1992	20.3	15.1
1993	19.8	14.4

Source: Pierre Tournier, "La délinquance des étrangers en France: Analyses des statistiques pénales," in *Immigrant Delinquency: Social Construction of Deviant Behaviour and Criminality of Immigrants in Europe,* ed. Salvatore Palidda (Luxembourg: European Commission, 1997), 133–162.

mained relatively stable in the period 1980 to 1990 (see table 5.1), the constancy of the involvement of immigrants in the criminal justice system when immigration violations are excluded suggests that the criminal involvement of immigrants in France has remained relatively constant over time.

These data do indicate that the control of immigrants by the criminal justice system has increased substantially, especially in the recent past. This may be part of the general increase in restrictiveness of immigration policies in France.

Public Opinion

As of 1993, the majority of French citizens believed there were "too many" or "a lot of" foreigners in France. In 1984, the following question was posed to French citizens:

Would you say that the proportion of immigrants in the French population is too small, too large, or not a problem?

	Percentage
Too small	2
Too large	58
Not a problem	33
Don't know	7

Source: American Institute of Public Opinion (Storrs: Roper Center, University of Connecticut, 1993).

More than half of the respondents believed that the proportion of immigrants was too large. In 1989, when French citizens were asked whether they were personally concerned with immigration in France, they responded as follows:

	Percentage
Yes	57
No	33
No opinion	10

Source: American Institute of Public Opinion (Storrs: Roper Center, University of Connecticut, 1993).

Again, more than half of the respondents said they were concerned with immigration in their country.

It is interesting that many of the negative reactions to immigrants stem from fear of the loss of a national identity and for personal safety, rather than concern about what immigrants are doing to jobs, unemployment, and education. The following attitudes, which were derived from national polls from 1985 through 1993, aptly demonstrate this point:

Immigrants do work the French refuse to do.

	Agree	*Disagree*	*Don't know*
1985	72%	24%	4%
1989	71	27	2
1993	76	23	1

In areas where there are many immigrants, one doesn't feel safe.

	Agree	*Disagree*	*Don't know*
1985	75%	17%	8%
1989	69	23	8
1993	75	17	8

If something isn't done to limit the number of immigrants, France risks losing its national identity.

	Agree	*Disagree*	*Don't know*
1985	68%	27%	5%
1989	74	24	2
1993	67	32	1

Immigrants play an important role in the development of the French economy.

	Agree	*Disagree*	*Don't know*
1985	29%	57%	14%
1989	44	46	10
1993	44	50	6

Every time a foreigner takes a job in France, a Frenchman is out of one.

	Agree	*Disagree*	*Don't know*
1985	45%	48%	7%
1989	32	63	5
1993	32	66	2

Immigrants are luck for France.

	Agree	*Disagree*	*Don't know*
1985	21%	66%	13%
1989	22	67	11
1993	32	62	6

Do you find the presence of foreigners disturbing?

	Percent
Yes	44
No	23
Don't know/ no answer	34

Note: This does not add up exactly to 100 percent due to rounding.

Do foreigners' children in schools lower the level of education?

	Percent
Yes	29.8
No	70.2

Do foreigner's increase our unemployment?

	Percent
Yes	35.8
No	64.2

Source: American Institute of Public Opinion (Storrs: Roper Center, University of Connecticut, 1993).

When asked for their views about whether immigrants should be under stricter police surveillance, strong majorities favored identity cards and the expulsion of illegals and convicted offenders:

The following are propositions concerning immigration. For each of them, tell me if you totally favor, somewhat favor, somewhat oppose or totally oppose it.

A. Totally favor
B. Somewhat favor
C. Somewhat oppose
D. Totally oppose
E. Don't know

	A	B	C	D	E
Have an unforgeable identity card	72%	22%	3%	2%	1%
Systematically expel illegal immigrants	54	25	15	5	1
Allow police to check IDs at any time	48	28	14	9	1
Systematically expel all immigrants convicted of crime	50	24	18	6	2
Limit the family by not allowing polygamy	48	22	14	11	5
Allow officials to deny fake marriages	41	22	18	15	4
Offer financial incentive for working immigrants to return	19	33	24	21	3

Source: American Institute of Public Opinion (Storrs: Roper Center, University of Connecticut, 1993).

France, like most other countries, has its "more" and "less" favored immigrants and, like other countries, immigrants who are most like the natives are viewed more positively than immigrants who have different ethnic, racial, and cultural backgrounds. We see in table 5.10 that north Europeans are the most liked of the immigrant communities and the Turks, North Africans, Asians, and black Africans are the least liked. The one group that does not fit this pattern are the West Indians, about whom 37 percent of the respondents say they "like," but West Indians comprise only a very small proportion of the immigrants who come to France.

Table 5.10 French Attitudes toward Particular Groups, 1994

Group	*Opinion*	*Percent*
South Europeans	dislike	5.0
	indifferent	56.0
	like	39.0
North Africans	dislike	33.9
	indifferent	52.0
	like	14.2
Turks	dislike	32.8
	indifferent	53.7
	like	13.5
Black Africans	dislike	20.7
	indifferent	61.7
	like	17.6
Asians	dislike	24.6
	indifferent	59.6
	like	15.8
Southeast Asians	dislike	20.4
	indifferent	58.0
	like	21.6
West Indians	dislike	9.2
	indifferent	53.7
	like	37.1
Jews	dislike	13.3
	indifferent	55.3
	like	31.4
North Europeans	dislike	4.8
	indifferent	47.9
	like	47.3

Source: Ira Gang and Francisco L. Riviera-Batiz, "Unemployment and Attitudes towards Foreigners in Germany," in *The Economic Consequences of Immigration in Germany,* ed. Gunter Steinmann and Ralf E. Ulrich (Heidelberg: Physica-Verlag, 1994), 141.

Note: Some of the columns do not add up exactly to 100 percent due to rounding.

In trying to assess whether French attitudes toward immigrants are moving in a more or less positive direction, we note that in December 1988 when asked if "France [is] a country that welcomes foreigners," 64 percent answered "yes." But in 1991, perhaps as the Le Pen movement gained more support and as former president d'Estaing warned of the imminent threat of an immigration invasion and called for the immediate closing of France's frontiers to all foreign settlers, attitudes shifted in a more anti-immigrant direction. Thus, in 1993, when asked whether foreigners from non-EEC countries are good or bad for their country, almost half the respondents who expressed an opinion said they were bad.

	Percent
Bad	17.9
A little bad	30.7
A little good	30.1
Good	9.4
Don't know/NA	11.9

Source: American Institute of Public Opinion (Storrs: Roper Center, University of Connecticut, 1993).

In the presidential elections held in 1995, Le Pen's anti-immigrant National Front Party gained 15 percent of the vote. The party won more than 25 percent of the vote in France's twenty largest cities. In the 1997 elections, the National Front Party had the support of more than 15 percent of the voters nationally. During the election campaign, the National Front voters blamed Africans and Arabs for their joblessness and crime and labeled them a threat to French bloodlines.

Summary

Although France does not share the aura of being a "nation of immigrants" such as the United States, Canada, and Australia, over the past one hundred or so years it has admitted, welcomed, naturalized, and married almost the same percentage of foreigners as some of the "immigrant" receiving nations. Underpopulation, rapid industrialization, and labor shortages (especially following World War I and II) were the major stimuli for France's immigration policy. Like the United States, France also has highly visible and vocal anti-immigrant groups who appeal to xenophobia and fear that foreign workers will change their culture, threaten their safety, and take jobs from natives. Unlike Germany and Britain, however, French rules about naturalization produce a much higher rate of naturalization than do either of the other European countries. Like the United States, France has more of a problem with illegal immigration than the other countries in the study.

As for criminal behavior, in 1991 immigrants accounted for three times the serious crime rate of French citizens. Drug offenses and trafficking are the crimes for which there is the biggest difference between French citizens and immigrants. French public opinion vis-à-vis immigrants manifests much the same combination of ambivalence, distrust, and anxiety expressed by respondents in all of the other countries, save that the French appear more concerned about losing their "national identity" to foreign influence than about such bread-and-butter issues as jobs and education. Some immigrants are more desirable than others, with Turks and North Africans occupying the bottom of the list and Europeans (northern and southern) occupying the top. It remains to be seen in the next few years, as the labor shortage declines and as the economy slows down, whether Le Pen's anti-immigrant movement gains in strength and has a strong impact on France's immigration policy.

Notes

1. James F. Hollifield, "Immigration Policy in France and Germany: Outputs versus Outcomes," The Annals of the American Academy of Political and Social Science, *The American Academy of Political Science* 485 (May 1985).
2. Hollifield, "Immigration Policy in France and Germany."
3. Hollifield, "Immigration Policy in France and Germany," 138.
4. Hollifield, "Immigration Policy in France and Germany," 144.
5. Hollifield, "Immigration Policy in France and Germany," 138.
6. Hollifield, "Immigration Policy in France and Germany."
7. David Jacobson, *Rights across Borders: Immigration and the Decline of Citizenship* (Baltimore, Md.: Johns Hopkins University Press, 1996), 28.
8. Gelles Verbunt, "France," in *International Immigration and Nationality Law: Immigration Supplement 2,* ed. Dennis Campbell and Joy Fisher (Boston: Nijhoff, 1993), 142.
9. Jacobson, *Rights across Borders,* 40.
10. Fabienne Daguet and Suzanne Thave, "La Population Immigree: Le Resultat dune Langue Histaire," *Insee Premiere* (Pris Insee) (June 1996).
11. Hollifield, "Immigration Policy in France and Germany," 140; and Isabelle Andre, "France," in *International Immigration and Nationality Law: Immigration Supplement 2,* ed. Dennis Campbell and Joy Fisher (Boston: Nijhoff, 1993), X1–X5.
12. Philip E. Ogden, "Immigration to France since 1945: Myth and Reality," *Ethnic and Racial Studies* 14 (July 1991): 294–318.
13. Verbunt, "France," 137.
14. Verbunt, "France," 138.
15. Andre, "France," V-3.

16. Hollifield, "Immigration Policy in France and Germany," 117.
17. Hollifield, "Immigration Policy in France and Germany," 117.
18. Verbunt, "France," 141–142.
19. Verbunt, "France," 150.
20. Verbunt, "France," 157.
21. Katrina Tomasevski, *Foreigners in Prison* (Helsinki, Finland: European Institute for Crime Prevention and Control, 1994).

6

Immigration in Germany

Like France, Germany has had a long tradition of immigration, but there is no ambivalence in that history. The admission of immigrants has always been clearly and closely tied to labor-market needs.[1] Foreign workers were admitted when labor was scarce and expelled or excluded when it was not. There were few efforts to assimilate these guest workers into German society and naturalization was and remains a rare event. Germany has always maintained that it is not an immigration nation. Since unification in 1989, anti-immigration sentiment and policies have increased dramatically. According to Philip Martin, over 60 percent of all Germans want immigration reduced or stopped.[2] Citing police reports, Martin states that there has been an average of fifty to one hundred antiforeigner incidents daily in 1992 and 1993. In 1992, major political parties agreed to limit the annual influx of ethnic Germans and, in 1993, they restricted the entry of applicants for asylum. The year 1999 marked a major shift in German legislation vis-à-vis immigration. On May 21, 1999, the German parliament introduced major changes in its citizenship laws. It cut the link between blood ties and nationality by granting automatic citizenship to anyone born in the country. The new legislation went into effect on January 1, 2000.

Historical Background and Major Legislation

During the period from 1871 to the beginning of World War I, Polish agricultural workers were admitted to help with planting and harvesting activities. This use of guest workers was only permitted in the agricultural sector. These workers were admitted after April 1 and had to return to Poland on or before November 1 of the same year. They were free to return the following year. The German government took no steps to accommodate Polish guest workers into German society. These immigrants were expected to speak German and otherwise adjust to their life in the host country. When World War I began, Polish guest workers in Germany were not allowed to leave and were used as captive labor to support the war effort.

The period 1918 to 1933 marked low levels of immigration due to the weakened state of the German economy. There was no need for foreign labor. Between 1933 and 1945, the demand for labor increased as the German economy geared up for the war effort, which required the replacement of German workers who were entering the military. Initially, the German government met this increased demand for labor by the repatriation of ethnic Germans. Later, with the Alien Decree, foreigners residing in Germany were pressed into service and the importation of captive labor from conquered nations began.

In the period immediately after World War II (1945–1955), Germany filled its labor needs by taking advantage of the massive population movements in the wake of the war. Previously forced laborers who wanted to reside in Germany, as well as refugees from the East, were guaranteed legal equity with Germans.

It was not until 1955 that the demand for labor prompted not only the admission, but the active recruitment of foreign labor.[3] It was clear, however, that these recruits were guest workers and not immigrants in the sense that they would become permanent residents who might acquire citizenship. This period of active recruitment persisted until 1973 when the German economy, like the economies in other European countries, began to slow. At that time, Germany began a policy of restricting the entry of foreigners and attempted to better integrate those guest workers who had become, effectively, immigrants. This policy continues to the present time.

The laws governing the admission and residence of immigrants in Germany are consistent with a guest-worker system. The laws allow admission for selected groups, but discourage permanent settlement. They also provide a great deal of administrative discretion to immigration authorities so that they may respond to labor-market needs swiftly. The rules on admissions also reflect the post-1973 change from a guest-worker policy to a policy of exclusion and integration. These rules made it more difficult to gain admission to Germany and offered secure residence only to those foreigners who demonstrated stability.

German immigration policy provides for a limit or quota on the admission of foreigners. These quotas are set jointly by the Bureau of Labor and the Ministry of Justice and can vary substantially from year to year. Preferences for admitting foreigners for extended stays fall into three categories: employment, family unification, and asylum. The relative emphasis given to each of these categories has varied over time.

Following the end of World War II and the adoption of a constitution for the Federal Republic of Germany (FRG), article 16, section 2 guaranteed the right of asylum to all victims of political persecution.[4] In 1951, the German government passed an act that guaranteed the legal equality of all persons who had done forced labor and had remained in the FRG. But as far as citizenship is concerned, the law that passed in 1913, which makes it very difficult for anyone who does not have German parents to become a citizen, is still operative.

In 1965, the Aliens Act was passed, which did not grant foreign citizens any legal rights of immigration or residence.[5] This meant that all foreigners who wanted to reside in or work in the FRG for more than three months had to possess a residence permit. A residence permit is issued at the discretion of immigration authorities, whose decision is based on the "interests" of the FRG.

During the period of heavy recruitment of guest workers, the customary duration of a residence permit was one year. These permits could be extended or renewed at the discretion of immigration authorities. In an effort to offer a measure of security to more stable foreign residents, longer-term residence permits are available to those who have spent a number of years in the country. After a minimum stay of five years, a permanent residence permit may be granted. The residence permit is not restricted as to duration or location but may be linked to certain other conditions. For example, foreigners are subject to expulsion if they violate the "considerable interests" of the FRG (e.g., through criminal actions, impoverishment, or immorality).

Citizens of the European Economic Community (EEC) member countries are entitled to residence without any restrictions on location and only minimal restrictions in duration.[6] They do not need a work permit; they merely need to prove that they are employed.

In 1978, the German government altered its regulations such that an indefinite residence permit might be issued after five years and a permanent residence permit after eight years if three conditions are met: adequate housing according to local standards, obligatory school attendance, and sufficient knowledge of the German language.[7]

Immigrants who want to work while in the FRG must also possess a work permit (they must have a residence permit in order to receive a work permit).[8] There are two types of work permits: specific and nonspecific. Specific permits are issued for jobs in a specific firm that no German can fill. To obtain such a permit, the worker must present evidence to the effect that there are no eligible German citizens. Nonspecific permits are not restricted to a specific job or to a particular firm. These permits can be obtained after eight years of residence and five years of uninterrupted work. A permanent work permit is only granted to immigrants with at least ten years of residence and five years of uninterrupted work.

In 1979, the following groups of persons were legally entitled to a nonspecific work permit: foreigners married to German citizens, political refugees, and the spouses of Greek, Spanish, and if employed before October 1978, Turkish immigrant workers who have resided in the FRG for at least five years. A recent addition to the nonspecific work permit category are citizens with European Union member status.

Some groups of immigrants are denied work permits of any kind. Specifically, arrivals after 1974 were not granted work permits. This policy was changed as the emphasis shifted from employment preferences to family unification preferences. Spouses joining foreign residents were allowed to obtain a work permit after residing in the country for four years. Children were eligible for these permits after residing in the country two years. Obviously, these policies made the process of family unification more difficult.

In December 1981, regulations were introduced that further restricted the relatively liberal immigration of family members.[9] Immigrant youths would be admitted if they were under sixteen. The immigration of children would be prohibited if only one parent lived in the FRG. Spouses would not be granted entry if they were married to persons who immigrated as children or were born in the FRG.[10]

These same regulations also began to restrict the right to asylum guaranteed in the constitution. The regulations required that applicants for political asylum must wait two (before it had been one) years before they were issued work permits. In July 1993, the asylum law was overhauled to require asylum seekers to demonstrate they risked political persecution. Economic persecution was no longer sufficient. The new law also added a clause that requires asylum applicants who arrive in the FRG through neighboring countries that also provide asylum to make their claim in those countries.[11]

Stock and Flow of Immigrants

Between 1950 and 1994, about 5 million persons, including over 3.3 million resettlers claiming German descent and about 1.67 million non-Germans (of whom 1.45 million were naturalized persons and 211,000 had been granted asylum), were admitted into the FRG. Between 1985 and 1990, the FRG admitted 1.1 million persons of German descent who lived in countries other than the former German Democratic Republic. As of November 1994, the number of foreigners in Germany increased to 6.9 million people, but their representation as a proportion of the population increased only 13 percent, from 7.5 to 8.5 percent of the population. Immigration increased the population at an average annual rate of 1.4 percent from 1962 to 1973, 2.5 percent in 1989, and 1.8 percent for each year from 1990 to 1992. In 1999, Germany was estimated to have 7.3 million immigrants, which comprised 9 percent of its population. Recall, however, that foreigners in Germany will include third- and even fourth-generation immigrants, while foreigners in the United States will be those who are foreign born only. The more comparable figure is the foreign born in both nations. Nonetheless, this very difference in the definition of immigrant reveals a great deal about the differences in immigration policy.

Between 1960 and 1973, some eighteen to nineteen million migrant workers were estimated to have worked in Germany. Of those, between four to five million stayed permanently. By the end of 1994, some 4.2 million guest workers or former guest workers lived in Germany. About 3.4 million have lived there more than ten years and have long-term residence rights and work permits. Turkish migrants and offspring represent the largest immigrant group, about 1.97 million. The next largest groups are 1.3 million from various communities of the former Yugoslavia, followed by Greeks (356,000), Spanish (132,000), and Portuguese (118,000). As of 1996, the share of foreign workers in the German labor force was 9.4 percent.

Between 1984 and 1989, there was an increase from 31 to 40 percent of the guest workers who expected to remain in Germany permanently—a decrease from 25 to 13 percent of those who came on a short-term basis.

Table 6.1 describes the occupational statuses of foreign workers in 1996.

The requirement of residence and work permits offers immigration authorities ample opportunity to monitor immigrant populations. When immigrants are first admitted, they must renew their residence permits annually. After three years of residence, an immigrant can obtain a residence permit

Table 6.1 Employed Foreigners in Germany by Economic Activities, 1996

Economic Activities	*Absolute*	*Percentage*
Agriculture, forestry, and fishing	27,272	13.4
Construction	196,070	12.7
Manufacturing	823,118	11.3
Services (restaurants, hotels, cleaning, and so on)	588,558	10.2
Transportation and communication	103,425	9.2
Commerce	217,282	6.7
Energy, mining of which 13.3% in 1995	21,899	5.9
Nonprofit organizations and private households	35,492	5.7
Local authorities and social insurance institutions	48,909	3.5
Banks and insurance companies	22,609	2.4
Total	2,084,634	8.1

Source: Christian Klos, "Employed Foreigners in Germany by Economic Activity, 1996," in *Information Chart* (Konstanz: Center for International and European Law on Immigration and Asylum, 1996).

for two years. After five years, immigrants can obtain an indefinite residence permit and, after eight years, a permanent permit. Even with these increases in the permanence of residence, the opportunity for monitoring immigrant populations through residence permits is substantial. In 1979, only 23 percent of all immigrants subject to residence permit requirements had received indefinite or permanent residence status. Hence, the vast majority of immigrants were still subject to these controls.

Work permits also afford the opportunity for control. Residence permits are required to obtain work permits, but residence permits do not guarantee work permits. Since new immigrants are not eligible for nonspecific work permits, they can only obtain specific work permits. These permits restrict the mobility of immigrants because they specify both a job and a firm. Changes in either require approval. This is another opportunity for immigration officials to exert control.

The substantial discretion allowed immigration authorities without judicial review also adds to the insecurity of immigrant populations. Administrative decisions not to renew work or residence permits are subject to review by administrative courts, but the appeal will not delay departure. Consequently, successful appellants may be out of the country when their petition is granted so that they must incur the cost of leaving and returning. This may be a powerful deterrent to appeals.

In addition, changes in the German asylum laws have had a noticeable impact on the flow of asylum seekers. In 1973, 57 percent of all applicants were granted refugee status. By 1980, only 12 percent of the almost 110,000 who applied were accepted. After the passage of the 1992 asylum laws, only 4 percent were accepted as political refugees of the 300,000 applicants. In 1994, about 7 percent had been granted sanctuary. At the same time, welfare payments available to asylum seekers while they await the asylum decision have been sharply curbed. In 1993, the amount of money involved in caring for refugees was estimated at $22 billion annually. The payment included monthly allowances, schooling, housing hostels or camps, health care, and cost of trials and extraditions.

Naturalization

Until January 1, 2000, becoming a naturalized citizen in Germany was not impossible, but it was extremely difficult. The rate of naturalization, at 3 percent, accurately reflected that policy. But at 3 percent, Germany's rate of naturalization is the same as Great Britain's and higher than France's. This despite the pre-2000 rules. On May 21, 1999, the German parliament gave final approval to a major overhaul of its 1913 citizenship laws. This new law, which went into effect on January 1, 2000, cuts the link between German blood ties and nationality by granting automatic citizenship to anyone born in the country. But the law also states that anyone born on German soil of a foreign parent must reject his or her parents' citizenship once he or she reaches his or her twenty-third birthday or forfeit his or her status as a German citizen. It also eased naturalization rules for long-time foreign residents. The time period for naturalization was shortened from fifteen to eight years.[12]

Until the passage of the 2000 act, there was no right to naturalization—it was purely at the discretion of immigration authorities. German law also distinguished between entitled naturalization, which was used mostly for spouses of German citizens, and discretionary naturalization, which applied to regular naturalization of immigrants. To be considered for naturalization, an immigrant had to:

1. Reside in the country for at least ten years
2. Hold a secure job
3. Renounce any other citizenship
4. Be fluent in German
5. Be legally competent with no police record

There was also a vague standard that allowed for considerable agency discretion. It stated that an applicant "support(s) and participate(s) in the national community" or must "have developed clear ties with and commitment to the community." In January 1991, a rule was enacted stating that offspring of labor migrants in Germany could become naturalized if they were between sixteen and twenty-three years old and had resided in Germany for at least eight years and had at least six years of schooling. They must also have given up any other citizenship. Persons over twenty-three years old needed fifteen years of residence and had to provide proof of guaranteed subsistence in Germany. Fewer than 20,000 immigrants each year became naturalized during the 1980s.

Demographic and Socioeconomic Characteristics of Immigrants

As of 1993, 10 percent of all marriages in Germany were between Germans and immigrants. In 1980, mixed marriages accounted for 7.7 percent, in 1985 for 7 percent, and in 1990 for 9.6 percent. Generally, the pattern was that the husbands were more likely to be foreign born than the wives.

A comparison of the fertility rates between native-born Germans and immigrants shows a consistently higher, but declining, rate for immigrant women, such that the difference between native-born women and immigrant women has grown smaller over the period 1975 to 1986. In 1975, the fertility rate for German women of child-bearing age was 1.34 compared to 2.64 for foreigners. By 1986, the fertility rates for Germans remained essentially stable at 1.31 while the rate for foreigners decreased to 1.76.

In 1991, 88 percent of foreign-born children between the ages of six and twenty were participating in education and vocational training, compared to 82 percent among German children. The federal government has instituted a program in which it pays 75 percent of the cost of German-language classes taken by foreigners. Other federal programs have been targeted to the children of immigrants where bilingual classes are offered to the children of foreign workers followed by mainstreaming in the older age groups. In 1980, vocational classes were offered for children of foreign workers. Youth who participated in these classes could waive the two-year waiting period required to obtain a work permit. The percentage of foreign students in academic programs is 10 percent compared to 24 percent of the German pupils. Whereas only 6 and 14 percent, respectively, leave school or vocational training programs without having reached a final degree, 20 and 34 percent, respectively, drop out of those programs before they have obtained their degrees.

Between 1960 and 1991, the percentage of immigrants in the German workforce increased from 1.5 to 8.5 percent. Table 6.2 describes the type of employment in which immigrants in Germany were engaged in 1983 and 1991.

Manufacturing, especially metal manufacturing, was the major category of work for immigrants in Germany. In 1991, 26.6 percent of foreigners worked in metal manufacturing compared to 15.8 of the German nationals (see table 6.3). Like the German nationals, however, 16.8 percent of the immigrants also worked in hotels, catering, and repairs.

Comparison of the unemployment rates between native-born Germans and immigrants from 1965 to 1993 shows that, beginning in 1975, the rate of unemployment increased at a higher rate for foreigners than for natives. In 1965, the unemployment rate for the total labor force was 0.7 percent and the unemployment rate for foreigners was 0.2 percent. By 1993, the total unemployment rate was 4.9 per 100 and the unemployment rate for foreigners was 12.7 per 100. The data in table 6.4 compare the contributions to social security insurance, tax payments, and various benefits received by German versus foreign households in 1984.

The data clearly indicate that while immigrants contribute more to the social security fund, they receive less than half the amount in benefits, especially pensions, than does the native-born population. The difference in the amount of taxes both groups pay is less than 1,000 deutsche marks (DM).

In 1989, immigrant workers contributed 12.8 billion DM to the state pension fund—7.8 percent of the total payment. As of 1989, only 3.43 billion DM—1.9 percent of the total pension volume—was paid to immigrants.

Table 6.2 Share of Foreigners in Total Employment in Germany, 1983 and 1991 (in percent)

Branches	*1983*	*1991*
00	2.1	3.0
10	8.6	9.4
20	11.2	12.4
30	13.8	13.5
40	11.6	11.6
50	9.5	9.6
60	7.1	8.6
70	5.7	6.7
80	3.1	4.1
90/1	1.6	1.7
90/2	6.7	7.3
Total (average)	7.4	8.0

Source: Organization for Economic Cooperation and Development, *Trends in International Migration, 1991* (Paris: Organization for Economic Cooperation and Development, 1992).

Note: 00 = agriculture, hunting, forestry, and fishing; 10 = energy and weather; 20 = extraction and processing of nonenergy-producing minerals and derived products, chemical industry; 30 = metal manufacture, mechanical, electrical, and instrument engineering; 40 = other manufacturing industries; 50 = building and civil engineering; 60 = distributive trades, hotels, catering, and repairs; 70 = transport and communications; 80 = banking and finance, insurance, business services, and renting; 90/1 = public administration, national defense, and compulsory social security, and diplomatic representation, international organizations, and allied armed forces; 90/2 = other services.

German immigration policy includes a number of programs designed to accommodate immigrants in German society. This is especially the case after 1973, when the thrust of immigration policy changed from one of a strict guest-worker system to one emphasizing the stabilization of the foreign population in the country. These special programs include educational, housing, and mental health services designed primarily to ease the transition. In addition, immigrants can avail themselves of the safety net of services open to native-born German citizens. This safety net seems ample relative to that available in other nations, such as the United States.

Criminal Involvement

In his chapter "Ethnic Minorities, Crime and Criminal Justice in Germany," Hans-Jorg Albrecht concludes that "foreigners do not create exceptional crime problems or pose special dangers."[13] But he also reports that a 1993

Table 6.3 Distribution of National, Foreign, and Total Employment between the Eleven Major Industry Divisions in 1991 in Germany (in percent)

Branches	*Nationals*	*Foreigners*	*Total*
0	3.7	1.2	3.5
10	1.6	1.8	1.6
20	4.9	7.5	5.2
30	15.8	26.6	16.7
40	9.5	13.4	9.8
50	6.7	7.7	6.8
60	16.6	16.8	16.6
70	5.8	4.5	5.7
80	8.8	4.0	8.4
90/1	9.1	1.6	8.4
90/2	17.5	14.8	17.3
Total	100	100	100

Source: Organization for Economic Cooperation and Development, *Trends in International Migration, 1991* (Paris: Organization for Economic Cooperation and Development, 1992).

Note: 00 = agriculture, hunting, forestry, and fishing; 10 = energy and weather; 20 = extraction and processing of nonenergy-producing minerals and derived products, chemical industry; 30 = metal manufacture, mechanical, electrical, and instrument engineering; 40 = other manufacturing industries; 50 = building and civil engineering; 60 = distributive trades, hotels, catering, and repairs; 70 = transport and communications; 80 = banking and finance, insurance, business services, and renting; 90/1 = public administration, national defense, and compulsory social security, and diplomatic representation, international organizations, and allied armed forces; 90/2 = other services. Some of the columns do not add up exactly to 100 percent due to rounding.

content analysis of print media in Germany shows that 40 percent of the articles related to immigrants highlight crimes committed by foreign minorities and that drug trafficking and organized crime were the subjects of approximately 60 percent of the mentions, outweighing all other types of crimes.

In the mid-1980s, one-third of all foreign suspects were guest workers. In 1992, 18 percent of criminal suspects were guest workers and 33 percent were asylum seekers. In 1993, 33.6 percent of persons suspected of crimes in Germany were foreigners. If immigration offenses are omitted, the percentage drops to 26.7. Almost half of the 46.5 percent of the eighteen- to twenty-year-old suspects were minority members, as were 34 percent of all juvenile offenders and 30.7 percent of all seven- to thirteen-year-old child offenders.

According to police statistics, immigrants are 2.3 times as likely as native-born German citizens of being suspected for a serious crime (see table 6.5). The overrepresentation of foreigners is most pronounced for

Table 6.4 Contributions to Social Security Insurance, Tax Payments, and Transfers, Deutsche Marks per Average Household, 1984

	Germans	*Foreigners*
Social Security Contributions	4,249	6,550
Unemployment insurance	560	874
Health insurance	1,435	2,159
Pension insurance	2,254	3,517
Tax Payments	8,051	7,129
Income tax	6,033	5,266
Value added tax	2,018	1,863
Selected Transfers Received	7,475	3,683
Unemployment benefits	463	1,140
Pensions	5,917	365
Children allowances	390	1,143
Social Security benefits	705	1,035

Source: Gunter Steinmann, "The Development of a Post-war Immigration and Refugee Policy," in *Immigration As an Economic Asset,* ed. Sarah E. Spencer (Sterling, Va.: Stylus, 1994), 74.

drug trafficking (4.0 to 1) and homicide (3.5 to 1), and lowest for assaults (2.2 to 1) and theft (2.1 to 1). The correctional data on foreigners in prison is consistent with the police data.

Immigrants are 1.9 times more likely to be incarcerated than native-born German citizens. The estimate of the criminal involvement of immigrants relative to the native population is somewhat lower when correctional as opposed to police data are used. This may be due to the use of summary deportation rather than imprisonment as a sanction for criminal offenses in Germany.

Table 6.5 Estimates of Offending by Citizenship and Type of Crime, Germany, 1985

	Foreigners		*Citizens*	
Offense	*Number*	*Per 100,000*	*Number*	*Per 100,000*
Homicide	662	13.66	2,221	3.95
Assaults	28,555	589.07	147,001	261.72
Drug offenses	9,320	192.26	4,124	73.41
Trafficking	5,406	111.52	15,967	28.43
Robbery	3,909	80.64	15,087	26.86
Burglary	NA	NA	NA	NA
Theft	87,018	1,795.11	468,011	833.24

Source: Bundeskriminalamt, *Polizeiliche Kriminalstatistik, 1985* (Weisbaden: Kriminalistiches Institut, 1986).

Table 6.6 Age-Specific Analysis by Citizenship and Gender of Total Suspects for Germany, 1984 and 1990

Age, Citizenship, Gender[a]	*1984 Population*	*1984 Arrests*	*1984 Rate*[b]	*1990 Population*	*1990 Arrests*	*1990 Rate*[b]	*Expected Arrests*	*Expected Change*	*Observed Change*
<18 FM	63,900	30,771	4,812	687,900	50,099	7,283	33,105	2,334	19,328
18–29 FM	516,700	72,026	13,940	723,700	145,645	20,215	100,881	28,855	73,619
30–49 FM	1,017,900	55,285	5,431	1,043,400	93,750	8,985	56,670	1,385	38,465
50+ FM	325,600	8,683	2,667	491,000	14,546	2,963	13,094	4,411	5,863
<18 FF	548,100	7,449	1,359	604,600	13,211	2,185	8,217	768	5,762
18–29 FF	413,700	14,450	3,493	575,200	32,528	5,655	20,091	5,641	18,078
30–49 FF	701,300	14,720	2,099	817,800	27,443	3,356	17,165	2,445	12,723
50+ FF	20,100	4,226	2,102	298,400	6,361	2,132	6,274	2,048	2,135
<18 GM	5,626,700	141,357	2,512	5,315,500	107,015	2,013	133,539	−7,818	−34,342
18–29 GM	5,660,600	302,101	5,337	5,705,600	302,586	5,303	304,533	2,402	455
30–49 GM	7,740,100	260,818	3,370	8,030,400	270,733	3,371	270,600	9,782	9,915
50+ GM	7,652,900	87,329	1,141	8,853,400	115,905	1,309	101,028	13,699	28,576
<18 GF	5,432,800	44,092	812	5,085,300	33,419	657	41,272	−2,820	−10,673
18–29 GF	5,397,400	74,257	1,376	5,471,000	78,396	1,433	75,270	1,013	4,139
30–49 GF	7,714,700	80,249	1,040	7,814,000	83,679	1,071	81,282	1,033	3,430
50+ GF	11,460,500	56,370	492	12,208,400	62,607	513	60,049	3,679	6,237
Total	60,293,000	1,254,183	2,080	63,725,600	1,437,923	2,256	1,323,070	68,857	183,710
Total observed increase		228,725							
Total expected increase[c]		77,548							
Percent explained		33.9							

Source: Hans-Jorg Albrecht, *Ethnic Minorities, Crime, Criminal Justice and Discrimination: The Case of the Federal Republic of Germany* (Dresden: Dresden University of Technology, 1996).

[a]FM = foreign male; FF = foreign female; GM = German male; GF = German female.

[b]Number per 100,000 population.

[c]To compute this total, the expected increase for a specific age group is limited to the observed increase for that group.

Table 6.6 describes the number and rate of criminal suspects in Germany in 1984 and 1990 by age, gender, and national origin. The data also show that about 60 percent of the total observed crime increases from 1984 to 1990 were the result of increases in the number of foreign male suspects. Another 15 percent was the result of increases in the number of foreign female suspects.

As of 1993, immigrants accounted for one-fourth of the prison population (including pretrial detainees and sentenced prisoners, youth and adult prisoners). Immigrants sentenced to imprisonment can be released after serving half of the prison sentence, under section 456a of the German procedural code, if deportation takes place immediately after release. Drug offenders account for a majority of the foreign inmates.

Public Opinion

Public opinion is an indicator of interest in, and support for or opposition to, a society's immigration policies. First, it is interesting to note that very few items bearing on immigration appeared in German national polls in the 1960s, 1970s, and 1980s. The typical question on polls that asked about immigration was whether foreign workers posed a serious problem. About a third of the public did not perceive the foreign workers as a serious problem, another third did perceive them as a problem, and all others either had no opinion or were undecided about whether foreign workers were a problem.

In 1974, German citizens were asked the following question:

If foreign workers want to stay here permanently should they be allowed to, or should they return to their home countries after a certain period of time?

	Percent
Allowed to stay	37
Should return	42
Undecided	21

Source: American Institute of Public Opinion (Storrs: Roper Center, University of Connecticut, 1974).

Thus, among those with opinions, a slightly higher percentage wanted foreigners to leave the FRG and return to their home countries. In addition, responses to the following question are:

Do you sometimes meet foreign workers, I mean on the job or otherwise? Are you friends with foreign workers, or do you at least know them well, so that sometimes you get together privately?

	Percent
Get together privately	13
Meet them, yet have no private contacts	32
Don't meet any	55

Source: American Institute of Public Opinion (Storrs: Roper Center, University of Connecticut, 1974).

Whatever their views, only a small minority (13 percent) of the German public had become familiar with the guest workers. In 1990, a united German public was asked: "Are you for a change of laws regarding political asylum so as to prevent many asylum seekers from coming into the country?" On this issue, there was much greater consensus. Sixty percent favored a change that would make it more difficult to receive political asylum, 24 percent opposed a change, and 16 percent were undecided.

In postunited Germany, surveys were conducted that asked about foreigners in general and their impact on unemployment and education and about particular types of foreigners. These were the same items that were included on national surveys in France and Great Britain. The German responses are reported in table 6.7.

Over 90 percent of native-born Germans believe there are "too many" or "a lot" of foreigners, although most Germans do not see them in their neighborhoods. Only 25 to 29 percent, respectively, believe the children of foreigners lower the level of education and that foreigners increase unemploy-

Table 6.7 German Attitudes toward Foreigners, 1989

Foreigners in our country[a]	too many	47.4
	a lot	44.8
	not many	6.9
Foreigners = presence disturbing	yes	16.9
	no	78.3
	don't know/NA	4.8
Foreigners in neighborhood	many	7.0
	few	52.1
	none	40.9
Foreigners = children in schools lowers level of education	yes	25.2
	no	74.8
Foreigners increase our unemployment	yes	29.0
	no	71.0

Source: Ira Gang and Francisco L. Riviera-Batiz, "Unemployment and Attitudes towards Foreigners in Germany," in *The Economic Consequences of Immigration in Germany,* ed. Gunter Steinmann and Ralf E. Ulrich (Heidelberg: Physica-Verlag, 1994), 141.
Note: Some of the columns do not add up exactly to 100 percent due to rounding.
[a]Percentage of foreigners in the population = 7.3; sample size = 858.

ment. As shown in their responses on table 6.8, the majority of Germans claimed they were "indifferent" toward all of the various racial and ethnic immigrant groups. But the north Europeans were the most favored followed by the south Europeans. Asians received the least positive reaction—almost one-third of Germans "dislike them."

On September 1, 1992, the *Guardian* reported the results of a national poll that found 78 percent agreed that immigration was Germany's most pressing problem, compared to 21 percent who cited unification.

Table 6.8 German Attitudes toward Particular Groups of Foreigners, 1989

Group	*Opinion*	*Percent*
South Europeans	dislike	9.1
	indifferent	49.9
	like	41.0
North Africans	dislike	22.7
	indifferent	59.4
	like	17.8
Turks	dislike	27.5
	indifferent	54.3
	like	18.2
Black Africans	dislike	26.3
	indifferent	55.9
	like	17.7
Asians	dislike	32.8
	indifferent	53.5
	like	13.8
Southeast Asians	dislike	25.4
	indifferent	56.2
	like	18.5
West Indians	dislike	18.4
	indifferent	60.0
	like	21.6
Jews	dislike	15.2
	indifferent	58.4
	like	26.5
North Europeans	dislike	4.7
	indifferent	37.3
	like	58.0

Source: Ira Gang and Francisco L. Riviera-Batiz, "Unemployment and Attitudes towards Foreigners in Germany," in *The Economic Consequences of Immigration in Germany,* ed. Gunter Steinmann and Ralf E. Ulrich (Heidelberg: Physica-Verlag, 1994), 141.

Note: Some of the columns do not add up exactly to 100 percent due to rounding.

Summary

Germany's history vis-à-vis immigration and the admission of foreigners has always been closely tied to labor-market needs. Thus, in recent times, following the end of World War II, Germany was the major recruiter of guest workers to help rebuild its war torn economy. But even during these periods of extreme labor shortage (some eighteen to nineteen million guest workers worked in Germany from 1960 to 1973), Germany maintained its policy of making it extremely difficult for immigrants to become German citizens or to remain in the country more than five years. Where Germany did depart from its history of not receiving immigrants or of refusing to convert foreigners to German citizens was in its asylum policy adopted following the end of the war in 1945. Between 1950 and 1994, some 5 million persons (3.3 million were resettlers who claimed German descent and 1.67 million were non-Germans) were admitted into the FRG. In May 1999, Germany passed a major immigrant act that cut the links between blood ties and nationality that had been in effect since 1913. Under the new law, citizenship is automatic for anyone born in the country.

Even though Germany made it very difficult for an immigrant to become a citizen (until the passage of the 1999 act), it does provide welfare and safety net benefits to its foreign workers. It pays for most of the language training for immigrants and vocational training programs for young immigrants. But a comparison of the amount of money immigrants pay in taxes and the amount they receive in benefits shows that foreign workers contribute more to the public coffers than they receive in children's allowance, social security, pension, and unemployment benefits.

The crime and corrections data indicate that foreigners are more likely to be suspects in serious crimes (e.g., homicide, robbery, assault, and drug offenses). And, like all of the other countries in this survey, the German public does not hold positive views toward immigrants, but perhaps because it knows they are a "temporary" presence the opinions expressed are less negative than in those countries that have histories and policies that welcome immigrants and grant citizenship relatively easily. Thus, in 1989 78 percent of the German public did not find the "foreigners' presence disturbing," and did not believe foreigners increased unemployment or lowered the levels of education in school. But in 1990, 60 percent of a united German public favored changing the political asylum law that would make it more difficult for persons to receive asylum and in 1992 78 percent agreed that immigration was Germany's most pressing problem.

Notes

1. Philip Martin, *Germany: Reluctant Land of Immigration* (Washington, D.C.: American Institute for Contemporary German Studies, 1988), at www.aicgs.org/publications/pubonline.shtml (accessed June 5, 1999).

2. Martin, *Germany,* 7.

3. Sarah Collinson, *European and International Migration* (London: Pinter, 1993), 51.

4. Munz Rainer and Rolf E. Ulrich, "Changing Patterns of Immigration to Germany, 1945–1997" (unpublished manuscript, 2000).

5. Rainer and Ulrich, "Changing Patterns," 10.

6. Christian Donle and Peter Kather, "Germany," in *International Immigration and Nationality Law: Immigration Supplement 2,* ed. Dennis Campbell and Joy Fisher (Boston: Nijhoff, 1993), X1–X5.

7. Christine Kreuzer, "Reforming Germany's Citizenship Law" (unpublished manuscript, 2000).

8. Donle and Kather, "Germany," VII.1.

9. Collinson, *European and International Migration,* 60.

10. Kreuzer, "Reforming Germany's Citizenship Law," 11.

11. Martin, *Germany,* 193.

12. Merih Asuly, "No More Foreigners? The Remaking of Naturalization and Citizenship Law, 1990–2000" (paper presented at the annual meeting of the American Political Science Association, San Francisco, September 7, 2001).

13. Hans-Jorg Albrecht, "Ethnic Minorities and Criminal Justice in Germany," in *Crime and Justice: An Annual Review,* vol. 21, ed. Michael Tonry (Chicago: University of Chicago Press, 1994).

7

Immigration in Japan

Of all the major industrial nations in the world, Japan has worked the hardest at maintaining a homogeneous, distinctive culture in which foreign influences and foreigners have been barely visible. Only following its defeat at the end of World War II and the subsequent establishment of U.S. military bases on its territory did Japan have to come to grips with Western culture and society. But the war ended over a half century ago and, although Japan did not close its doors to foreigners as effectively as it had in earlier periods, compared to European nations and to Australia, Canada, and the United States, it has nevertheless actively discouraged immigration. Even following the end of the Vietnam War, when thousands of refugees were seeking safe havens and Japan was a relatively close haven, the government and people of Japan withstood international pressure and accepted very few refugees.

However, beginning in the early to mid-1990s, it must be noted that as a result of "demographic changes and the refusal of increasing affluent and well-educated Japanese youth to perform dirty, dangerous and difficult jobs, the native born workforce became unable to meet the rising demand for unskilled labor."[1] As a result, greater numbers of migrant workers mainly from East and Southeast Asia and Latin America began entering the country. By the mid-1990s, there were around 800,000 unskilled foreign workers in Japan.

Historical Background and Major Legislation

The legal basis for Japanese immigration policy is the Immigration Control and Refugee Recognition Law (ICRRL), which was last amended in 1993.[2] This law requires that all immigrants must enter Japan as visitors. There are seven different kinds of visas under which visitors can enter the country: diplomatic, official, transit, short-term visit, work, general, and unspecified. Each type of visa specifies the purpose of the visit and the period of stay. There are twenty-seven categories of residence status, each of which specifies the duties of that class of immigrant. Activities that are not covered in one of these twenty-seven classes of residence status cannot be a legitimate purpose for entering Japan.

There are sixteen classes of work-related visas and twelve categories of nonwork visas. The work-related visas include diplomacy, official business, professorships, art, religion, journalism, investment and business management, legal and accounting services, medical services, research, instruction, engineering, humanities and international services, intracompany transfers, entertainment, and skilled labor. The requirements for each of these classes of work visa are described in greater detail in table 7.1. Nonwork visas include those for cultural activity, temporary visits, university study, preuniversity study, training, dependent, a designated activity, and personal status. Included in this last category are permanent residents, spouse or child of a Japanese national, spouse or child of a permanent resident, and long-term residents. The requirements for these nonwork classes of residence are also described more fully in table 7.1.

In 1992, entertainers (82,253 foreigners) were the largest class to enter Japan under work-related visas. At a conference on human trafficking held in Japan in January 2000, the senior state secretary for foreign affairs acknowledged that "Japan is a destination country for trafficking in persons" and "it is difficult to determine if women are entering Japan to join the sex trade." How many of the 85,000-plus entertainers who enter Japan annually are in fact trafficked to work as prostitutes is not known. The next largest group was translators and other international services (46,422), followed by investors and business managers (29,911), intracompany transfers (20,227), engineers (12,988), instructors (11,924), skilled laborers (7,279), researchers (2,401), law and accounting professionals (426), and medical professionals (329). In that same year, 150,000 immigrants of Japanese descent entered the country to work largely as unskilled laborers. The vast majority of these came from South America. As of January 2000, there were 1.5 million registered foreigners in Japan.

Although there is a residence status for permanent residents, Japan does not allow entry for the purpose of permanent residence. A person desiring permanent residence must enter the country under one of the other residence statuses described earlier and then apply for permanent resident status. This request is granted at the discretion of the Ministry of Justice. Article 22 of the ICRRL requires that applicants for change in status demonstrate good behavior and conduct and have the ability or assets to make an independent living. The applicant's permanent residence must also be in the Japanese national interest.

Table 7.1 Residence Statuses and Authorized Activity, Japan

Status	*Activity*
Work-Related Visas	
Diplomacy	Authorized to engage in diplomatic and consular activities for foreign governments for the duration of his or her mission. Family members and others who enjoy diplomatic privileges and immunities under law are also eligible.
Official business	Authorized to engage in official business of a foreign government or an international organization that is recognized by the Japanese government for the duration of the mission. Family members are also eligible.
Professorship	Authorized to engage in research and education in universities and equivalent institutions for a period of stay of three years, one year, or six months.
Art	Authorized to engage in artistic activities with remuneration for a period of stay of three years, one year, or six months. Artistic activities in public performance for audiences are not included. Music composers, painters, sculptors, and artists who engage in creative activities or in artistic instruction are eligible. Artists who engage in research and education in universities and equivalent institutions are not eligible.
Religion	Authorized to engage in missionary and other religious activities for stays of three years, one year, or six months. Clergy, ministers, preachers, priests, evangelists, bonzes, and other religious leaders are eligible. Activities as mere believers are not sufficient.
Journalism	Authorized to engage in news coverage and other journalistic activities for foreign journalistic organizations. The journalist must be under a contractual relationship with a foreign newspaper, news agency, broadcasting company, or other journalistic organization.
Investment and business management	Alien is authorized to commence the operation of, invest in, operate, or manage international trade or other business for a period of stay of three years, one year, or six months. Aliens applying for this status of residence must have three years of experience or more and must receive no less remuneration than comparable Japanese nationals.

continued

Table 7.1 Residence Statuses and Authorized Activity, Japan (continued)

Status	*Activity*
Legal and accounting services	Authorized to engage in legal and accounting services to be performed by legally qualified legal and accounting professionals for a period of stay for three years, one year, or six months.
Medical services	Authorized to engage in medical services performed by medical professionals for a period of stay of one year or six months. Medical doctors, dentists, midwives, nurses, assistant nurses, and other medical professionals who are qualified under the relevant Japanese laws are eligible when they receive no less remuneration than comparable Japanese nationals.
Research	In this category for researchers, an alien is authorized to engage in research under contract with public and private organizations for a period of stay of one year or six months. Unless the applicant for this status of residence works for government agencies and other designated institutions, he or she must have certain experience and receive no less remuneration than comparable Japanese nationals.
Instruction	Authorized to engage in education in elementary school, junior high school, senior high school, advanced vocational school, vocational school, or in other educational institutions of equivalent levels for a period of stay of one year or six months.
Engineering	Authorized to offer services in engineering and other natural science fields under contract with public and private organizations in Japan for a period of stay of one year or six months. The applicant for this status of residence must have a certain educational background or job experience and receive no less remuneration than comparable Japanese officials.
Humanities and international services	Authorized to offer services that require knowledge in law, economics, sociology, or other human science fields for a period of stay of one year or six months. The applicant must have a certain educational background or job experience and receive no less remuneration than comparable Japanese nationals.
Intracompany transfers	Authorized to engage in the same activities authorized under the category for engineering and

Table 7.1 Residence Statuses and Authorized Activity, Japan (continued)

Status	*Activity*
	humanities and international services in Japanese offices and transfers from foreign offices of the same public or private organizations for a period of stay of one year or six months.
Entertainment	Authorized to engage in theatrical, artistic, and music performances, sports, or other entertainment performances for a period of stay of one year or three months. The applicant must have relevant experience of two years or more in foreign countries.
Skilled labor	Authorized to engage in activities that require experience and skills in special industrial sectors under contract with public and private organizations in Japan for a period of stay of one year or six months.
Nonwork Visas	
Cultural activities	Authorized to engage in academic or artistic activities without remuneration, specialized research in Japanese art and culture experts for a period of stay of one year or six months. University students and trainees are not eligible.
Temporary visits	Alien is authorized to engage in sightseeing, recreation, sports, visiting relatives, inspection tours, attending conferences, making business contacts, or other similar activities for a period of stay of ninety or fifteen days.
University study	Alien is authorized to study in a university, in university-equivalent educational institutions, in specialized courses of advanced vocational schools, or in schools designed for the preparation of those who have had twelve years of education in foreign countries to enter Japanese universities for a period of stay of one year or six months.
Preuniversity study	Authorized to study in high school, in higher or general courses in an advanced vocational school, in vocational school, or in an equivalent educational institution for a period of stay of one year, six months, or three months.
Training	Authorized to learn and acquire technology, skills, or knowledge in public or private organizations in Japan for a period of stay of one year, six months, or three months. The applicant for this status must

continued

Table 7.1 Residence Statuses and Authorized Activity, Japan (continued)

Status	*Activity*
	be accepted by an organization and cannot engage in self-training. There are specific qualifications for the training and the accepting organizations. The alien with this residence status is not allowed to engage in remunerative activities and cannot be hired for labor. The organization may pay the trainee alien the training expenses, but the amount paid must not exceed actual expenses.
Dependent	With this status of residence, an alien is authorized to engage in daily family activities as a spouse or a child of an alien whose status of residence is not "diplomacy," "official business," or "temporary visit" for a period of stay of three years, one year, six months, or three months. If an alien stays in Japan on dependent status, he or she needs to obtain proper alternative residence status in order to engage in other independent activities.
Designated activities	With the status of residence for designated activities, an alien is authorized to engage in specific activities that the minister of justice designates individually for a period of stay of three years, one year, or six months. The designated activities include those of the Taiwanese and the Palestinian Liberation Organization representatives and their families, those of aliens on working holiday programs, and those of amateur athletes.
Personal status	Unlike the other categories of residence status, an alien may fit within the following four categories not on the basis of the activities he or she engages in but, rather, based on personal status or in his or her family relationship to a Japanese national or a permanent resident. There is no restriction under the immigration law on the activities of holders of these categories of residence status, and the holders may work unless otherwise prohibited by other laws.
Permanent Residents	
Spouse or child of a Japanese national	Authorized to reside in Japan for a period of stay of three years, one year, or six months. A foreign spouse must be formally married to a Japanese national, and there must be a genuine marital relationship as demonstrated by a shared abode. A foreign child must have been born to a Japanese national or have been adopted by Japanese nationals.

Table 7.1 Residence Statuses and Authorized Activity, Japan (continued)

Status	*Activity*
Spouse or child of a permanent resident	Authorized to reside in Japan for a period of stay of three years, one year, or six months. A foreign spouse must be formally married to a permanent resident, and there must be a genuine marital relationship as demonstrated by a shared abode. For a child to qualify, he or she must have been born to a permanent resident and have been residing in Japan ever since.
Long-term residents	With this status of residence, an alien is authorized to reside in Japan for a designated period of stay by special consideration of the minister of justice. There have to be humanitarian and other special reasons to obtain this status of residence.

Source: Akio Shimizu, "Japan," in *International Immigration and Nationality Law: Immigration Supplement,* vol. 2, ed. Dennis Campbell and Joy Fisher (Boston: Nijhoff, 1993).

According to Sumikazu Taguchi, "no matter how long a foreign national resides in Japan, he/she is still regarded both legally and socially as an alien."[3] A foreign national can never become a citizen. But the Japanese Nationality Law passed in 1950 and last amended in 1984 defines the following as persons who are Japanese citizens: a person whose father or mother was a Japanese national at the time of birth, a person whose deceased father was a Japanese national at the time of his death, and a person born in Japan whose parents are either both undetermined or stateless. The law also defines the classes of persons eligible for Japanese citizenship. They include a child under the age of twenty who is legitimized by marriage or acknowledgment, if the father or mother was a Japanese national at the time of the child's birth and is currently a Japanese national or was so at the time of his or her death. Persons in this category must apply for citizenship by presenting the relevant facts to the Ministry of Justice. Citizenship can also be obtained through naturalization.

For an immigrant to be naturalized, he or she must satisfy the following requirements:

1. Continuous residence in Japan for five or more years or temporary residence for ten years
2. Twenty years of age or older and mentally competent
3. Demonstrates good behavior or conduct
4. Financially supported by skills or assets or those of a relative in the same household
5. Relinquish any other citizenship
6. Not involved in activity that attempts or advocates the overthrow of the constitution or the government by violence

Any modification in the activity pursued or other conditions of the residence status must be approved by the Ministry of Justice.

A foreign national who engaged in a remunerative activity not allowed by his or her status of residence would be penalized under the new law, as would persons who offered employment to persons engaged in illegal work. The law also allowed third-generation Nikkei (foreigners of Japanese ancestry) and non-Nikkei married to second-generation Nikkei to obtain long-term resident status. This portion of the 1990 act was aimed at promoting the introduction of Nikkei as an effective source of unskilled labor.

In April 1993, the Japanese government introduced the Technical Intern Training Program. This program opened the door for Japanese employers to accept trainees, many of whom then worked as unskilled workers under the name of "on-the-job training."

In 1993, Nikkei workers were heavily concentrated as laborers mostly in the automobile and electrical appliance industries. Foreign students were more likely to be found in white-collar positions, especially as language teachers and interpreters, and clandestine workers[4] were employed in a variety of unskilled occupations, especially construction.[5]

Stock and Flow of Immigrants

As of 1994, there were 1.4 million registered immigrants in Japan, constituting 1.1 percent of the population. Koreans were the most prevalent nationality of foreigners with 693,000, followed distantly by China with 171,000, Brazil with 119,000, the Philippines with 62,000, and the United States with 42,000. Survey data indicate that most clandestine workers remain in Japan long enough to earn the maximum income possible doing unskilled manual work and then return to their home country. These workers do not come with the intention of settling in Japan and most do not remain.

Between 1995 and 2000, Japan's population grew at the lowest rate since the end of World War II, according to Takeyuki Tsuda, the associate director of the Center for Comparative Immigration Studies at the University of California, San Diego.[6]

The proportion of workers of age fifteen to twenty-nine peaked in 1998 and will decline from 24 to 18 percent of all workers by the end of this decade. Japan is currently tied with Italy as the country with the oldest population and has the most rapidly aging populace in the world. In addition, the labor force is estimated to contract by 10 percent in 25 years (the entire population itself is projected to decline by 21.6 million during the next 50 years), requiring Japan to import over 600,000 immigrants *per year* simply to maintain its present workforce or face a 6.7 *annual* drop in gross domestic product.

As of 1999, there were 1.6 million foreign residents in Japan and in 2000 the numbers increased to 1.7 million. The estimated number of illegal foreign residents at the end of 1999 was in the 400,000 to 500,000 range. Most of them came from China followed by South Korea. Tsuda believes that "the Japanese government will soon need to reconsider and change its restrictive immigration policies and admit larger numbers of foreign workers to sustain its economy or be faced with an increased deluge of illegal immigrants."[7]

Refugees

In 1972, there were only 773 Vietnamese in Japan and they were mostly students. Following the fall of South Vietnam, the number of Vietnamese refugees in Japan increased to 3,132. As of 1982, there was a total of 4,003 refugees in Japan, most of whom did not wish to remain permanently.

Deportation

Immigrants admitted to Japan can be deported if their stay violates immigration law or if their conduct is otherwise unacceptable. Activity that violates immigration law and would warrant deportation include:

1. Entering without a valid passport
2. Landing without landing permission
3. Staying in excess of the period of stay without the requisite renewal or change of period
4. Violating the conditions of temporary landing
5. Not leaving Japan despite orders to leave when permission to land is not granted

Additional misconduct that could result in deportation includes aiding other immigrants to enter illegally, engaging in income-generating activity not specified under a person's residence status, being a convicted offender, prostitution, attempting the violent overthrow of the government, and committing harmful acts against national interest or public safety.

The number of immigrants deported by Japan has increased greatly in the recent past—from 10,573 in 1986 to 66,892 in 1993. Most of the persons are deported for exceeding their allowed period of stay. Of the 36,364 persons deported in 1990, 32,647 overstayed their visa, 2,320 were illegal entrants, and 751 engaged in some income-generating activity not specified in their visa.

The Japanese Immigration Bureau estimated, by comparing legal entry and exit records, that there were 295,096 visa overstayers in Japan in November 1993. Government officials assumed that over 90 percent of these overstayers were in the workforce. Table 7.2 describes the estimates of visa overstayers and their country of origin from July 1990 to November 1993. We see that the number has nearly tripled between 1990 and 1993.

In February 2000, a law took effect that prevents foreigners who have been deported from reentering Japan for five years. The previous law imposed a one-year ban. Another change in Japan's immigration statutes applies penalties, including a fine of $2,800 or up to three years in prison or both, to people who enter the country illegally.

Crime

Studies of the criminal involvement of immigrants in Japan are few and far between. According to Wayne Cornelius, Philip Martin, and James Hollifield, media reports on crime statistics often focus on the number of crimes committed by foreigners, especially South Koreans and Iranians.[8] However, there is no evidence that foreign workers are, as yet, a major source of urban crime.

In 1994, the Ministry of Justice issued a report on crime by immigrants.[9] The report states that of the 297,725 offenders identified as committing penal offenses in 1993,[10] 12,182 were immigrants.[11] Of these immigrants, 7,276 were visiting foreigners (i.e., persons other than the permanent residents and U.S. Army personnel and families) and 4,906 were other foreigners. Japanese penal code offenses include serious crimes such as homicide, assault, robbery, bodily injury, larceny, forgery, and gambling. Violations of the immigration laws are not penal offenses in Japan and do not contribute to these offender counts. Immigration law offenses are classified with other lesser infractions as "special offenses." Most of the crimes in this class would be considered public order offenses, such as prostitution and morals charges in the United States and European countries, but Japan also includes drug sales and drug use in this category.

In 1993, an estimated 675 immigrants were identified as offenders in drug crimes solved by the police.[12] When these drug charges are added to the penal code offenses, the number of arrested foreigners becomes 12,857. These counts of offenders were divided by the respective populations at risk: the stock populations of foreigners and the stock population of native-born Japanese. The resulting crime rate for foreigners was 9.3 per 1,000 for foreigners and 2.3 per 1,000 for citizens. The offender rate for foreigners is more than three times that for Japanese citizens.

Table 7.2 Estimates of Unauthorized Visa Overstayers, by Nationality, 1990–1993

Nationality	*July 1, 1990*	*May 1, 1991*	*Nov. 1, 1991*	*May 1, 1992*	*Nov. 1, 1992*	*May 1, 1993*	*Nov. 1, 1993*
Thailand	11,523 (10.8)	19,093 (12.0)	32,751 (15.1)	44,354 (15.9)	53,219 (18.2)	55,383 (18.6)	53,845 (18.2)
South Korea	13,876 (13.0)	25,848 (16.2)	30,976 (14.3)	35,687 (12.8)	37,491 (12.8)	39,455 (13.2)	41,024 (13.8)
China	10,039 (9.4)	17,535 (11.0)	21,649 (10.0)	25,737 (9.2)	29,091 (9.9)	33,312 (11.2)	36,297 (12.2)
Philippines	23,805 (22.4)	27,228 (17.0)	29,620 (13.7)	31,974 (11.5)	34,296 (11.7)	35,392 (11.9)	36,089 (12.2)
Malaysia	7,550 (7.1)	14,413 (9.3)	25,379 (11.7)	38,529 (13.8)	34,529 (11.8)	30,840 (10.3)	25,653 (8.7)
Iran	764 (0.7)	10,915 (6.8)	21,719 (10.0)	40,001 (14.3)	32,994 (11.3)	28,437 (9.5)	23,867 (8.0)
Peru	242 (0.2)	487 (0.3)	1,017 (0.5)	2,783 (1.0)	6,241 (2.1)	9,038 (3.0)	11,659 (3.9)
Bangladesh	7,195 (6.8)	7,498 (4.7)	7,807 (3.6)	8,103 (2.9)	8,161 (2.8)	8,069 (2.7)	7,931 (2.7)
Taiwan	4,775 (4.5)	5,241 (3.3)	5,897 (2.7)	6,729 (2.4)	7,283 (2.5)	7,457 (2.5)	7,677 (2.6)
Pakistan	7,989 (7.5)	7,864 (4.9)	7,923 (3.7)	8,001 (2.9)	8,056 (2.8)	7,733 (2.6)	7,414 (2.5)
Myanmar	1,041 (1.0)	1,676 (1.1)	2,712 (1.3)	3,661 (1.3)	4,149 (1.4)	4,511 (1.5)	4,686 (1.6)
Others	17,305 (16.2)	21,645 (13.5)	28,236 (13.1)	32,290 (11.6)	36,005 (12.3)	37,511 (12.3)	38,954 (13.1)
Total	106,104	159,443	215,686	277,849	291,515	297,138	295,096

Source: Brian Bailey, "Japanese Laws and Policies Concerning Immigration (Including Refugees and Foreign Workers)" (senior thesis, George Washington University, 1996). Statistics are derived from computerized cross-checking of individual entry and exit records. Because of several potential sources of error in this methodology, the figures should be regarded as best estimates rather than precise statistics. The figures do not refer to unauthorized immigrants who have been apprehended by the immigration authorities, but only to those whose presence in Japan has been detected by the government through the cross-checking of records. The assistance of Kiriro Morita (University of Tokyo) and Katsuhiko Fujimori (Fuji Research Institute, Tokyo) in obtaining the latest data from 1993 is gratefully acknowledged.

Note: Figures in parentheses are percentages of the estimated total of visa overstayers. Some of the columns do not add up exactly to 100 percent due to rounding.

Table 7.3 Percentage Distribution of Offenses for Foreigners and Japanese Citizens

	Type of Penal Code Offense			
Population Group	*Homicide*	*Other Crimes*	*Property Crimes*	*Forgery/Gambling*
Foreigners	0.001	0.051	0.854	0.040
Japanese citizens	0.004	0.096	0.784	0.051

Source: Ministry of Justice, *Summary of the White Paper on Crime, 1993* (Tokyo: Ministry of Justice, 1994).

The distribution of types of crimes differ somewhat for native-born Japanese and immigrants. Immigrants, for example, commit a greater proportion of property offenses. More than 85 percent of the crimes committed by immigrants are property crimes, whereas slightly more than 78 percent of the crimes known to be committed by Japanese citizens are property crimes. A greater proportion of native-born Japanese are charged with violent crimes other than homicide, but foreigners commit a greater proportion of homicides (see table 7.3). As in the case of most of the other countries included in this study, foreigners in Japan are arrested for drug offenses at higher rates than native-born citizens. The drug offender rate for foreigners is 0.6 per 1,000 while the rate for citizens is 0.1 per 1,000.

Public Opinion

The first national survey on the attitudes of the Japanese public toward immigrants was conducted in 1980. This was a period when large numbers of Vietnamese and Cambodians were seeking places of refuge and the Japanese government stated it would accept five hundred refugees. After being informed that the number admitted was five hundred, the Japanese public responded to the following question:

Do you think that Japan should accept more refugees or not?

	Percent
Should accept more	38
Should maintain the present number	38
Should not accept more	10
No opinion	14

Source: American Institute of Public Opinion (Storrs: Roper Center, University of Connecticut, 1993).

Most respondents supported the government's policy. Among those who said "should accept more," almost 90 percent based their response on "humanitarian reasons" and because "as a member of the international community, we are responsible for them." Nine years later, in 1989, the following items about refugees appeared in national polls:

Refugees from Vietnam and China are pouring in. Those who leave because of difficult living conditions, in other words economic refugees, are included. Do you think these economic refugees should be allowed to enter or not?

	Percent
Should be allowed to enter	32
Should not be allowed to enter	52
Other/no answer	16

Is it accurate or inaccurate to say that with respect to the acceptance of refugees from other countries, Japan lacks understanding and closes its doors?

	1989	*1990*
Accurate	49	49
Inaccurate	38	38
Other/no answer	13	13

Source: American Institute of Public Opinion (Storrs: Roper Center, University of Connecticut, 1993).

While half the respondents believed that their country lacked understanding, a majority nonetheless favored maintaining the almost "closed door" policy.

In 1993, a national survey stated: "Local conflicts and struggles based on nationalism or religion treat people who want to move to other countries as refugees. What do you think Japan should do for these people?" The following responses indicate that, in 1993, there was some shift in the thinking of the Japanese public. While most respondents did not support admitting refugees into their country, over 80 percent seemed to recognize a "moral obligation" to help these people and a strong minority were willing to admit more refugees than were currently accepted.

	Percent
Should accept as many people in cooperation with other countries	36
Should cooperate financially rather than accepting refugees	46
Need not cooperate any more than at the present level	9
Other/don't know	9

As far as the immigrants generally are concerned, the following survey data show little interest or moral compulsion to increase immigration. Between

October 1987 and March 1993, the following items appeared on national polls in Japan:

There is a trend toward the increase of foreign workers in Japan. What do you think of the increase?

	October 1987
Current level is fine	42%
Increase is desirable	31
Increase is undesirable	18
Don't know	9

Source: American Institute of Public Opinion (Storrs: Roper Center, University of Connecticut, 1993).

Then, in 1988, 1989, 1990, and 1993, the Japanese public was asked:

Do you support or oppose allowing foreign laborers to work in Japan?

	December 1988	*January 1990*
Support	14%	17%
Support somewhat	31	34
Oppose somewhat	35	29
Oppose	13	15
No opinion	7	5

The government has a policy of not allowing foreigners to enter for the purpose of finding unskilled employment. Do you think that the policy of not admitting those people should be continued? Or do you think they should be admitted with various restrictions?

	October 1989
Continue policy of not admitting	33%
Admit, but with restrictions	56
Other/no opinion	11

What do you think should be done about foreigners who are currently breaking the law by engaging in unskilled labor?

	Percent
Change the law, so they can work legally	45
Enforce the law strictly	34
Be lenient as long as they are not undesirables (e.g., criminals)	16
Other/no opinion	5

Under present laws, foreigners are not allowed to stay in Japan to work as untrained workers in factories or building sites. However, some companies suffering from a lack of workforce are arguing that they should be able to hire foreigners as untrained workers. Do you agree with this opinion?

	March 1993
Yes (for hiring untrained workers)	64%
No (against hiring untrained workers)	21
Don't know/no answer	15

(If "Yes"): Why do you think so? Choose as many as you like from the answers below.

	Percent
Foreigners will help to solve the problem of a lack of workforce	50
Foreigners will work for lower ranges	21
Acquiring skills in Japan, they can make use of them when they return home	42
You cannot stop foreigners who want to work in Japan	11
It is a common trend worldwide that anybody can work in any country	61
Japanese will have the chance to know foreign countries and their people	33
Other/don't know	2

(If "No"): Why do you think so? Choose as many as you like from the answers below.

	Percent
The number of unemployed Japanese will increase	53
The wages of Japanese workers who do the same jobs as foreigners will stay low	18
The atmosphere of the region will change when there are many foreigners	33
Foreigner-related crimes may increase	59
Companies will be spoiled and will not try to introduce new technology to save labor	8
It is more necessary to help them build industry in their countries so that they can work in their home countries	30
Other	3
Don't know	3

Source: American Institute of Public Opinion (Storrs: Roper Center, University of Connecticut, 1993).

The responses describe a divided public with a plurality, and by 1993 a majority, who favored allowing unskilled workers to enter legally but with restrictions on length of stay, type of work, and number admitted. The responses also show that a plurality did not favor increasing the number of skilled workers permitted to enter.

In 1989 and 1992, the following questions take the issue a step further by asking:

If foreign workers were to be admitted it is possible that they may come with hopes of bringing their families and becoming permanent residents. What do you think of this?

	1989
It would be fine to allow them to bring families and become permanent residents	19%

They should be allowed to live with families while they are in Japan, but they should not be allowed to become permanent residents	33
Only the individual workers should be allowed in Japan	37
Other/don't know	12

Note: This doesn't add up exactly to 100 percent due to rounding.

If a foreign worker hopes to settle in Japan permanently, get married, have children, etc., would you oppose?

	1992
Yes	71%
No	19
No opinion	10

Source: American Institute of Public Opinion (Storrs: Roper Center, University of Connecticut, 1993).

On the issue of the permanent status of immigrants and their families, the large majority of Japanese agreed: they were opposed. Quite consistently, in 1991 and 1992, two-thirds of the Japanese public said they believed "certain conditions and limits are necessary."

	1991	*1992*
Conditions/limits necessary	62%	66%
Not necessary	16	14
Difficult to say	18	17
No opinion	4	3

What do you think about foreigners living in Japan? Which is close to your idea, A or B?

	1993
A. As long as they are living in Japan, people from any country should be guaranteed the same rights as Japanese	28%
B. Even if they are living in Japan, foreigners are not Japanese nationals, so it is natural that their rights are limited	21
Inclined to A	24
Inclined to B	18
Hard to say/no answer	8

Source: American Institute of Public Opinion (Storrs: Roper Center, University of Connecticut, 1993).
Note: This does not add up exactly to 100 percent due to rounding.

The question was then posed in more personal terms: "How would you feel if a foreign worker or a refugee were to move into your neighborhood?" When so phrased, the Japanese, like Americans and perhaps people everywhere, had a greater acceptance and a willingness to be hospitable:

Would help them adjust to the new society	47%
It would be a good opportunity to be exposed to another culture	11
Would like to avoid them as much as possible	20
Would like them to move elsewhere	10
Other/no answer	12

Source: American Institute of Public Opinion (Storrs: Roper Center, University of Connecticut, 1993).

In sum, the data show a public divided on whether unskilled laborers should be allowed to work legally in Japan. But the data also show a Japanese public that exhibits greater consensus in its opposition to allowing foreign workers to have permanent status in Japan and to bringing their families with them.

But one indication that some degree of assimilation is possible is the rate of intermarriage between Japanese and Koreans, Filipinos, and Latin American Nikkeijen. Quoting Cornelius, Martin, and Hollifield, "about 80 percent of permanent resident Koreans now are marrying Japanese."[13] And marriage between Japanese and Filipinos and Japanese and Latin American Nikkeijen has also become increasingly common.

Summary

If we were writing before the mid-1990s, we would have summarized Japan's immigration policy as follows: Japanese immigration policy is restrictive in terms of admissions. No one is admitted for the purpose of permanent residence. Every immigrant enters Japan as a guest. Transition from guest status to naturalized citizen is at the discretion of immigration authorities in the Ministry of Justice. The laws governing eligibility for citizenship status and permanent residence status are not very different than they are in other countries examined in part I. The rules governing the passage from visitor to permanent residence status are less visible, however. This decision seems to be purely at the discretion of the Ministry of Justice. The low naturalization rate in Japan may be due to the discretionary judgments made when application is made for permanent residence status.

The restrictions placed on immigrants while they are in Japan are comparable to those of France or Germany. Permanent residents have no restrictions on their activity other than those of Japanese citizens. Other immigrants, however, must adhere to the conditions of their visa. Any change in employment or activity must be approved by the Ministry of Justice. Failure to do so can result in deportation. Immigrants (other than permanent residents) must also register with local authorities when they change residence. Finally, there are no government programs or policies designed to integrate permanent residents or other classes of immigrants into Japanese society. This is entirely consistent with a policy that does not encourage entry for the purpose of permanent settlement.

But the last few years have produced drastic changes in Japanese society. As a function of a very low birthrate (the lowest in the world) since 1995 and an increasing unwillingness of educated Japanese youth to work as laborers (skilled or unskilled), Japan has become more dependent on foreign workers. Thus, while one cannot characterize Japan as "a country of immigrants," its restrictive policies have and are continuing to change in the direction of making it much more open to foreign workers.

Notes

1. Takeyuki Tsuda, "Reluctant Hosts: The Future of Japan As a Country of Immigration," Center for Comparative Immigration Studies at the University of California, San Diego, November 2001.
2. Brian Bailey, "Japanese Laws and Policies Concerning Immigration" (senior thesis, George Washington University, 1996), at www.ufj.gol.com/newsletter/japan_immgration.html (accessed June 20, 1996).
3. Sumikazu Taguchi, "A Note on Current Research of Immigrant Groups in Japan," *International Migration Review* 17, no. 4 (1983): 1.
4. A clandestine worker is a person who overstays his or her tourist visa and is working without authorization.
5. Brian Bailey, "Japanese Laws and Policies Concerning Immigration (Including Refugees and Foreign Workers)" (senior thesis, George Washington University, 1996).
6. Tsuda, "Reluctant Hosts."
7. Tsuda, "Reluctant Hosts."
8. Wayne Cornelius, Philip Martin, and James Hollifield, eds., *Controlling Immigration* (Stanford, Calif.: Stanford University Press, 1994).
9. Ministry of Justice, *Summary of the White Paper on Crime, 1994* (Tokyo: Ministry of Justice, 1994).
10. Ministry of Justice, *White Paper*, 40, table I-1.
11. Ministry of Justice, *White Paper*, 118, table VI-1.
12. Ministry of Justice, *White Paper*, 120, table VI-4.
13. Cornelius, Martin, and Hollifield, *Controlling Immigration*.

PART II

CROSS-NATIONAL COMPARISONS

8

Comparative Immigration Policy

The term "immigrant nation" is commonly used to refer to a country that accepts, even encourages, immigration to the point where immigrants figure prominently in the population, the culture, and the mythology of that nation. If there are immigrant nations, then there must be "nonimmigrant nations" that do not accept immigrants, where relatively small proportions of the population are immigrants or are of immigrant stock and where immigrants have not had much impact on the culture and mythology of the nation. In the foregoing chapters, we have reviewed singly the policies and practices of nations that are commonly regarded as immigrant nations and others that are generally regarded as nonimmigrant nations. In part II, we explicitly compare these policies and practices to see how they differ across nations and whether these differences are consistent with the popular preconceptions of these nations.

Dimensions of Immigration Policy

Although we have used the term "immigrant nation," we have never explicitly defined what immigration policy would look like in such a country and how it would differ from that of a nonimmigrant nation. Certainly, one earmark of an immigrant nation would be an *unrestrictive immigration policy.* This would mean a formal recognition that the nation will allow persons to enter the country for the purpose of permanent residence and ultimately citizenship. It would also mean that the number of immigrants admitted would be relatively high given the size of the population. The admissions policy of an immigrant nation would also impose fewer preconditions on those who want to immigrate, so that language facility, employment, or other conditions would not be a prerequisite for entry. It is also essential that the implementation of admissions policy be consistent with the formal rules and laws governing admissions.

An immigrant nation would also have a less stringent naturalization policy than a nonimmigrant nation. Again, an immigrant nation would clearly and explicitly acknowledge the right of immigrants to become citizens. The conditions imposed on those applying for citizenship status, such as periods of residence or language facility, would be less extensive in immigrant as opposed to nonimmigrant nations. Again, practice should reflect formal policy such that nations that have few formal restrictions should not use these few restrictions in an aggressive way to deny large proportions of applicants for citizenship. It is less clear that an immigrant nation should have a high proportion of immigrant admissions who ultimately become citizens. While policy and its implementation clearly influence the rate at which applications for citizenship are granted, they do not necessarily determine who will apply for citizenship. Other factors such as the proximity of the immigrant's nation of origin or whether he or she has a family will influence this complex decision. Nonetheless, it can be argued that immigration policy has a strong influence on the decision to apply for citizenship. Policies that facilitate permanent settlement, for example, by making family unification easy, do undoubtedly affect the decision to apply for citizenship. We would expect, therefore, that an immigrant nation would have a higher proportion of admitted immigrants that ultimately become citizens than nonimmigrant nations.

An immigrant nation would impose few restrictions on the actions of resident aliens that are not required of citizens. They would not be required to register periodically with immigration authorities or asked to apply for approval for changes in residence or employment.

Immigrant nations would administer policy in an open and public manner. The discretion allowed administrative agencies would be substantially less than it is in nonimmigrant nations. Admission limits or targets would be set in legislative bodies rather than by immigration officials. Discretionary decisions made by immigration officials would be relatively few and these would be reviewable by both administrative courts and courts of general jurisdiction.

It is not entirely clear how an immigrant nation would approach the issue of policies that foster the social integration of immigrants, such as language or job training. At first blush, these policies can be seen as helping immigrants adapt to their host society. From another perspective, these efforts can be seen as an attempt to mold and control these new arrivals since they are designed more to protect the culture and social structure of the host society than to assist immigrants. In the end, the meaning of these programs may turn on how they are administered rather than whether they exist. Programs that are more voluntary or that involve immigrant organizations in their recruitment and administration increase social integration without requiring cultural homogeneity.

Finally, any characterization of immigration policy must come to grips with the issue of illegal immigration. A description of formal policies and even their implementation is meaningless in the face of high levels of illegal immigration. How does one characterize a nation with a very restrictive immigration policy that permits the entry of illegal immigrants in numbers many times that of the formal quota. In terms of social impact, this would be an immigrant nation. Even if we consider policy as an expression of the intent of a nation toward immigration and immigrants, the tolerance of large numbers of illegal immigrants perennially implies consent. It would not be tolerated if there was no support for it. Hence, the existence of a large number of illegal immigrants can be seen as the earmark of an immigrant nation.

It is also important to distinguish nations that have large numbers of illegal immigrants because of the volatility that this brings to the political debate surrounding immigration policy. Whatever one's stand on the benefits of legal immigration, illegal immigration introduces the complexity of admitting that a government does not have control over its borders. Persons who embrace legal immigration may, on these grounds, oppose illegal immigration. The presence of large numbers of illegal immigrants often confuses the policy debates such that attributes that may characterize illegal immigrants, for example, that they do not have respect for the laws of the host country, are applied to the total immigrant population. The added complexity that high levels of illegal immigration brings increases the rancor of policy debates and lessens the stability of immigration policy.

Immigrant nations then should have immigration policies and practices that encourage admission and naturalization. These policies and practices should be debated publicly and implemented with a minimum of administrative discretion. Once immigrants are in the country, immigrant nations would impose few restrictions on their behavior that are not imposed on citizens.

Characterizing Immigration Policies across Nations

Among the nations we examined, there are substantial differences in immigration policies and practices. Australia, Canada, and the United States appear to conform to the profile of immigrant nations. In contrast, Germany, at least until January 2000, and Japan, until even more recently, have had very restrictive immigration policies and fit the profile of nonimmigrant nations. Great Britain and France have policies that share some of the attributes of immigrant nations and some of the attributes of nonimmigrant nations, while at the same time being quite different from each other.

Admissions and Preferences

Australia, Canada, and the United States admit annually a large number of immigrants to their population. Australia, for example, admits approximately 120,000 persons annually and has a population of 13 million persons. This yields an admissions ratio of about 0.0092 percent. In Canada, the number of immigrants admitted annually varies substantially from year to year. Approximately 150,000 entered in 1987, over 250,000 entered in 1993 then decreased to 174,000 in 1998 and increased to 227,000 in 2000. If we said that in the recent past on average 200,000 persons enter Canada in a given year, then the admissions ratio for Canada would be about 0.0075. The United States admitted about 880,000 legal immigrants in 1992 and 191,000 refugees in the same year, and has an admissions ratio of approximately 0.0044. When rough estimates of illegal immigration are included in these calculations, the Australian admissions ratio becomes 0.013, the Canadian is 0.011, and the United States is 0.0061. These indicators of the flow of immigrants are much higher than those of other nations examined here. Great Britain, for example, allowed 96,850 persons to enter for the purpose of permanent residence in 1996 for an admissions ratio of 0.0019. France had an admissions ratio of 0.003 even when illegals are included. In the late 1990s, between 200,000 and 300,000 newcomers entered Germany. This includes family members of guest workers, asylum applicants, and ethnic Germans. Japan allows no admissions for the purpose of permanent residence. All persons enter as visitors. Before the mid-1990s, the number of entrees was about 365,000 annually. Between 1995 and 2000, the number has increased to about 600,000 annually. A very small proportion of these visitors later apply for and receive permanent resident status.

Illegal Immigration

Illegal immigration is much greater in the United States than it is in the other nations studied here. The flow of illegal immigrants is about one-third that of legal immigrants annually in the United States. Canada has lower rates of illegal entry than the United States and France, but higher rates than the other nations. Illegals are relatively rare in Japan, England, Australia, and Germany. In the case of England, Japan, and Australia, the fact that they are island nations makes illegal entry more difficult. Those who wish to enter illegally must be able to afford transport to these nations. The number of ports of entry are more limited and therefore easier to control. Canada and Germany are not island nations. They share long land borders with other nations. In the case of Canada, that border is with the United States and there is little difference in the standard of living in the two nations. This may discourage massive illegal movement from the United States into Canada. Germany's shared borders are with nations of the formerly communist Eastern bloc that have much lower standards of living, therefore there are greater incentives to cross into Germany illegally. Perhaps, the strict border controls and internal controls on foreigners in Germany discourage illegal entry. This may also be a contributing factor to Japan's low rates of illegal immigration.

The high rates of illegal immigrants in France and the United States are due in part to their proximity to nations with much lower living standards—North Africa and Mexico, respectively. The cost of travel from these poor nations to these affluent ones is not great. In the case of the United States especially, there are numerous points of entry that cannot be easily monitored. Internal controls in the United States are very weak and so the likelihood of apprehension is not great. Moreover, the penalties for apprehension are not great. The volume of persons attempting illegal entry is too great to permit imprisonment in every instance, so that the only penalty is immediate deportation. More importantly, in both of these nations there has been a historical tolerance of illegal immigration largely because the official policies failed to serve the needs of certain regional economies or specific industries. These interests needed labor and if the official policies would not allow for that labor to legally enter the country, they would ignore the immigration laws. In some cases, these demands for labor still exist. In other cases, the habit of ignoring immigration laws has become institutionalized such that it persists even in the absence of the need for labor.

The U.S. and French responses to illegal immigration have also been remarkably similar. Both nations have tried amnesties and employer sanctions to stop illegal immigration, and both have been unsuccessful. The similarity of the U.S. and French experiences with illegal immigration in light of their differences in internal controls suggests that societal ambivalence toward illegal immigration coupled with the geographic proximity of affluent and poor nations has a lot to do with the magnitude of illegal immigration.

Preferences and Exclusions

While Canada and Australia admit more people in proportion to their population than the United States, they appear to screen these admissions more extensively than the United States and even some nonimmigrant nations. Canada, for example, employs a point system to determine which persons will be admitted first in the economic immigrant category and then in the nonimmediate family class. This point system gives precedence to persons with skills that will facilitate their assimilation into Canadian society: persons with more education receive more points than those with less education;

those with occupational skills that are in demand get more points than those without these skills; younger applicants are favored over older applicants; and those with English- and French-language facility are preferred relative to those without these language skills. Applicants deemed "personally suitable" are preferred to those deemed less so. The maximum number of standard points is 100 with the potential of a 10-point bonus for a guarantee of assistance by relatives currently in Canada. The minimum acceptable standard for admission is 70 points and preference is given to persons with the highest number of points.

The Australian system is similar but less elaborate. Foreigners seeking admission as economic immigrants or nonimmediate family members receive points for language proficiency, the demand for their job skills, and the willingness of family members in Australia to "underwrite" the acquisition of English-language skills.

In contrast, the United States does not have a point system. Quotas are established by the purpose of the application, for example, family unification, economic, and by country of origin. Within these classes, however, there are no distinctions made for language proficiency, age, or other attributes of applicants. People are admitted on a first come, first served basis. Within the purpose categories, country quotas are used to queue applicants for admission. These quotas have been used as a way of admitting persons more similar to the native population, but more recently they have been allocated in terms of the demand for admission. Countries with greater demand get more visas. There are ceilings set for any nation in an effort to promote equity. These quotas, then, are more for establishing equity and diversity in admissions than for screening the applicant pool for more assimilable candidates.

The nonimmigrant nations employ much more elaborate and specific preference systems. France and Germany require specific work and residence permits as a precondition of admission. This approach to preferences, as opposed to those employed by Canada and Australia, is taken because France's and Germany's policies grew out of guest-worker systems. These nations are less concerned about the assimilation of those admitted than they are about the ability of those admissions to fill labor-market needs. Hence, preference is given to those persons who have a place to go in the society rather than those who can "fit in" to the society more generally. England gives preference according to nativity and indirectly by race. The distinction between patrials and nonpatrials clearly limits the admission of nonwhite persons from the New Commonwealth nations (that are largely nonwhite) and favors applicants from the Old Commonwealth nations (that are largely white). Family unification policies circumvent these preference schemes, but the preferences do affect admissions for persons who do not have family members who are British citizens or permanent residents. These race-based preferences are intended, presumably, to make immigrants more similar to the British population racially and culturally.

It is very difficult to assess the preferences applied to persons who request permanent residence in Japan. Since all admissions to Japan are by definition visitors, the whole notion of admission preference does not seem to apply. It is at the point where visitors apply for permanent residence that the notion of preferences becomes applicable. This decision appears to be a purely administrative one in which immigration officials have a great deal of discretion. In some sense, the invisibility of this process makes it all the more exclusionary.

Naturalization

Australia and Canada also have high rates of naturalization. In Australia, more than half of the immigrants admitted in a given year had become naturalized citizens within ten years of their arrival. After twenty years, 73 percent had done so. In the United States, 35 percent of persons admitted for permanent residence in 1977 were naturalized by 1991. France's naturalization rate is about 38 percent. Canada has the highest rate of naturalization of all the countries studied: As of 1991, 81 percent of all those eligible to become citizens had done so. In 1996, 43,000 persons were granted citizenship in England. The number of naturalizations has remained relatively constant at about 45,000 since 1992. Germany at 3 percent and Japan at less than 1 percent have the lowest naturalization rates.

Internal Regulation of Immigrants

Once immigrants enter one of the immigrant nations, they are almost entirely free of regulation by the government. They can change residence or employment without regulation or registration. This is the case for Australia, Canada, and the United States. Britain also has the same laissez-faire approach to the regulation of immigrants once they are admitted into the country. This suggests that the absence of extensive internal controls is more a feature of common-law nations rather than a characteristic unique to immigrant nations. The common-law tradition minimizes the regulatory power of the state relative to citizens. It affords the state fewer opportunities to intrude into the lives of citizens. So, for example, civil-law countries such as France or Germany have internal passports or identity cards that all citizens are required to carry or produce on demand. Similarly, citizens (and foreigners) are required to notify the police after a change of address. This type of "intrusion" would not be acceptable in common-law countries. The absence of internal controls on immigrants in immigrant nations is more the result of common-law legal institutions and the social organization of the justice system than it is immigration policy per se. In order for internal controls on foreigners to be effective, they must be administered in the context of controls over the movements and behaviors of citizens. Otherwise, it would be difficult to know when aliens are avoiding controls. Citizens of common-law countries are unlikely to accept the restrictions on their behavior that would be required to implement strict internal controls on alien populations. This problem becomes even more complex in the case of illegal immigration.

France, Germany, and Japan have much more stringent control requirements for aliens. In Germany, for example, guest workers must apply for residence and work permits. These permits must be renewed after a change of employment or residence. These episodic checks give immigration authorities the chance to intrude into the lives of immigrants. Although the likelihood of interference may be small, there is the chance that the required permits may not be renewed and the foreign national will be required to leave. This uncertainty reinforces the perception that foreigners are outsiders. The internal controls on foreigners that exist in Germany lessen with length of residence, such that recent arrivals must renew their permits at more frequent intervals than persons who have lived in Germany for longer periods of time. The French and the Japanese have similar control arrangements where immigration authorities have numerous opportunities to intrude into the lives of immigrants and the discretion to affect a foreigner's ability to remain in the country.

Discretion in the Implementation of Immigration Policy

The amount of discretion afforded immigration authorities also varies between immigrant and nonimmigrant nations. In immigrant nations, there is much more oversight of immigration authorities than there is in nonimmigrant nations. In the United States, immigration quotas are set by Congress annually and the president determines the level of refugees that will be admitted within limits set by Congress. The Immigration and Naturalization Service does not set these limits. Moreover, there is extensive administrative review of discretionary decisions made by immigration officials with regard to exclusions or deportations. The procedures followed in Canada and Australia give slightly less opportunity for immigration to become a highly politicized issue. Annual admissions quotas are proposed by immigration authorities whose head is appointed by the leader of the majority party in Parliament. These proposals are commented on by the legislature, but without very strong opposition, and they become policy for a given year. The decisions of individuals can be appealed even to courts of general jurisdiction.

In contrast, the level of foreigners admitted to nonimmigrant nations is set by immigration officials with little legislative oversight and there is no extensive opportunity for judicial review of the decisions made by individual immigration officials. In Germany, for example, the number of foreigners admitted in a given year is set by immigration authorities without substantial legislative oversight.

Policies for the Social Integration of Immigrants

The extent of government policies designed to facilitate the assimilation (or acculturation) of immigrants into the host society varies across the nations studied. Japan does the least to integrate foreigners into its society. This is in keeping with the underlying premise of Japanese immigration policy, which is that all foreigners who enter Japan are visitors and not immigrants. The United States would be second in terms of doing little to integrate foreigners into society. Refugees from Cuba, and later from Vietnam, were the only groups that were given assistance in the settlement process. Britain's approach to assimilation is quite similar to that of the United States. There are very few government programs to facilitate the transition into British society. The United States and Britain are followed distantly by Canada and France. The governments of Australia and Germany do the most to ease the movement of foreign residents into the host society. Recall that the foregoing discussion refers to the government policies designed to facilitate the assimilation of immigrants. This should not be confused with the ability of the society to absorb foreign residents.

The Japanese government does nothing to facilitate the accommodation of foreign residents into Japanese society. It does not provide language classes, job training, temporary housing, or other assistance. Foreigners in Japan are, however, entitled to many of the same social welfare benefits as citizens. For example, the health care benefits that are available to citizens are available to foreign visitors while they are in Japan. This is consistent with an immigration policy in which all admissions are visitors. There is no reason for a nation to invest in the assimilation of persons who will only be in the country for a short period of time. That small proportion of visitors who ultimately do change their status to permanent resident are so few as not to warrant, from a nation's point of view, an extensive investment in assimilation.

The lack of attention to government-sponsored integration programs in the United States is not due to the low volume of immigrants, but to the relatively minimal role that government plays in social policy more generally. There are many areas in which the U.S. government does not get involved in the lives of its citizens when most other countries do. The government involvement in the provision of basic health care, for example, is much more extensive in the other nations studied here than it is in the United States. While language classes for nonnative speakers can be offered by local governments and voluntary organizations, there is little or no funding for these services coming from the federal government. The only exception to this general rule has been for Cuban and Vietnamese refugees. Here, the Office of Refugee Resettlement has provided language and job training as well as cash payments to ease the transition into American society.

Britain takes much the same attitude toward assimilation policies as the United States. There are no government programs to ease the transition of immigrants into society. The volume of immigration into Britain is relatively low so that there may be less perceived need for assimilation efforts. It is also the case that while the role of government in the provision of services generally is greater in Britain than it is in the United States, this role is still more minimal than it is in other nations examined here. Finally, it may be that the British truly do not see themselves as an immigrant nation and they do not feel that extraordinary efforts should be made to assist the adjustment of foreigners. Indeed, extraordinary efforts on behalf of immigrants may engender hostility among the native population and as a result these efforts are avoided by the government. The emphasis on civil rights as an approach to dealing with the accommodation of culturally dissimilar groups is consistent with this view.

Australia has and continues to have a policy that helps immigrants adjust to their new society. At one point, temporary housing was provided to newcomers on arrival until they could find housing on their own. Language classes were provided as well as job training. This direct governmental assistance has been replaced by grants to ethnic voluntary associations that may provide these or other services to immigrants. The cost of language training has been passed back to the immigrant and the screening achieved by the point system has lessened the need for remedial services after admission. Nonetheless, the Australian government appears to take a more active role in the assimilation of immigrants than other nations examined here. This active involvement with the integration of immigrants is certainly promoted by the sheer volume of immigrants relative to the population. Also, the prevalence of the public provision of service is greater in Australia than in nations such as the United States. Finally, the rapid transition from the whites-only policy to the "Australian miracle"[1] could be very traumatic for such a relatively homogeneous society. Policies to accommodate this heterogeneity such as screening applicants for "assimilability" and policies for the provision of remedial services after admission are essential.

Germany also invests in policies designed to provide guest workers and their families with the skills to survive and flourish in the new society. Particular emphasis has been given to language training and vocational education. This is consistent with an overall immigration policy that does not encourage permanent residence or permit naturalization. Foreigners should be given the skills required to survive in and contribute to German society, but no extraordinary steps should be taken to ease the transition into German society or to change that society to be more accommodating.

The contrast between Germany and Australia is informative. While both nations take steps to integrate foreign residents into society, they are substantially different in the degree and nature of that assistance. The Australians are concerned with transforming foreign residents into citizens and so the assistance afforded is more varied and not restricted to language and vocational skills. Moreover, foreign residents have some control over the determination of what services will be afforded and who will provide them. The German policies do not allow for the participation of foreign residents in this essentially political process (see table 8.1).

Immigration Policy in Immigrant Nations

The foregoing discussion suggests that the immigration policies in those countries traditionally considered immigrant nations differ in dramatic ways from those regarded as nonimmigrant nations. The former have admissions, naturalization, and control policies that are more inviting of immigrants than the latter. More immigrants enter immigrant nations than nonimmigrant nations relative to the size of the native population. The preconditions for admission or the preferences afforded applicants are fewer in immigrant nations and more often based on the achieved characteristics of the applicant than the needs of the host nation. The internal controls imposed on resident aliens are usually less in immigrant nations than nonimmigrant nations.

It is also clear from the earlier discussion of immigration policies that the designation of "immigrant" and "nonimmigrant" nation is much too simple. There is considerable variation in goals and policies within immigrant and nonimmigrant nations. These variations may be consequential for the social integration of immigrants in these societies. It may be better to expand this dichotomy into a typology that would allow for ambivalent nations as well as for different strategies within an overall orientation. So, for example, we would characterize the United States, Canada, and Australia as immigrant nations, Japan and pre-2000 Germany as nonimmigrant nations, and Britain and France as ambivalent nations. Within the immigrant nations, the U.S. policy would be characterized as laissez-faire, while Canada and Australia would be referred to as controlled pluralism. The entire policy typology is presented in table 8.2.

Immigrant Nations: Laissez-Faire and Controlled Pluralism

Although the U.S. policy is similar in many respects to that of other traditional immigrant nations, it differs from them in important ways. Specifically, the United States does not screen admissions as assiduously as these other nations on the basis of cultural compatibility with the host country.

Table 8.1 Dimensions of Immigrant Policy by Nation

Policy Area	*Australia*	*Canada*	*United States*	*France*	*England*	*Germany*	*Japan*
Admit policy	liberal		liberal	moderate	restrictive	restrictive	restrictive
	open	liberal open	open	open	closed	closed[a]	closed
Admit practice	liberal		liberal	liberal	restrictive	restrictive	restrictive
	open	liberal open	open	open	closed	closed[a]	closed
Naturalization policy	liberal	liberal	liberal	liberal	liberal	restrictive[a]	restrictive
Naturalization rate	high	high	high	high	moderate	low	low
Control policy	minimal	minimal	minimal	substantial	minimal	substantial	substantial
Administration discretion	minimal	minimal	minimal	moderate	minimal	substantial	substantial
Public integration efforts	moderate	moderate	low	moderate	low	high	low
Illegal immigration	low	low	high	high	low	low	low

[a]Pre-January 2000.

Table 8.2 A Typology of Immigration Policies

Type	*Attributes*	*Countries*
Immigrant nations: laissez-faire pluralism	• Right to permanent residence and citizenship • High levels of immigration • Little selectivity on basis of cultural compatibility • Few internal controls • Government does not engineer integration • Tolerance of illegal immigration	United States
Immigrant nations: controlled pluralism	• Right to permanent residence and citizenship • High levels of immigration • High levels of selectivity in admissions based on cultural similarity • Few internal controls • Government efforts to foster assimilation • Low illegal immigration	Canada and Australia
Ambivalent nations: conflicted pluralism	• Right to citizenship but not permanent residence • Moderate levels of immigration with high illegal entries • High selectivity on labor-market needs but massive family unification entries	France
Ambivalent nations: default pluralism	• Right to citizenship and permanent residence • Low levels of immigration • High selectivity on cultural compatibility • Few internal controls • Laws to prevent discrimination but no government efforts to foster integration	Britain
Nonimmigrant nations: contained pluralism	• Until 1999, very restricted rights to citizenship and permanent residence • Very low levels of immigration • High selectivity on admissions based on nativity • Strict internal controls	Germany

continued

Table 8.2 A Typology of Immigration Policies (continued)

Type	*Attributes*	*Countries*
	• Some government efforts to integrate resident aliens • Little illegal immigration	
Nonimmigrant nations: nonpluralism	• Very restricted rights to citizenship and permanent residence • Very low levels of immigration • High selectivity on admissions based on nativity • Strict internal controls • No government efforts to foster social integration • Little illegal immigration	Japan

Moreover, persistently high levels of illegal immigration suggest further that a more open and less filtered admissions policy is tolerated, if not embraced. In contrast, the point systems employed by Canada and Australia are designed to screen out those persons least likely to be absorbed into the society. The preference system used in the United States does not serve this screening function. Illegal immigration is relatively low in Canada and Australia. Related to this are differences in government-sponsored programs for the social integration of immigrants. The United States provides little in the way of language classes and other mechanisms for integrating immigrants into the society, while Australia and Canada provide various programs to promote language facility, housing, and employment. As we noted earlier, this assistance can be considered a humane gesture meant to ease the transition into a new society or a form of cultural imperialism meant to protect the host society from foreign influences.

These differences in immigration policy are substantial and may be very consequential for the social integration of immigrants. The laissez-faire approach employed in the United States may complicate or slow the process of assimilation or accommodation, while the selectivity and acculturation efforts of Canada and Australia may accelerate these processes. Conversely, the laissez-faire policy may promote a process of natural selection in which only those immigrants who can adapt to the host nation remain, while those who cannot thrive unaided leave. Alternatively, the absence of cultural selectivity and acculturation efforts in the United States can, by promoting culturally diverse enclaves, offer opportunities that are unique to specific immigrant groups and thereby promote some form of accommodation. For example, the persistence of culturally diverse immigrant groups in a society perpetuates the demand for group-specific products and services that only immigrants and their immediate progeny can supply. Providing these goods and services gives members of the immigrant group both a livelihood and a place in the community. It is not clear which, if any, of these processes are operating. It is important, however, to keep these distinctions in mind as we move to comparisons of the social integration of immigrant groups in subsequent sections.

Ambivalent Nations: Conflicted Pluralism and Default Pluralism

France and Britain are labeled "ambivalent nations" because their immigration policies include contradictory elements that suggest simultaneous acceptance and rejection of immigrant nation status. France, for example, has very strict internal controls on immigrants, yet there is a massive illegal immigrant population. Britain has a very restrictive immigration policy based on cultural background, but once a person is admitted for permanent residence great pains are taken to see that he or she is treated as a citizen would be. These aspects of policy are not necessarily inconsistent with themselves, but they are inconsistent with the stereotype of immigrant and nonimmigrant nations.

The ambivalence of these nations is due in part to the fact that they do not view themselves as immigrant nations. Unlike Australia, Canada, and the United States, Britain and France were both exporters of immigrants not importers. For several centuries, both of these nations had extensive empires from which they could get both raw materials and labor without bringing the laborer to the host country. Special relationships developed between the colonies and the mother countries such that colonial peoples considered themselves citizens of the mother country and often the mother country regarded them similarly. With the collapse of their empires and the expansion of their economies, Britain and France were inundated with applicants and arrivals from their former colonies. The British response was to shut down immigration from the New Commonwealth by redefining the "special relationship" that existed between these former colonies. The French instituted a guest-worker system. Both of these were attempts to come to grips with the fact that these nations were becoming unwillingly immigrant nations.

The ambivalence in British immigration policy comes from the ruthless and racist manner in which immigration to Britain was curtailed and the subsequent efforts to prevent discrimination against culturally dissimilar residents of Britain. While these two aspects of policy are not inconsistent, they do send radically different messages to immigrants. The exclusionary admissions policies underscore the fact that nonwhite people are not welcomed in Britain. At the same time, the increasingly stronger legal protections against discrimination suggest that the government will prevent that exclusion from becoming unequal treatment. These apparent contradictions are a special case of a much broader tension in British society: the tension between cultural homogeneity (even imperialism) and a free market society with a strong tradition of rule of law. Britain is not in its mind a pluralistic society. There is one dominant culture in Britain and one set of social institutions: traditional British institutions. Much of day-to-day life in Britain transpires smoothly because of the broad acceptance of these institutional arrangements. The reliance on minutely specified rights and duties in legal codes appears not to be as prevalent in Britain as, say, in the United States. Nonetheless, laws set limits for custom. It is unclear just how far law will go in replacing custom as the basis for social interaction in Britain.

One outcome of the current British immigration policy would be the gradual absorption of immigrants and their children into British society—they will become "Englishmen." This is likely because the decreasing flow of new arrivals should lessen the ability of ethnic enclaves to persist. The demise of ethnicity, however, could give rise to racial distinctions and groupings that would perpetuate the exclusion of immigrant groups.

The nature of French ambivalence is quite different from that of the English because it is fundamentally contradictory in every respect. At its root is the fact that the French have never decided if they have a guest-worker policy or an immigration policy. While the large waves of foreigners entered France as guest workers, subsequent waves of immigration emphasized family unification. Many of the guest workers stayed to become citizens because French law or policy permitted it. There were a large number of illegal immigrants who through amnesties and other means have been allowed to remain in France permanently. Children of immigrants, legal and illegal, could obtain French citizenship. So, while the formal immigration policy was a guest-worker policy, the actual practice was that of an immigration policy. Once people gained admission to France, it was relatively easy to stay permanently. Indeed, the formal guest-worker policy may have made more palatable high levels of immigration that would have been opposed had they been justified as such.

The ambivalence of French immigration policy does not seem to provide a logical model for resolving the tensions that immigration brings. Admitting a large number of guest workers and then making it possible for many of them to stay permanently has created a situation in which there is a sizable group of immigrants and children of immigrants who are culturally distinct from the native population. This distinctiveness is constantly reinforced by continuous flows of new immigrants. The sometimes restrictive regulation of guest workers, for example, the creation of hostels for guest workers, has contributed to the concentration of immigrants in certain sections and the maintenance of separation. It is not clear how French immigration policy would contribute to the reduction of or the accommodation to this separation. It is possible that the French would take a page from the book of immigrant nations and assume that a laissez-faire approach would result in the natural progression of immigrant groups from concentrated areas of first settlement to greater diffusion in society and greater assimilation or acculturation. This model may not be as realistic in a centralized and homogeneous society like France as it was in a country like the United States. The notion of apportioning power to ethnic groups as a means of maintaining the polity is at variance with the French emphasis on individualism and equality.

Nonimmigrant Nations: Contained Pluralism and Nonpluralism

Japan is not and Germany was not an immigrant nation. The ability of foreign-born people to become citizens in Japan and until 1999 in Germany, is extremely restricted. The number of foreigners admitted for long stays or permanent residence is extremely low, and restrictions on them while they are in these host countries are relatively high. Despite these similarities, the immigration policies in these nations are different in important ways. Specifically, the German immigration policy is sufficiently porous to allow a reasonably large number of foreigners to enter the country and stay. Until the 1999 change, these foreigners could never become German citizens nor could they enter the political process, but they could enjoy most of the rights of citizenship. Japanese immigration policy has been more absolute in its exclusion of foreigners for the purpose of permanent settlement.

The term "contained pluralism" is appropriate for the German policy because although Germans have let foreigners into the country, they have clearly and effectively limited the extent to which foreign residents can participate in the society. The message seems to be that one may live in German society, but one will not transform German society. Foreign residents of Germany are strongly encouraged and assisted in learning German and in acquiring job skills. They are entitled to the same social welfare benefits as citizens. The regulations to which foreigners are subject decrease with time in the country. Those who engage in socially undesirable behavior can be summarily deported. German immigration policy, then, makes it easy to reside in Germany as long as foreigners are productive members of society. At the same time, these foreigners and their German-born offspring, until 1999, could not become citizens or engage in the political process. These latter exclusions were designed to limit the extent to which foreigners (including those who are German born) could affect the distribution of power in Germany society and the formulation of public policy.

The Germans and the French found themselves in ostensibly similar positions in the early 1970s. They both had admitted a large number of guest workers who were becoming entrenched in their respective societies. Both countries restricted their admissions in response to slowing economies. The

French were less successful in terminating admissions because of illegal immigration and family unification. Moreover, the ability of foreigners to naturalize and of their children to become French citizens ensured that immigrants would become a force in national politics. This further increased the ambivalence of immigration policy because immigrants had a voice in the shaping of that policy. The exclusion of foreigners from citizenship, and thereby the political process, in Germany minimized the ambivalence in the German's response to immigration. It may have permitted a long-term stability in immigrant policy that was not possible in France.

Theoretically, then, German immigration policy would allow for the indefinite residence of foreigners in German society. As long as foreigners are productive members of society, they will be allowed to stay. Their exclusion from the political process should lessen the perception of threat of the native population. With the reduction in the arrival of new foreigners, the foreign residents of Germany should become more similar to the German population and gradually merge into German society. It remains to be seen if this approach to immigration facilitates social integration or whether, as cultural differences decline, racial differences become more salient.

Japan never allowed a large number of foreigners into its country for the purpose of permanent residence, or even as guest workers. Some Koreans were admitted to fill labor needs and a portion of these have remained as permanent residents. Another small group of Latin Americans of Japanese ancestry were admitted and many became naturalized citizens of Japan. Otherwise, visitors to Japan remain just that—visitors. Their stay is tied to a specific purpose and their length of stay is prescribed. It can only be altered or extended at the discretion of immigration authorities. The controls on foreigners are such that those who overstay their visas are easily identified and deported. The opportunity to appeal these deportation decisions is minimal. Immigration in Japan is so limited that the social integration of these groups is simply not a major concern or an object of policy. The small Korean minority can be excluded from mainstream Japanese society without repercussion. As noncitizens, they cannot vote or engage in political processes. Moreover, those other few foreigners who remain in Japan have enough corporate or familial ties that social integration is not a problem.

Note

1. "Australian miracle" refers to the transformation of Australia from a largely white and British society to a multicultural one.

9

Criminal Involvement among Immigrants and Natives across Countries

Crime figures largely in almost any discussion of immigration. The almost universal popular conception is that immigrants engage in crime in much higher proportions than the native populations. The descriptions presented in the foregoing chapters, however, indicate that it is extremely difficult to know the extent to which immigrants engage in crime. This makes one wonder about the source of this almost universal preconception. Moreover, the limited assessments that we can make about the criminal involvement of immigrants suggest that it varies substantially across nations. Immigrant nations have low rates of criminality among their immigrants as opposed to their native populations, while nonimmigrant nations have higher rates of criminal involvement among their immigrants than among their native populations. The level of crime by aliens differs within nations by type of immigrant. In a number of nations, refugees and asylum seekers have higher rates of criminal involvement than immigrants who have moved for economic or family reasons. Finally, the one universal that has emerged from the data is that the criminal involvement of aliens is higher for drug offenses than for other types of crime. There is good reason to believe, however, that this finding is due to the involvement of visiting foreigners rather than immigrants.

Complexities in the Comparison of Crimes

Before reporting the crime data, it is important that we discuss the limitations and complexities involved in making cross-national comparisons of crime and particularly crime involving immigrants. First of all, it is difficult to assess the volume of crime in large measure because the concept is so variable across nations. There are minute legal definitions of criminal behavior and these definitions can vary substantially across nations (and in some cases within nations). In England and Wales, for example, the forcible entry into an "outbuilding" such as a barn or garage (as opposed to a residence) would be classified as a burglary while in the United States it would not.[1] These differences in the legal definition of criminal acts will complicate cross-national comparisons. Even when the legal definitions of crime are similar, the procedures used to identify, label, and count criminal behavior as criminal can introduce differences across nations.[2] Police statistics in a very decentralized police system like the United States will clearly be more variable than countries with more centralized police systems such as France.[3] Victimization surveys are another common source of data on crime, but they too can employ variable procedures that can affect crime counts cross-nationally.[4] Many of these problems in the nonuniformity of crime statistics cross-nationally are made less damaging if we compare the ratio of the criminal involvement of aliens to the criminal involvement of the native-born population or of citizens. To the extent that differences in crime statistics are constant across the foreign and native population within countries, then these differences should not affect cross-national comparisons.

It is not clear how tenable this constancy assumption is. Nations with very restrictive immigration policies and especially those with a great many internal restrictions on aliens may be more likely to detect and record the criminal involvement of aliens as opposed to that of citizens. Our review of immigration policies indicated that nonimmigrant nations have closer supervision of noncitizen residents than countries with less restrictive policies. This could account for higher rates of criminal involvement of aliens relative to citizens in France, Germany, and Japan as compared to the United States, Australia, and Canada. It is important to note, however, that these nations also have many more restrictions on their citizens than immigrant nations do, such as internal passports. This should reduce artificial discrepancies between estimates of the criminal involvement of aliens and those for native populations.

The influence of data collection procedures on cross-national comparisons can also be reduced by restricting comparisons to more serious or detectable crimes where administrative discretion is less than for minor crimes.

A more major problem in identifying crimes committed by aliens is the identification of criminals as aliens. In a large proportion of crimes, the offender is not known and, therefore, his or her citizenship cannot be determined. Consequently, we are restricted to comparisons of offenses where the offender is known. Even when the offender is known, his or her citizenship may not be. An even more difficult distinction must be made between foreigners involved in crime and immigrants involved in crime. Immigrants are foreigners who come to the host nation with the intention to stay. Many more foreigners enter host countries for other purposes such as business meetings, conferences, or tourism, with no intention of permanent residence. These "sojourning residents" will be recorded in unknown proportions as "foreigners" in police and correctional statistics. To the extent that these sojourning foreigners are included in the numerator of crime rates, they must also be included in the denominator of those rates. In many countries, it is difficult to enumerate the number of sojourning foreigners in the country at any given time. Immigration services, for example, may count border crossings but not link those crossings to individual persons. Consequently, one person can account for numerous border crossings. Using crossings or entries would provide a substantial overcount of sojourning foreigners in any given period.

Another problem posed by sojourning foreigners is the fact that nations do not always keep detailed data on how long these visitors stay in the host nation. This is important for the computation of crime incarceration rates in that persons at risk, for example, foreigners, should figure in the denominator in proportion to their exposure. Since immigrants or permanent residents are in the country 365 days a year while sojourning foreigners usually have much shorter time in exposure, it would not be appropriate to weigh sojourning foreigners and immigrants equally.

Fortunately, the participation of sojourning foreigners in criminal activity is likely to be heavily concentrated in drug crimes rather than other types of common-law crimes. A central feature of the drug trade is moving the merchandise across borders. Much of this moving is done by tourists and other sojourning foreigners who are detected at the airport or other ports of entry. It is less likely for foreigners to cross borders for the purpose of committing assaults or street robberies. Hence, the distortions introduced into crime and incarceration rates by sojourning foreigners should be lessened if drug offenses are not included in rate comparisons.

Finally, there is the problem of citizenship and nativity that confounds many of the cross-national comparisons of statistical data. Some nations identify offenders or inmates by nation of birth while others distinguish persons according to citizenship. It is possible that definitions of foreigners based on nativity would include persons who have been in the country longer than groups defined by citizenship status. This would result in lower rates of crime or incarceration for foreigners based on the nativity criteria than those defined by citizenship.

While all of these problems complicate cross-national comparisons of crime by immigrants and natives, making these comparisons with the available data are still worthwhile. Only after these comparisons are made can we assess the likelihood that the observed differences are due to noncomparabilities in the data. In some cases, likely errors in the data may be in a direction that could not possibly explain the differences observed. In that event, these flawed data can still be used to inform the issues addressed here.

Comparative Crime Rates

The most consistently available data on criminal involvement of aliens cross-nationally comes from incarceration rates. This is the case because there is generally more information available on persons at the time of incarceration than at earlier stages in system processing, such as arrest. Consequently, we are better able to determine who is a citizen and who is not at the incarceration stage, although some nations do have data on citizenship status at the arrest stage.

Comparing incarceration rates, the pattern that emerges across the seven nations is that overall immigrants in the United States, Canada, and Australia, the traditional immigrant receiving countries, have lower crime rates than natives, and that immigrants in Great Britain, France, Germany, and Japan have higher crime rates than natives. In Japan, foreigners have higher crime rates for property offenses and homicides, but not for other violent offenses. Great Britain is in between immigrant and nonimmigrant nations but closer to immigrant nations in the ratio of immigrant-to-native rates of incarceration (see table 9.1).

There is one type of offense, however, for which immigrants in all seven of the countries have higher incarceration rates than natives: drug offenses. Table 9.2 compares the ratios of incarceration rates for immigrants to those for natives across nations for drug crimes and other serious offenses.

Table 9.1 Incarceration Ratios for Immigrants and Nonimmigrants by Nation and Year

Nation[a]	*Ratio*
France (1993)	6.01
Japan (1993)	3.83[b]
Germany (1990)	1.90
Great Britain (1992)	1.29
Australia (1985)	0.68
United States (1991)	1.13
Canada (1989)	0.58

Source: James P. Lynch and Rita J. Simon, "A Comparative Assessment of Criminal Involvement among Immigrants and Natives across Seven Nations," *International Criminal Justice Review* 9 (1999): 1–17.

[a]This is the ratio of the population-based stock incarceration rate for foreigners to the same nation.

[b]This is the ratio of offender rate for foreigners to the offender rate for citizens. Offender rate is the ratio of persons known to police over total persons in that category.

Table 9.2 Criminal Involvement Ratios for Immigrants and Nonimmigrants by Type of Offense, Nation, and Year

Offense	*Australia (1985)*	*United States (1991)*	*France (1993)*	*Germany (1990)*
Violence	0.78	0.83	3.35	2.33
Property	0.64	0.62	4.83	2.15
Drugs	2.29	2.37	NA	2.61
Drug trafficking	3.02	1.48	11.06	4.0

Source: James P. Lynch and Rita J. Simon, "A Comparative Assessment of Criminal Involvement among Immigrants and Natives across Seven Nations," *International Criminal Justice Review* 9 (1999).

Note: The data for Australia, France, and the United States are incarceration rates. These data were used for Germany because there were no readily available, nationally representative data on offense-specific incarceration rates for immigrants and natives.

In every country, immigrants are overrepresented relative to natives in drug offenses. In the United States in 1991, immigrants were 2.37 times more likely than natives to be incarcerated for drug offenses. In Australia in 1992, 1995, and 1997, immigrants were incarcerated for drug offenses at 2.4, 3.3, and 4.0 times the rate of natives. In France, this ratio was 4.0 and in Germany 2.6. In Canada in 1991, among all the imprisonments for drug offenses, 67 percent were natives and 33 percent were immigrants, a much higher percentage than the latter's representation in the country. In Great Britain in 1995, 98 percent of all incarcerated immigrants had been convicted of drug offenses. In Japan, the incarceration rate for drug offenses by immigrants was 0.6 per 1,000 compared to 0.1 per 1,000 natives.

While immigrants are consistently overrepresented in drug crimes across nations, the representation in other types of offending varies substantially by country. In the traditional immigrant receiving countries of the United States, Canada, and Australia, the rate of incarceration for most other types of crimes is lower for immigrants than for natives. For example, see the data in table 9.3 for Australia, in table 9.4 for France, in table 9.5 for Germany, and table 9.6 for the United States.

By contrast, rates of criminal involvement for nondrug offenses in traditionally nonimmigrant nations are much higher than those of the native population. As of 1993, immigrants in France were arrested for violent crimes at a rate 3.18 times that of natives and for property crime at a rate 2.73 times that of natives. The same was the case in Germany in 1990 where the arrest rate of immigrants for violent crime was 2.33 times that of natives and for property crime 2.15 times that of natives. Incarceration rates for the foreign born in Australia convicted for drug offense were almost four times that of native-born Australians (table 9.3). Offense-specific information is not available for Japan and Great Britain.

Table 9.3 Offense-Specific Stock Incarceration Rates per 1,000 by Country of Birth, Australia, 1992, 1995, 1997

	Type of Crime								
	Violence			*Property*			*Drugs*		
Country of Birth	*1992*	*1995*	*1997*	*1992*	*1995*	*1997*	*1992*	*1995*	*1997*
Australia	0.40	0.49	0.53	0.29	0.29	0.32	0.06	0.07	0.06
Other	0.32	0.41	0.43	0.21	0.20	0.22	0.15	0.21	0.23
Ratio of Other to Australian	0.81	0.84	0.80	0.75	0.71	0.69	2.42	3.28	3.92

Source: Satyanshu Mukherjee, *Ethnicity and Crime* (Canberra: Australian Institute of Criminology, 1999).

While the overrepresentation of immigrants in drug crimes is universal, the relative involvement of immigrants and natives in other crimes varies considerably by nation and by immigration policy. Immigrants have lower rates of involvement in nondrug crimes than the native population in traditionally immigrant nations and higher rates of involvement in traditionally nonimmigrant nations.

There are a few countries for which arrest data are available in which immigrants or foreigners and natives or citizens are identified. In table 9.4, such data are described for France. Overall, the offender rate for foreigners, based on police-recorded serious crimes, was approximately three times that of French citizens. As shown in table 9.4, the differences were smallest for burglary and greatest for drug trafficking.

In Germany in 1993, 26.7 percent of persons suspected of crimes (not including immigration offenses) were foreigners. According to police statistics, foreigners are 2.3 times more likely than German citizens of being suspected of a serious crime (see table 9.5). The overrepresentation of foreigners is most pronounced for drug trafficking (4.0 to 1) and homicide (3.5 to 1), and lowest for assaults (2.2 to 1) and theft (2.1 to 1).

For the United States, the empirical evidence on the relative criminal involvement of aliens and citizens in the United States is reasonably consistent (see table 9.6). In general, aliens are involved in criminal activity at a much lower rate than citizens of the United States. This is the case for every type of serious crime except drug offenses. This seems to be the case even when attributes of immigrants and aliens that may account for differences in criminal involvement, such as race or educational attainment, are held constant.

Table 9.4 Estimated Offenses by Citizenship and Types of Crime, France, 1991

Offense	*Number of Foreigners*	*Per 100,000*	*Number of Citizens*	*Per 100,000*
Homicide	5	0.49	1,191	2.09
Attempted homicide	149	4.13	826	1.45
Assaults	6,813	188.78	4,275	60.24
Drug offenses	12,090	335.00	47,612	83.69
Trafficking	3,530	97.81	6,551	11.51
Robbery	2,966	82.18	12,899	22.67
Burglary	5,097	141.23	44,219	77.72
Theft	34,096	944.75	181,496	319.01

Sources: Aspects de la criminalité et de la délinquance constates en France en 1991 (Paris: La Documentation Français, 1992). Estimation of foreign population from Sarah Collinson, *Europe and International Migration* (London: Pinter, 1993).

Table 9.5 Estimates of Offending by Citizenship and Type of Crime, Germany, 1985

	Foreigners		*Citizens*	
Offense	*Number*	*Per 100,000*	*Number*	*Per 100,000*
Homicide	662	13.66	2,221	3.95
Assaults	28,555	589.07	147,001	261.72
Drug offenses	9,320	192.26	4,124	73.41
Trafficking	5,406	111.52	15,967	28.43
Robbery	3,909	80.64	15,087	26.86
Burglary	NA	NA	NA	NA
Theft	87,018	1,795.11	468,011	833.24

Source: Bundeskriminalamt, *Polizeiliche Kriminalstatistik, 1985* (Weisbaden: Kriminalistiches Institut, 1986), 49.

Summary

This pattern between the inclusiveness of immigration policies and the criminal involvement of aliens suggests that the more restrictive the policy, the greater the criminal involvement of foreigners. It is somewhat ironic that exclusiveness should breed crime when undoubtedly its intent is to reduce it. But this pattern is not perfect. The disproportionate involvement of foreigners in crime in France, for example, is much greater than that existing in Ger-

Table 9.6 U.S. Incarceration Rates and Ratios for Aliens and Citizens by Types of Offense, 1991

	Citizenship Status		*Alien-to-Citizen*
Offense	*Alien*	*Citizen*[a]	*Ratio*
Violence	109.4	120.7	0.91
Homicide	38.7	29.7	1.30
Sexual Assaults	20.6	26.4	0.78
Robbery	26.6	41.6	0.64
Assault	23.5	23.0	1.02
Property	43.8	69.6	0.63
Burglary	26.9	34.8	0.77
Larceny	7.9	13.7	0.58
Drug Offenses	141.7	59.8	2.37
Other Offenses	22.2	20.5	1.08
Total	317.1	270.6	1.17
Total Less Drugs	175.4	210.8	0.83

Source: Bureau of Justice Statistic, Survey of Inmates in State and Federal Correctional Facilities, 1991 (Washington, D.C.: Bureau of Justice Statistics, 1991); and from the Current Population Survey public use data files.

[a]Citizen = native born and naturalized.

many or Japan, while the latter nations have much more restrictive immigration policies than the former. Nonetheless, the differences between the criminal involvement of foreigners in immigrant nations is substantially and consistently less than the native population in nonimmigrant nations.

This pattern may be an artifact of the data used and the variable definitions of immigrant that are employed in those data. The immigrant nations with the lowest ratio of immigrant-to-native crime (Australia and Canada) are also the nations where the term "immigrant" is defined as "foreign born." The foreign born can include a large number of persons who are naturalized citizens as well as noncitizens. One could argue that these naturalized persons have a greater commitment to the host country and are generally more stable than noncitizens. Including both noncitizens and naturalized citizens in the definition of immigrant would reduce criminal involvement rates relative to nations that define immigrant in terms of noncitizens only. It is also likely that the foreign born will include a higher proportion of older persons than noncitizens, which would also reduce the relative rate of criminal involvement among the foreign born.

It is unlikely that the large differences in the criminal involvement of immigrants in immigrant as opposed to nonimmigrant nations is due entirely to differences in the definition of immigrant. In the United States, the data on immigrants pertains to noncitizens, not the foreign born. Nonetheless, the criminal involvement rates of noncitizens in the United States is substantially lower than the rates of criminal involvement for noncitizens in France. This large difference is not a statistical artifact. Similarly, the ethnicity-based definition of immigrant employed in Germany is much more inclusive than the foreign-born definition employed in Australia and Canada. It includes persons born in Germany and also persons whose families have resided in the host nation for several generations. If the foreign-born definition of immigrant would capture very stable groups with low criminal involvement rates, then this ethnicity-based definition should include even more of these settled groups, thereby depressing these rates further. This is not the case. The criminal involvement of immigrants in Germany is much higher than it is in Australia and Canada. Again, this suggests that differences in the definition of immigrant across nations does not account for the large differences in the relative criminal involvement of immigrants and natives observed earlier.

The pattern of criminal involvement of aliens across nations may also reflect the use of the law as a means of harassing or controlling immigrants. There is certainly some evidence that in France, for example, that the enforcement of immigration laws has become much more aggressive throughout the 1990s and that this has increased the appearance of immigrants in police records and in the justice system as a whole. The discretion of the police, however, is limited by the severity of the crime. While there is extensive discretion in the enforcement of immigration laws and drug laws, there is much less discretion in responding to serious violence and theft. In the case of these serious crimes, the discretion of the police is scrutinized more extensively by judicial officials and others because the implications of prosecution and conviction are so severe. Moreover, in these types of crime there is a complainant who is interested in the outcome of the case and who can hold the police accountable. The fact that the patterns in the criminal involvement of aliens across nations persist for serious crimes indicates that these patterns are unlikely to be due wholly to harassment and the labeling of immigrants by the police and others in the criminal justice system.

If we can assume, then, that this relationship between immigration policy and immigrant criminal involvement is real, it may not be due to immigration policy per se, but to other features of the nations that are correlated with a more or less restrictive immigration policy. Most of the nonimmigrant nations, for example, are culturally homogeneous and social control within those nations depends on that homogeneity. Many of the norms that govern daily interaction are so ingrained that they need no explicit mention. Residents would not even think to do otherwise. In these nations, broad discretion is allowed the police and other agents of the government under the assumption that these powers will seldom be used or abused. In contrast, immigrant nations rely less on shared culture and prefer to make expectations explicit through formal rules of law. The discretion of government agents who can use coercive force are explicitly and minutely circumscribed by constitutions. In nonimmigrant nations, therefore, it is easy for persons who are not integrated into the culture to run afoul of cultural norms and become involved with the police. Presumably, this is less likely in immigrant nations that rely less on cultural norms as the basis for social control.

If we also assume that this pattern is due in a more direct manner to immigration policy, we could speculate that it operates through a process of selection or integration. Immigrant nations select persons with the self-professed desire to become a permanent resident or citizen. This commitment "up front" may exclude those who have more tenuous attachments to the host country. The higher the proportion of these "unattached" foreigners in the population, the higher the rates of criminal involvement in that population. This particular explanation does not fit the observed pattern perfectly. This selectivity argument would account for the relatively high rates of criminal involvement of foreigners in Japan and Germany where foreigners are virtually excluded from citizenship and where they are (or have been) recruited explicitly to fill labor-force needs. This is not consistent with the very high rates of criminal involvement in France where population maintenance has competed with labor-force needs as the driving force behind immigration policy. Immigration for the purpose of permanent residence has figured more prominently in France than in Germany and Japan. Great Britain has also emphasized family unification in its immigration policies, yet it has rates of criminal involvement for foreigners that are greater than those of the native population. When we exclude drug crimes (and presumably sojourning foreigners), however, the criminal involvement of foreigners in Great Britain resembles that of immigrant nations. This would support the selectivity explanation.

Social integration explanations for the pattern of immigration policy and criminal involvement of aliens would emphasize what happens to immigrants once they arrive in the country as opposed to the motivation that they have when they come. To the extent that immigrants are allowed to participate in all of the major social institutions in the society, they will form bonds with legitimate groups in that society and refrain from criminal involvement. So, if immigrants can find jobs, can form families or bring their families, can own property, can vote, and can conduct their daily lives without overt discrimination, then they will be less involved in criminal activity in the host nation. This speculation is consistent with the very high rates of criminal involvement of foreigners in Germany and Japan where foreigners are excluded from major social institutions such as voting and citizenship. It is less compatible with the high rates in France where naturalization is broadly available. There are other aspects of French policy such as the concentration of guest workers in hostels and public housing outside of major cities that are less inclusive. Moreover, public opinion data in France indicate that the French are afraid of "losing their culture," which suggests a cultural exclusion of immigrants (and particularly North Africans), if not an exclusion based on policy. This would make the higher rates in France somewhat more compatible with the social integration explanation.

The selectivity argument receives some additional support from data on legal as opposed to illegal immigrants in the United States. To the extent that legal immigrants, unlike those who enter illegally, know that they are welcomed (at least in a formal sense that they do not have to worry about being deported or being under surveillance) and that they come with the expectation of staying, then the fact that illegal immigrants have much higher rates of criminal involvement than legal immigrants seems more consistent with the selectivity explanation. People who come voluntarily with the expectation of staying are less likely to be involved in criminal activity than those who regard themselves as temporary residents, regardless of the social integration of immigrants after entry.

It is likely that if immigration policy has any direct effect on the criminal involvement of aliens, both selectivity and integration processes are involved. We do not have the detailed information required to sort these and other issues out. It is sufficient here to demonstrate that immigration policies and the criminal involvement of foreigners are related. Much more fine-grained and careful work must be done to determine if this pattern is causal or spurious, and if causal, to disentangle the processes by which it occurs.

Notes

1. P. Mayhew, *Residential Burglary: A Comparison of the United States, Canada, England, and Wales* (Washington, D.C.: National Institute of Justice, 1985).

2. A. D. Biderman and J. P. Lynch, *Understanding Crime Incidence Statistics: Why the UCR Diverges from the NCS* (New York: Springer-Verlag, 1991); A. D. Biderman, "Social Indicators and Goals," in *Social Indicators,* ed. R. Bauer (Cambridge: MIT Press, 1965); and J. P. Lynch, "A Comparison of Imprisonment in the United States, Canada, England, and West Germany: A Limited Test of the Punitive Hypothesis," *Journal of Criminal Law and Criminology* 79, no. 1 (1988).

3. D. Bayley, *Patterns of Policing: A Comparative International Analysis* (New Brunswick, N.J.: Rutgers University Press, 1969); and P. Rechiel, *Comparative Criminal Justice Systems: A Topical Approach* (Englewood Cliffs, N.J.: Prentice-Hall, 1995).

4. J. P. Lynch, "Secondary Analysis of International Crime Survey Data," in *Understanding Crime: Experiences of Crime and Criminal Control,* ed. A. del Frate, U. Zvekic, and J. van Dijk (Rome: UN Inter-Regional Crime and Justice Research Institute, 1993); and R. Block, "Measuring Victimization: The Effects of Methodology, Sampling and Fielding," in *Understanding Crime: Experiences of Crime and Criminal Control,* ed. A. del Frate, U. Zvekic, and J. van Dijk (Rome: UN Inter-Regional Crime and Justice Research Institute, 1993).

10

Public Opinion toward Immigrants

This chapter compares public opinion toward immigrants over approximately the past twenty-five years for the United States, Canada, Australia, Great Britain, France, Germany, and Japan. Although we recognize that the public opinion data are not uniform and comparisons must therefore be made with care, the surveys can nevertheless be used to provide a general idea of how positively or negatively the public views the issue of immigration and the admission of specific groups of immigrants. Moreover, the specific questions that are unique to particular nations give us some insight as to why the respondents of that nation feel the way they do. The one major and consistent theme that is sharply and clearly defined in each country's responses is that in no country—those that have long histories of admitting immigrants, those that have more restrictionist policies, and those that have consistently kept a lock on their doors—do a majority of the respondents have positive feelings about their current cohort of immigrants or the desirability of allowing more immigrants to enter than current regulations permit.

The United States

As we noted in the United States chapter, until the late 1990s, the physical image that best described the American public's attitude toward immigrants is that they were viewed with rose-colored glasses turned backwards. In other words, those immigrants who came earlier, whenever "earlier" happened to be, were viewed as having made important and positive contributions to our society, economy, and culture, but those who are coming now, whenever "now" happens to be, are viewed, at best, with ambivalence and more likely with distrust, fear, and hostility.

There are some indications, as shown in responses to national surveys from the mid-1990s through 2000, that the glasses may be turning around and immigrants currently entering the United States may be receiving a warmer welcome. Again, we emphasize that the data and analysis are pre-September 11, 2001. We review some of the earlier and most recent survey results in this chapter.

In 1993 and 1997 when two national polls asked "Was immigration a good thing or a bad thing for this country in the past?" 59 and 65 percent of the respondents said it was good thing. But when asked whether immigration is a good or a bad thing today, only 29 and 45 percent said it was a good thing.

On the theme of whether immigrants are good or bad for the country on specific issues, note the following results:

Which of the following statements comes closer to your views (in percent):

	1993	*1999*	*2000*
Immigrants mostly take low paying jobs Americans don't want	67	71	75
Immigrants mostly take jobs that American workers want	23	16	13
Both/neither	8	8	8
No opinion	2	5	4

Source: American Institute of Public Opinion (Storrs: Roper Center, University of Connecticut).

We see that in 2000 75 percent of the respondents believed immigrants mostly took low-paying jobs American's did not want. Only 13 percent believed immigrants competed with American workers for jobs Americans wanted. And when asked whether they thought immigrants mostly helped or hurt the economy by driving down wages for many Americans, the percentage who answered "mostly help" increased from 28 to 44 from 1993 to 2000.

Responses to the question "Should immigration be kept at its present level or should immigration be increased or decreased?" that was asked on at least fourteen national polls from 1946 through 2000 show that during periods of economic expansion or recession or during periods of heightened or relaxed tension among the major powers, between 4 and 13 percent of the public favored increasing immigration. But we noted that in 1999 and 2000 more respondents favored keeping immigration at its present level or increasing it than at any other previous time. At no time in the fifty-plus years that the question was asked did a majority favor those two categories.

We warned, however, about the danger of exaggerating the strength of the positive shift by showing that in March 2000 when asked which statement most clearly represented their feelings—immigrants strengthen or weaken the American character—58 percent said it weakened compared to 44 percent who said it strengthened. And when asked to choose between which is the greatest threat to the United States remaining a major world power in the next century, almost four times as many respondents answered too much immigration from foreign countries as opposed to population growth within the United States.

Canada

In Canada, citizens were asked the following question on ten national polls from 1975 to 1993: If it were your job to plan an immigration policy for Canada at this time would you be inclined to increase immigration, decrease immigration, or keep the number of immigrants at about the current level? Over the almost twenty-year time span, at most, 17 percent of the Canadian public favored increasing immigration and between 32 and 55 percent favored decreasing the number of immigrants permitted to enter.

In 1957, 95 percent of the 282,164 immigrants who came to Canada were Europeans and Americans. In 1987, of the 152,098 immigrants who entered Canada almost 75 percent came from Asia, the West Indies, and other mainly Third World countries. In 1993, Canadian citizens were asked: How do you view the increase in the number of immigrants arriving in Canada from Asia, the West Indies, and other mainly Third World Countries? Twenty percent said it was a good thing.

In the matter of refugees, most Canadians believe that their country is doing *more* than its share vis-à-vis the admission of refugees, compared to other countries. In 1986 and 1989, 72 and 74 percent, respectively, thought Canada was doing more than its share. Also in those years, most Canadians (58 and 59 percent, respectively) thought Canada should accept fewer refugees than its policies then supported.

Australia

We found a similar pattern in Australia where government policies also seem to be more proimmigrant than public opinion supports. Between 1988 and 1991, when the Australian public was asked whether it favored admitting more, the same, fewer, or no immigrants into the country, less than 10 percent of the Australian respondents favored admitting more and about two-thirds favored admitting fewer or no immigrants.

As discussed in chapter 3, the big story about Australian public attitudes toward immigrants began in 1958 when there was a dramatic shift from negative attitudes toward non-European immigrants. In 1954, 61 percent opposed admitting non-Europeans. By 1965, only 16 percent opposed admission of non-Europeans.

But in more recent years, Australia's attitudes toward non-European immigrants have become similar to those expressed by the Canadian and American respondents. Immigrants from Britain, Ireland, and western Europe are clearly preferred over other parts of the world. Immigrants from the Middle East are least "desired," followed by Asians and Africans. Immigrants most favored by the Australian public are those who bring with them skills useful to Australia.

We see that Australia, like the other "traditional" immigrant receiving countries, is clearly ambivalent about welcoming new immigrants. Most of the respondents favor admitting fewer immigrants than the government's targeted number and most prefer immigrants with skills as opposed to the government's policy of favoring immigrants who have families in the country.

Great Britain

Although Great Britain has not been one of the major immigrant receiving countries, British attitudes are similar to American, Australian, and Canadian attitudes. For example, in response to the same item asked of the Americans, Canadians, and Australians about preferences for admitting more, the same, or fewer immigrants, most of the British public (between 53 and 62 percent) in 1989, 1992, and 1993 believed too many immigrants were being admitted. Only 6 percent thought "too few" were allowed to come in and between 23 and 28 percent believed the right number were being admitted.

On the basis of responses to national polls from 1983 to 1989, we saw that the British public exhibited a stronger preference for "white" immigrants, from Australia and New Zealand and from European common-market countries, than it did for Indians, Pakistani, and West Indians. Without specifying any particular types of people, when asked between 1983 and 1989 about the families (husbands, wives, children, and parents) of people who have already settled in Britain—"Would you say in general that Britain should: be stricter in controlling the settlement of closer relations, be less strict, keep the controls about the same?"—the majority of respondents (58 percent) favored keeping the controls as they "are."

For those Asians and West Indians already in the country, a large majority of the British public believed that they should be treated no differently than other British citizens. When specific questions were asked about policies that should be used to ensure equal treatment, however, public support declined substantially. The British public seems to favor equal treatment more in principle than in specific practice.

Like the major immigrant receiving countries, Britain is also ambivalent about "its immigrants." It clearly does not want more immigrants to come to its shores and it prefers immigrants from Australia and New Zealand to those "colored" immigrants from the New Commonwealth and the West Indies. But once in the country, most British citizens favor fair and equal treatment toward all immigrants, regardless of color or country of origin, at least in principle.

France

France, and especially Germany, the two European countries that sought the greatest number of guest workers to help rebuild their economies after World War II, do not have a history of receiving and welcoming immigrants. Today, the majority of the French public believe there are too many immigrants in their country. Much of the French public's negative reactions to immigrants stem from fear of the loss of a national identity and for personal safety, rather than concern about what immigrants are doing to jobs, unemployment, and education. When asked for their views about whether immigrants should be under stricter police surveillance, strong majorities favored identity cards and expulsion of illegals and convicted offenders. Over 50 percent also favored offering financial incentives for immigrants to leave their country.

France, like most other countries, has its "more" or "less" favored immigrants and, like the respondents in the other countries, immigrants who are most like the natives are viewed more positively than immigrants who have different ethnic, racial, and cultural backgrounds. Thus, north Europeans are the most liked of the immigrant communities and the Turks, North Africans, Asians, and black Africans are the least liked. It is interesting to note that even though the French express at best ambivalent attitudes toward immigrants on many specific issues, when asked, in December 1988 if "France [is] a country where one welcomes foreigners or a country where much remains to be done in this area," 64 percent perceived France as a country that welcomes foreigners. But as the movement led by Jean-Marie Le Pen gains more supporters, as recent articles in the French and American press claim it is doing, so are more antiforeign sentiments likely to be expressed publicly. For example, in a 1991 poll 71 percent of the French public complained that "there are too many Arabs here." In a 1991 article in the *Economist,* former president Valey Giscard d'Estaing is quoted as describing the imminent threat of an immigrant invasion and as calling for the immediate closure of France's frontiers to all new foreign settlers. D'Estaing also advocated a return to the concept of strict consanguinity (instead of place of birth) as the basis for French citizenship. In the 1995 and 1997 elections, Le Pen's National Front Party gained 15 percent of the vote.

Germany

Very few items bearing on immigration appeared on national polls in the 1960s, 1970s, and 1980s in the Federal Republic of Germany (FRG). When a question did appear, it usually was about foreign workers and whether they posed a serious problem. The responses indicated that about a third of the public did not perceive the foreign workers as a serious problem, another third did perceive them as a problem, and all others either had no opinion or were undecided about whether foreign workers were a problem.

In the united Germany, surveys were conducted that asked about foreigners in general and specifically about their impact on unemployment and education levels, and about particular types of foreigners. For example, in September 1992 the results of a national poll found that 78 percent believed immigration was Germany's most pressing problem compared to 20 percent who cited unification. Although the majority of Germans were "indifferent" toward the various racial and ethnic immigrant groups, north Europeans were the most favored followed by south Europeans. Asians received the least positive reaction with almost one-third of Germans disliking them. In regard to political refugees, when the German public was asked in 1990 whether it favored a change of laws regarding political asylum so as to prevent many asylum seekers from coming into the country, 60 percent favored a change that would make it more difficult to receive political asylum, 24 percent opposed a change, and 16 percent were undecided.

Japan

Finally, we come to Japan, a country in which the concept of immigration does not exist in fact and perhaps not in law. The "immigration" issues posed on national surveys were either very narrow or hypothetical. They are about admitting foreign laborers and refugees.

The first national survey was conducted in 1980. This was a period when large numbers of Vietnamese and Cambodians were seeking places of refuge and the Japanese government stated it would accept 500 refugees. When the public was asked whether Japan should accept more refugees, and before being asked respondents were told that the number admitted was 500, 38 percent of the respondents said Japan should accept more, 38 percent said they should accept the present number, and 10 percent said they should not accept more. The others had no opinion.

On the issue of admitting foreign laborers, in 1987 42 percent believed the current level was fine, 31 percent thought an increase would be desirable, and 18 percent thought an increase would be undesirable. And in 1988 and 1990, 45 and 52 percent said they "supported" or "somewhat supported" allowing foreign laborers to work in Japan, while 48 and 44 percent "opposed somewhat" or "opposed" having foreign laborers work in Japan. The other 7 and 5 percent had no opinion. The public was ambivalent about allowing foreign workers to work in Japan, but a strong majority opposed increases in admissions and favored maintaining reductions.

On the whole, the Japanese responses describe a divided public with a plurality, and by 1993 a majority favored allowing unskilled workers to enter legally but with restrictions on length of stay, type of work, and number admitted. But a strong majority did not want foreign workers to have a permanent status in their country.

In Japan, as in the other nations examined here, there is a disjuncture between policy and public opinion, but in the case of Japan the public seems to be in favor of increasing the admission of foreigners, not opposed to it. Remember, however, that the favored increase is not an increase in immigration since these foreigners would still be visitors and not immigrants. There is no assumption that these foreign workers would or should remain in Japan permanently.

Cross-National Comparisons

It is difficult to explicitly compare and evaluate public attitudes toward immigrants across nations because the questions asked and the contexts vary over time and country. In some cases, respondents are asked about admissions policies, in others they are asked whether they like or dislike specific immigrant groups, and in still others they are asked if the admission of these groups has been good for the country. Nevertheless, the kinds of questions that are asked do generally assess the positiveness or negativeness of attitudes toward immigrants. Small differences in the responses to these questions may not be noteworthy, but large differences should not be dismissed as artifact.

The data on public preferences regarding immigration policy suggest that these preferences are not closely related to the openness of immigration policy in a given nation. The proportion of respondents favoring a decrease in immigration are not radically different in immigrant nations like the United States than they are in more ambivalent nations like Great Britain. There is a slight tendency for lower proportions of respondents to favor decreasing immigration in Canada and Australia than in Britain. Given the procedural differences in the data across countries, not too much should be made of these differences. It is also interesting to note that even in immigrant nations a large minority and in some years a majority of respondents favor decreasing immigration in any given year. And, as shown by the Australian responses between 1988 and 1991, roughly 45 percent favor decreasing immigration.

There is considerable variability in the desire to restrict immigration over time within nations. In the United States, for example, the proportion advocating decreases in admissions varied between 33 and 66 percent over a fifty-year period. In Canada, the proportion varied from a low of 32 percent to a high of 55 percent. Since the length of the period for which data are available varies across nations, comparisons should be restricted to roughly similar periods. When this is done, the variability in support for decreases in immigration is still greater in the United States than it is in Canada. It is also greater than the variability in the proportion supporting decreases in Australia and Great Britain.

Again, the variability in support for limiting immigration does not seem to be simply related to the general openness or restrictiveness of the nation's immigration policy. Volatility of the attitudes toward immigration policy in the United States may reflect the greater decentralization of policy making with regard to immigration across the countries in question. The setting of quotas and the changes in immigration law are much more open in the United States than in some of these other nations. Congress sets the quotas and the legislative body is intimately involved in the process of setting immigration policy. This is less the case in Canada, but the general decentralization of the political process in Canada makes more public the setting of policy. The relative centralization of the policy-setting process may give greater stability to public attitudes in Australia and Britain relative to the United States and Canada.

In addition to the questions asked about immigration policies, there were roughly comparable questions asked about feelings toward various immigrant groups in each nation. Comparing these questions across nations indicates something about attitudes toward immigrants in general and attitudes toward groups in particular. When attitudes toward specific groups are aggregated across these groups to compute an "average" attitude about immigrants, we see that there is substantial variation across nations. The United States has the greatest "average" proportion (43 percent) expressing positive attitudes toward immigrants. The United Kingdom is second (40 percent) followed by Germany (36 percent). The Australians and the French express the lowest level of positive attitudes toward immigrants with 24 and 27 percent, respectively. It is interesting to note that in no country do the majority of citizens express positive attitudes to immigrants on average.

Given the "immigrant ethos" in the United States, it is not surprising that attitudes in the United States are relatively positive. But positive attitudes toward immigrants in Germany and the United Kingdom do not seem consistent with their relatively restrictive immigration policy. While the relatively more negative attitudes toward immigrants would be expected in France, given that immigration has become a hot political issue, it would not be expected in Australia with its large proportion of foreign born and its open immigration policy.

This distribution of "average" positive evaluations of immigrants does not seem to be consistently related to the openness of a nation's immigration policy. Indeed, attitudes about policies (i.e., decreases in admissions) do not seem to be consistently related to attitudes about immigrants. The demand for decreases in admissions is relatively high in the United Kingdom, for example, but attitudes toward immigrants are relatively positive. In other cases, such as Australia, high demand for decreases in admissions is correlated with negative attitudes toward immigrant groups. These comparisons suggest that policies, public opinion about policies, and public attitudes toward immigrants are neither monolithic nor related in a simple fashion.

The distribution of attitudes toward immigrants (as opposed to attitudes about policies) across nations does suggest that attitudes toward immigrants may be related to the stability or consistency of immigration policy rather than its openness. While the United Kingdom and Germany have relatively restrictive policies, these policies have been set in place and have been adhered to for many years. In France and Australia, in contrast, immigration policy and immigration practice have undergone rapid and substantial change. The fundamental ambivalence in the French government's immigration policy may be a source of instability. Relatively restrictive formal immigration policies coexist with substantial illegal immigration and liberal naturalization policies. This ambivalence can contribute to negative attitudes toward immigrants. Similarly, there has been a massive shift in Australian immigration from a whites-only policy to a more open immigration policy. This shift has been followed by a change in the nature of immigration to Australia, from white and European, to Asian. This change could be at the root of the relatively negative attitudes toward immigrants observed among Australians. Of course, both ambivalent policies and negative or unstable public attitudes may be manifestations of a more fundamental ambivalence about immigration.

Negative attitudes toward immigrants vary substantially within countries for specific immigrant groups. In general, attitudes are more positive for groups most culturally and racially similar to the citizens of the host country. So, north European immigrants are regarded more positively by citizens of all the nations examined here except Japan where the questions about immigrants were not asked. Immigrants from non-European nations are regarded more negatively. These differences in the attitudes toward specific groups may be a reflection of the social distance between the immigrant groups and the majority population of the host nation or it may be due to recency of the arrival of the immigrant groups. In almost every instance, those most culturally dissimilar to the host nation are also the most recently arrived group.

While the social distance between the host nation and the immigrant groups seems to be related to negative attitudes toward the group, this does not seem to be the only determinant of the relative position of groups. In France, for example, West Indians are regarded more positively than North Africans even though the former are racially more dissimilar from the French than the latter. In the United States, gradations are made between Asian immigrants (37 percent positive) and West Indian or Caribbean immigrants (10 percent positive), while in Germany the level of positive attitudes is quite similar for Asians (13 percent), North Africans (17 percent), and black Africans (17 percent). While social distance is strongly related to negative attitudes toward immigrant groups, the specific dimension of social distance that is operating, that is, race versus culture, is not clear. Moreover, other features of the groups such as its sheer size and thereby the threat that it poses to the dominant group may explain the distributions that we see here.

There are several major points that this review of the public opinion data allow us to make. The first is that countries that have major differences in statutes, policies, and practices vis-à-vis immigration and in the number and types of immigrants they admit per year, nevertheless share a great many attitudes and beliefs about immigrants. While allowing for some differences, there is more consensus than descensus about how the publics in those countries feel about immigrants. Most respondents want their country to accept fewer immigrants than the law permits, place more restrictions on immigrants of color, and give priority to immigrants with special skills as opposed to family unification. The second point is that these opinions about immigration policy vary over time within countries; and it is unclear at this time exactly what drives this variability. There is not a ready fit between history, population density, and economic conditions and the demand to reduce immigration. The variability in the support for restricting immigration seems to differ across nations. The third point is that attitudes toward policy and immigration do not appear to be monolithic. The desire to restrict immigration is not closely related with negative attitudes toward migrants more generally. Finally, negative attitudes toward specific immigrant groups seem to be generally related to the social distance between the group and the host society. This relationship is far from perfect, however, and can mask other factors such as the size of the group that might account for this observed pattern.

Immigration is an important and hotly debated issue for most of the societies included in this study. Public opinion surveys are often used in these debates to fan the flames. In such uses, public opinion is treated as an unambiguous ratification of one side of the debate or the other. This limited review of public policies toward immigration and public opinion on immigrants suggests that these links between policy, public attitudes toward policy, and public attitudes toward immigration are anything but unambiguous and consistent. More work needs to be done to disentangle this web. Most especially, greater attention must be given to identifying the various dimensions that should be used to characterize public opinion concerning immigrants and immigration.

11

Social Integration of Immigrants in Host Societies

While it is universally recognized that it is beneficial to include immigrants in the host society, there is much less consensus over what this means and how much inclusion is desirable. Inclusion can mean the total absorption of the immigrant population both in terms of culture and social structure or it could mean more limited involvement as in the case where immigrant groups participate in the major social institutions but still retain their cultural distinctiveness. At the other extreme, immigrant groups are excluded from the host society both in terms of culture and participation in major social institutions. This exclusion would mean that they are not allowed to assimilate and efforts are made to suppress the cultural distinctiveness of the immigrant group.

There is a great deal of disagreement over which of these strategies is morally correct or wise. Some consider total absorption or "assimilation" desirable, while others believe that some diversity or pluralism is preferable. In this chapter, we try to avoid normative judgments about the appropriateness of these various strategies of inclusion. Rather, we attempt to describe the nature and degree to which immigrant populations are included in the various societies addressed in the previous chapters. This description is juxtaposed to the previous characterization of immigration policies. In this framework, policies are seen as encouraging or discouraging social integration.

Japan has been excluded from this discussion of integration largely because the Japanese do not acknowledge immigration. While there is a large and growing number of "guests" who stay and of foreign workers, they are not acknowledged as permanent residents. Consequently, very little systematic data are collected on their social integration, and it is difficult to characterize the status of these "guests" relative to immigrants in other nations.

Dimensions of Social Integration

The description of social integration distinguishes between inclusion in the major social institutions such as the labor force and educational institutions, and cultural matters such as language, choice of marital partner, religion, and other beliefs. In this way, we will be able to determine whether the cultural and social structural aspects of social integration function independently. We also examine the relationship between inclusion and participation in negative behaviors such as welfare and crime. While there may be legitimate disagreement over the desirability of assimilationism and pluralism, there is much more agreement about the inappropriateness of dependency and criminal activity. To the extent that patterns of assimilation are related to these patterns of negative behavior, we may be able to make some statements about the desirability or wisdom of these various strategies for dealing with immigrant populations.

Cultural Integration

The cultural integration of immigrant groups refers to the extent to which they share the same basic values as the citizens of the host society. These values would include religious principles, beliefs about family or gender roles, or the values concerning private property. In some cases, these values are manifest in attitudes while in others they are expressed as behavior. Immigrants can demonstrate their beliefs by professing these beliefs, as in the case where they agree with the native born on rights of private property. They can also demonstrate their beliefs in action, as in the case where fertility rates for immigrants and for the native population reflect the beliefs of these groups regarding children, gender roles, and family size.

Social Structural Integration

Social structural integration refers to the extent to which people resident in a nation participate in the major social institutions of that country. These social institutions are normatively prescribed persistent patterns of interaction. They include the labor force, educational institutions, political institutions (such as parties or the electoral process), voluntary associations, and the military. Participation means that residents are actively involved in these institutional arrangements. People who work, for example, are participating in the labor force and perhaps in trade union organizations. Those who attend or have attended school participate in educational institutions. Voting involves participation in political institutions and so on. It is also possible to distinguish degrees of participation in these institutions. So, for example, people who have progressed farther or spent more time in school have participated more in educational institutions than people who have attended school for fewer years. Persons who vote only are less involved in political institutions than those who vote and belong to a political party and so on.

It is widely believed that participation in these major institutions is good for the nation. This belief in the desirability of social integration is apparent in statements that bemoan the low rates of participation in the electoral process in industrialized democracies. Low school dropout rates and unemployment are similarly regarded as indications that a society is in good health. If, however, participation in these institutions prompts fears of being overrun by immigrants, then high levels of participation may not be desirable.

Patterns of Social Integration across Nations

The patterns of social integration across the nations that we have examined are very complex and differences in the organization of these institutions across nations make comparisons difficult. The concept of the "drop out" in the United States, for example, is quite different from the concept of "school leaving" in England. The former is much more indicative of an absence in social integration than the latter. As with other cross-national comparisons we have made in this book, these must be done with caution and sensitivity to these differences.

The general pattern that emerges from comparisons of social integration across nations is that the social integration of immigrants is more extensive in immigrant nations than nonimmigrant nations. Immigrants in the United States, Canada, Australia, and Great Britain participate more extensively in major social institutions than do immigrants in France and Germany. Again, there is also variation within immigrant and nonimmigrant nations with regard to participation. The extent of participation in Canada, for example, is much greater than it is in the United States or Australia.

Naturalization

One of the most fundamental ways that immigrants can participate in a host society is to apply for and be granted citizenship. This allows immigrants full participation in the legal and political institutions in the society. When a large proportion of newcomers apply for and are granted citizenship, it is a presumably a sign of mutual commitment.

The data that we have on naturalization is not consistent across nations. In some cases, we only have the number of persons granted citizenship in a year or some other unit of time, for example, one decade. When we divide this figure by the number of immigrants admitted in that unit of time, then we get a naturalization rate. If the rate of naturalization is stable over time and if the number of admissions is also stable over time, then this rate will be reasonably accurate. In other cases, we have the proportion of the foreign-born population living in the host nation that has been naturalized. This method will always produce a high estimate of the naturalization rate because persons who remain in the nation to be interviewed are more likely to naturalize. Immigrants who have left the country before the interview are not included in the base of the naturalization rate. The best data on naturalization rates comes from cohorts of admissions who are followed until they naturalize.

Australia and Canada stand out as nations with the highest naturalization rates. In Australia, 50 percent of persons admitted naturalize within five years and 73 percent take Australian citizenship within twenty years of admission. Canada does even better with 88 percent of admissions becoming citizens within twenty years. Great Britain, the United States, and France have considerably lower rates of naturalization than Australia and Canada. Estimates of the naturalization rate in Great Britain vary between 35 and 45 percent.[1] In the United States they range from 34 to 39 percent,[2] and in France the best data suggest a naturalization rate of about 38 percent. Germany and Japan have very low naturalization rates, 3 percent and less than 1 percent, respectively.

This ranking of naturalization rates is somewhat consistent with the leniency of policies governing naturalization. The Australians and Canadians do not have onerous requirements for becoming a citizen, whereas Japan and Germany (less so as of January 2000) do. Great Britain, France, and the United States have longer waiting periods than the Canadians and the Australians. Other factors can also be operating such as the proximity of sending nations. The United States, for example, has a long land border with Mexico where a large proportion of the immigrant population originated. It is simple to maintain ties to the sending nation when it is so proximate. The same is true for the French and the North Africans. Home is a short boat ride away. In contrast, the major sending nations for Australia and Canada are quite distant from these host nations. This explanation does not fit the British situation, however.

Economic Institutions

There are a number of ways to participate in economic institutions. Being in the labor force is perhaps the most common form of participation, although those engaged in entrepreneurial activity are also engaged in production. We can also distinguish the degree of participation in economic institutions according to the income that people earn and the occupational prestige that they attain. The higher the income or the occupational prestige, the greater the level of participation.

On these criteria, immigrants in Canada, Australia, and the United States have the greatest involvement in economic institutions. The labor-force participation rate for immigrants in these nations is very similar to that of the native-born population. In Australia, 61.6 percent of the immigrants are in the workforce compared to 60.6 percent of the native born. In the United States, the comparable figures are 76.9 and 74.2 percent and for Canada 74.5 and 76.4 percent. In contrast, the labor-force participation rates for immigrants are significantly lower than the native born in Great Britain, France, Germany, and Japan. In Great Britain, for example, the labor-force participation rate for the native born is 67 percent compared to 54 percent for immigrants.

The unemployment rates tell a similar story. In Canada, the unemployment rate for the foreign born is lower than that of the native population. In Australia, Great Britain, and the United States, the unemployment rate of immigrants is slightly higher than that of the native population. Immigrants in Germany and France have substantially higher rates of unemployment than the native population with the differential being the greatest in France.

In Germany, 6.3 percent of the German citizens were unemployed in 1999 compared to 10.9 percent of foreigners. In France, these figures were 6.3 and 11.3 percent, respectively.

The picture is similar, if slightly more complex, when we examine indicators of the degree of participation in economic institutions. Again, immigrants in Canada, Australia, Great Britain, and the United States have incomes equal to or slightly lower than that of the native population. The per capita annual income of the foreign born in the United States, for example, was $15,033 compared to $14,637 for the native born in 1999. The household income of immigrants ($28,300), however, was slightly lower than that of the native born ($30,100). The annual income of the foreign born was $30,871 in Canada and the income of native-born Canadians was $31,250 in 1996. In France and Germany, the income of the foreign born is substantially lower than that of citizens.

There also appears to be greater concentration of immigrants in lower-prestige occupations in nonimmigrant nations compared to immigrant nations. While the overrepresentation of immigrants in lower-status occupations is universal, the underrepresentation of immigrants in higher-status occupations seems to be greater in nonimmigrant nations. In the United States, for example, 27.4 percent of the foreign born are operatives or laborers compared to 18.1 percent of the native born. The representation of the two groups is more similar for professional and managerial occupations with 21.2 of the foreign born in these occupations and 25.9 percent of the native born. In contrast, 47.1 percent of foreigners are in extraction and manufacturing occupations in Germany compared to 30 percent of German citizens. The representation of German citizens (23.7 percent) in communications and finance occupations, however, is substantially greater than that of foreigners (10.1 percent). The picture is similar in France where 21.8 percent of the employed foreigners are in construction compared with 6.8 percent of French citizens. In both countries, immigrants appear to be concentrated in manufacturing and other manual occupations.

Educational Institutions

The distribution in the participation of immigrants in educational institutions across nations is similar to that found for economic institutions. The educational attainment of immigrants is higher than that of the native population in Great Britain, Canada, and Australia. The average years of schooling for the foreign born in Great Britain is 13.9 years (13.6 if the Irish are included) compared to 11.9 for the native-born population.[3] In Canada, the comparable figures are 13.33 for foreign-born and 12.56 for native-born Canadians.[4] The same is true in Australia where the average years in school is 13.13 for the foreign born and 12.29 for the native born.[5] The educational distribution of immigrants in all three nations tends to be bimodal with more highly educated and more persons with less education than the native population. Approximately 12 percent of native-born Canadians, for example, have a college degree as compared to 17 percent of the immigrant population. But, 11 percent of the native-born population have nine years of education or less compared to 17 percent of the foreign born.[6]

In the United States, the educational attainment of the immigrant population is substantially lower than that of the native population. The average years of schooling for the native born is 13.24 and for the foreign born 11.7. Here, too, the educational distribution is bimodal. Forty-one percent of the immigrant population of the United States has less than a high school education, while only 23 percent of the native population has less than a high school education. At the same time, the proportion of immigrants with a doctorate is higher than that of the native population.

In Germany, the rate at which immigrants attend school is quite high, but a much smaller proportion of immigrants go on to universities than the native population. A much larger proportion of immigrants receive vocational education than the native population. In France, the educational attainment of the immigrant population is substantially less than the native population at all levels.

Patterns of Cultural Integration Cross-Nationally

Patterns of cultural assimilation are somewhat different from those in social structural integration. Cultural integration is higher in Canada and Germany than it is in the United States, Australia, and France.

Language Facility

The language facility of the immigrant population varies substantially across nations. Variation in the ability to speak or read the language of the host country is not neatly split across immigrant and nonimmigrant nations. The language ability of immigrants in Canada is very high. Less than 4 percent of immigrants were reported as not having conversational ability in English or French.[7] In Australia, somewhat more of the immigrant population reported having no English-speaking ability, about 9 percent. A much higher percent of the immigrant population in the United States could not speak English—about 23 percent. In Great Britain, the proportion of immigrants with limited English facility was approximately 39 percent.[8]

The differences in language facility of immigrants across nations tend to diminish over time in the country, but they do not disappear. The differences among Canada, Australia, and the United States in the percent speaking the host language well or quite well are much less for immigrants in the country for twenty-nine years or more. Ninety-nine percent of these immigrants in Canada are fluent, compared to 95 percent in Australia and 91 percent in the United States. The differences in fluency are greatest among the recent arrivals for whom 92 percent of Canadian immigrants spoke the official languages well compared to 82.4 percent of Australian immigrants and 61.3 in the United States.[9] These high rates of language facility for recent arrivals in Canada may be due to both the point system used to select from among applicants for admission and the emphasis on language acquisition in immigrant integration programs.

Intermarriage

The data on intermarriage cross-nationally suffers from many of the same problems as the data on naturalization or language fluency. The information on intermarriage is generally cross-sectional and not longitudinal. We have the rate of intermarriage at a given point in time and not the proportion of an entering immigrant cohort that marries natives of the host country at some point in their life. The longitudinal data on intermarriage is a much clearer indicator of integration than the cross-sectional data because the latter can be affected by the ebbs and flows of admissions as well as the propensity of groups to intermarry. Presumably, even the relative size of the immigrant and native groups will affect the rate of intermarriage.

The available information on intermarriage between immigrants and the native population suggests that Canada has the highest rates of intermarriage. Eighteen percent of the marriages in Canada in 1996 involved persons born outside of Canada and native-born Canadians. In France and Germany, 10 percent of marriages involved foreigners and citizens. In the United States, only 5 percent of marriages involved the foreign and the native born.[10]

It may be more appropriate in comparing intermarriage rates if these rates took account of the differences in the size of the foreign-born population. Presumably, the probability of intermarriage should be greater if the proportion of the population that is foreign born is greater. In a nation with a population that is 10 percent foreign born, we would expect that the probability of a foreign-born man marrying a native-born woman would be 0.1 times 0.9 or 0.09. The probability of a foreign-born woman marrying a native-born man would also be 0.09. The probability of intermarriage in this nation would be the sum of these probabilities or 0.18. A nation would have a high intermarriage rate if it exceeded that expectation and a low rate if it was less than this expectation. If we express the observed rate of intermarriage as a ratio of the observed to the expected, then the rank order of the nations changes. In this case, Germany has a higher rate of intermarriage. It is 84 percent of what we would expect given the percent of foreigners in Germany. Canada has the next highest rate at 0.61 followed by France at 0.55 and the United States at 0.27

For both France and Germany, the percentage of intermarriage has increased from 1980 to 1993. In France, the intermarriage rate for immigrants increased from 6.2 percent in 1980 to 10.6 percent in 1990. In Germany, it increased from 7.7 percent in 1980 to 10.0 percent in 1993.

Fertility Rates

Fertility rates of the immigrant population are higher than the native population in all of the countries for which data are available. But the magnitude of the differences between the fertility rates of the native and immigrant populations differ substantially across nations. The differences are smallest in Canada where the fertility rate of the immigrant populations is 1.86 per 1,000 and that for the native population is 1.73 per 1,000—a difference of 6 percent in the rates. In the United States, the difference between the fertility rates of native-born and naturalized women is similarly small—2.24 for native born and 2.33 for the foreign born. These differences between the fertility rates of the native and foreign born are much greater in Great Britain, France, and Germany. In 1975, the fertility rate for immigrants in Germany was roughly twice that of the native population—2.64 per 1,000 to 1.34 per 1,000. By 1986, the difference between the fertility of foreigners and natives decreased to 1.76 and 1.31, respectively. Immigrants in Great Britain had a fertility rate of 4.0 in 1970 compared to a rate of 2.4 for the native population. The fertility rates for both the native and immigrant populations declined in Great Britain to 2.8 and 1.7, respectively. While the rates of fertility decreased in both countries for the native and foreign populations, the relative position of immigrants and natives stayed the same in Great Britain, but foreigners and Germans became more similar over time. Foreigners in

France had a fertility rate of 2.8 per 1,000, compared to a rate of 1.7 per 1,000 for French citizens. The disparity in immigrant and native fertility rates is greatest in France (a rate ratio of 1.74) followed closely by Great Britain (1.64) and more distantly by Germany (1.34). Immigrant and native-born fertility are not very different in the United States and Canada (1.04).

Table 11.1 summarizes the relative position of nations on these various indicators of social integration.

Comparing the Social Integration of Immigrants across Nations

The nations examined differ in terms of the degree and nature of immigrants' integration into the host societies. Canada is at one extreme. Immigrants to Canada participate in social institutions at a rate that is equal to or higher than the native population and often higher than the participation of immigrants in other nations. Germany and Japan are at the other extreme with immigrants participating in major institutions at rates lower than the native populations and lower than immigrants in other nations. The remaining countries are in between these extremes, some closer to the Canadian pole, and others more similar to Germany and Japan.

Immigrants in Canada are also more culturally similar to the native population than immigrant groups in other nations. Canadian immigrants nationalize at very high rates. They participate in the labor force at rates similar to the native population; their unemployment is lower; their occupational prestige is similar; and their income is the same as the native population. The educational attainment of immigrants in Canada is higher than that of the native population. In terms of indicators of cultural integration, immigrants to Canada are similar to the native population. The language facility of immigrants is very high at admission and it becomes higher with time in the country. Fertility rates are very similar to the native population and intermarriage rates between the native and the foreign born are high relative to other nations. In every respect, immigrants in Canada appear to be integrated both culturally and structurally into Canadian society.

The situation in Australia is quite similar to that in Canada, only slightly less so. Naturalization rates in Australia are quite high, but not as high as those in Canada. Employment of immigrants is high and unemployment is about the same as that of the native born, as is their income. The educational attainment of immigrants is higher than that of the native population, but the difference is not as great as it is in Canada. In terms of occupational prestige, immigrants to Australia are overrepresented in lower-status occupations relative to the native born to a greater extent than immigrants in Canada and they are not overrepresented in the higher-status specialties to the extent that

Table 11.1 Social Integration of Immigrants by Nation

Social Integration	*AUS*	*CAN*	*USA*	*FR*	*UK*	*GER*	*JAP*
Naturalization[b]	high	high	moderate	moderate	moderate	low	low
Labor force[a]	same	same	same	lower	lower	lower	NA
Unemployment	same	lower	same	higher	same	higher	NA
Income[a]	same	same	same	NA	higher	NA	NA
Job prestige[a]	same	same	same	lower	same	lower	NA
Education[a]	higher	higher	lower	lower	higher	lower	NA
Dependency[a]	lower	lower	same	NA	lower	lower	NA
Language fluency[b]	high	high	moderate	NA	moderate	low	NA
Fertility rates[a]	NA	same	same	higher	higher	moderately higher	NA
Intermarriage[b]	NA	high/moderate	low	moderate	NA	moderate/high	NA

[a]Comparisons made to the native-born population.
[b]Comparisons made across nations.

immigrants are in Canada. The same is true with respect to cultural indicators. Australian immigrants are not as integrated as their Canadian counterparts. The language facility of Australian immigrants is high, but not as high as that of immigrants in Canada.

The United States is further down on the inclusion continuum. Naturalization rates in the United States are substantially lower than in Canada and Australia. Rates of labor-force participation for immigrants in the United States are very similar to those of the native born and their income is similar. Immigrants in the United States are overrepresented in lower-prestige occupations to about the extent of Australian immigrants, but they also do not have parity with the native born in the higher-status occupations. Their representation in these higher-status specialties is not quite up to that of the native born. The educational attainment of immigrants in the United States is substantially lower than that of the native-born population. The indicators of cultural integration are also lower in the United States than in Canada and Australia. English-language facility is much lower among immigrants to the United States than it is for immigrants in Australia and Canada. Rates of intermarriage between immigrants and the foreign born are lower than those in Canada. Fertility rates for immigrants, however, are very close to those of native born in the United States.

Great Britain is quite similar to the United States in terms of social integration. Naturalization rates are moderate. All of the indicators of participation in economic institutions for immigrants are similar to those of the native born. Labor-force participation and unemployment rates for immigrants are similar to those for the native population. Income is somewhat higher and the distribution of immigrants across occupations is more like that of Australia than the United States. Immigrants are overrepresented in lower-status jobs, but are represented in roughly the same proportion as the native population in higher-status occupations. The educational attainment of immigrants in Great Britain is substantially higher than that of the native born. In terms of cultural integration, immigrants in Great Britain are less integrated than those in the United States, Canada, and Australia. The level of language facility among immigrants is lower in Great Britain than in these other nations, even lower than the United States. Fertility rates of immigrants in Great Britain differ from the native population fertility rates of immigrants in the United States and Canada. Great Britain, then, seems to have slightly higher rates of immigrant participation in economic and educational institutions than immigrants in the United States but larger differences in terms of cultural indicators.

France is further down the inclusion continuum than the United States and Great Britain. Naturalization rates for immigrants in France are moderate, at about U.S. and British levels. Their participation in economic institutions is substantially less than the native population. Unemployment rates of immigrants are much higher than the native born and immigrants are more overrepresented in lower-status occupations and underrepresented in higher-status occupations than is the case in Australia, Canada, Great Britain, and the United States. The educational attainment of immigrants is lower than the native population. The cultural indicators suggest that immigrants are still somewhat different from the native population. French-language facility is moderate among immigrants in France. Fertility rates are much higher for immigrants than in the native population. The intermarriage rate, however, is moderately high. Immigrants in France have lower rates of participation in major social institutions than natives and they remain culturally distinct from them in some ways.

Germany appears similar to France in terms of the social integration of immigrants, but the de sanguine definition of immigrant used in Germany (until recently) makes a precise comparison complex. It would seem appropriate to view Germany's score on these indicators of social integration as a best-case scenario, since we would assume that the fourth-generation Turks who are considered immigrants would be more integrated than the foreign born in France or the United States. Naturalization rates in Germany are much lower than those of other nations described here. The participation in economic institutions is similar to that observed for France. Unemployment is much higher for immigrants than for natives and immigrants are substantially overrepresented in lower-status occupations and underrepresented in higher-status occupations. The indicators of cultural integration in Germany suggest relatively high levels of integration. The fertility rate of immigrants is higher than that of German citizens but not nearly to the degree that it is in France or even in Britain. This appearance of integration is due less to the ability of Germany to absorb immigrants than to the increasingly higher representation of the German born in the "foreigner" population. In a sense, this strategy is the antithesis of integration.

Immigration Policy and Patterns of Social Integration

These patterns of social integration are the product of policy and happenstance. In general, nations with more open immigration policies have more integrated immigrant populations. These policies, in turn, are driven by characteristics of the host nation and the immigration populations residing there. In nations where the immigrant population poses a threat to the dominance of the native born, for example, immigration policies are more restrictive than in nations where immigrant groups do not pose a threat. Similarly, host nations that rely more heavily on shared values to maintain social control will be more resistant to immigration and social integration than those less dependent on consensus.

Immigration Policy and Integration

Immigration policy facilitates the social integration of immigrants through admission policies, naturalization policies, and control policies. Admissions policies can assist integration as well as the perceived threat posed by immigrant groups. It seems that the sheer number of immigrants admitted is a poor predictor of social and cultural integration, since nations with the highest levels of immigration like the United States, Australia, and Canada have the highest levels of social structural integration. Canada also has very high levels of cultural integration. Admissions policies could account for this pattern in that the Canadian immigration policy employs a point system that emphasizes the "assimilation potential" of the immigrant. This kind of selectivity can facilitate the social integration of immigrant groups by only admitting "good risks." The United States does not employ such an admissions policy and the social structural and cultural integration of immigrants is somewhat lower than in Canada. Australia also employs a point system but it is not as straightforwardly organized to pick the most easily assimilated groups as the Canadian system is.

Admissions policies can also affect social and cultural integration by determining the mix of groups that are allowed to enter. The immigrant nations are distinctive in the variety of groups admitted relative to nonimmigrant nations such as France and Germany. In the latter nations, the overwhelming majority of immigrants are from one or two nations. In France, for example, North Africans from Algeria and Morocco constitute the overwhelming majority of immigrants. In Germany, the Turks and Yugoslavs constitute the majority of admissions. It is conceivable that the diversity of the immigrant population (as engineered through admissions policies) facilitates integration. The country quotas employed in the United States can be seen as an attempt to diversify the immigrant pool. This can occur in part because diversity diffuses the focus and the fear of native-born populations. This, in turn, lessens the demand for further controls and impediments to social integration in the name of protecting the native culture or preserving jobs of the native born. This is consistent with the pattern wherein the nations with the least diversity in their immigrant pool have the lowest levels of social structural integration.

Patterns of social integration are also influenced by immigrant control policies and integration policies. Germany, for example, followed a very restrictive admissions policy after the mid-1970s. At the same time, the government pushed the acquisition of language skills for immigrants and education with an emphasis on vocational education. Restrictive naturalization policies excluded immigrants from meaningful direct political participation. These policies worked together to produce an immigrant population that is culturally integrated (through intermarriage and other processes) but socially marginal. Without replacement, the immigrant population becomes increasing more similar to the native population culturally but further social assimilation is slowed by limited access to university education. Great Britain took a similar approach to the restriction of admissions in the early 1970s, but it did not have the same investment in social integration programs and it took a more liberal attitude toward naturalization. About the same time, access to university education in Great Britain was expanded with the rise of the "red brick" universities, thereby offering more universal access to further social mobility for immigrant groups. The result was a less culturally integrated immigrant population in Great Britain than in Germany even though its admissions policies were somewhat similar relative to those of other nations.

The contrast between Canada and Australia also suggests the influence of integration policies. Canada invests heavily in language programs and in other activities to help integrate immigrants into society. Australia makes less of an investment in these programs and the United States even less. The social integration of Canadian immigrants is marginally greater than immigrants to Australia.

Naturalization policies can also contribute toward social integration. Where naturalization policies are the most open, immigrants will invest more in the society with the expectation that they will reside there permanently. This contributes to social integration in several ways. First, demonstration of productivity and social involvement in the host society are often required for naturalization. Second, the opportunity to be accepted for full citizenship encourages full participation as a form of reciprocity. Third, citizenship can often remove legal barriers to fuller participation as in the case where certain jobs, for example, government employment, are restricted to citizens or loans are more easily obtained by citizens than noncitizens. This is consistent with the fact that immigrant nations that have the least restrictive naturalization policies also have the highest levels of social integration. But that pattern is not perfect, for example, in that France has relatively permissive naturalization and low levels of social integration. Other factors may be at work here that will be discussed.

The differences observed here in the social integration of immigrants across nations suggest that immigration policies can make a difference in the integration of immigrants. They suggest that big differences in policies, such as that between a guest-worker policy and an immigration policy, will make a difference. They also indicate that small differences, such as the use of point systems of various types or language programs, may also affect integration.

Happenstance

Policies that inhibit or facilitate the integration of immigrants are often shaped by a complex mix of physical, social, and economic forces the effects of which are screened through the political process in each nation. In addition to the influence of these larger social forces on policy and thereby the social integration of immigrants, they can also exert a direct effect on integration. One would expect, for example, that a nation sharing a long land border with another will be less likely to integrate culturally immigrants from its neighbor. Since it is easy to move back and forth across the border, many of the customs and other aspects of culture will be brought back and forth and the cultural distinctiveness of the immigrants will be preserved. In countries like Germany or Canada where the distance between sending and host countries is great, cultural integration should be easier than in France or the United States where principal sending nations are more proximate.

Among the factors that can lead to policies that restrict the social and cultural integration of immigrants, the perceived threat of the immigrant group is perhaps the most important factor. The perceived threat posed by immigrants is a function of the size and homogeneity of the group and the importance of cultural homogeneity for social control within the host nation. Where immigrant groups constitute a large portion of the population, then the perceived threat will be great as will the demand for exclusionary policies. This can be seen in the variation of immigration policies within the United States over time. The greatest change toward restrictiveness in U.S. policies occurred in 1921 soon after the greatest surge in immigration ever experienced in that nation. The same type of restriction occurred in France, Germany, and England where a surge of immigrants in the 1960s was followed by severe restrictions in policies in the 1970s.

When immigrants are homogeneous among themselves, it will take fewer of them to create the perception of threat. This seems to be the case when we compare France with the immigrant nations. The sheer volume of immigrants is greater in the immigrant nations than it is in France, but the fact that the vast majority of immigrants to France come from Morocco and Algeria enhances the perception of threat and the demand for restrictive policies. The diversity of the immigration to Canada, Australia, and the United States defuses the demands for more exclusionary policies. As Mexican immigrants (both legal and illegal) grow as a proportion of immigrants to the United States, the demand for restrictions grows in the United States. As Chinese and other Asians become a greater proportion of immigrants to Australia, the demand for more restrictive policies increases.

Finally, the perception of threat will be felt first by those nations that rely on cultural homogeneity to maintain order in the society. The Japanese may be the most extreme example of this. Here, shared understandings of what is and is not appropriate are almost unfathomable to anyone not reared in the culture. Many of the public policies that would be the subject of adversarial debate in other nations are negotiated privately in Japan. The importance of shame in social control assumes a high level of consensus over what is right, otherwise shame cannot work. While Japan is the most extreme case of a society that virtually requires homogeneity, Germany and England and to a lesser degree France also require high levels of cultural homogeneity to preserve order in their society. In contrast, the immigrant nations, because of their tradition of accepting newcomers, rely on vast amounts of space and the decentralization of authority. Conflict among diverse groups is not minimized by common cultural understandings of what is appropriate. Rather, heterogeneous groups are separated in space to minimize their contact. Decentralized governmental units like states or counties allow different groups to be a majority locally while they are a minority nationally. This allows for an ordered segmentation that is not available in nations that are more densely settled and more centralized politically. With these ecological and governmental arrangements, social order can be preserved with greater diversity in immigrant as opposed to nonimmigrant nations. Consequently, smaller numbers of immigrants and less diverse immigrants will pose a greater real and perceived threat to social order in nonimmigrant as compared to immigrant nations.

The degree to which immigrants are integrated into their respective host societies is affected by the confluence of both policy and happenstance in complex interaction. This comparison does not include enough nations with sufficiently different policies to isolate the influence of any particular dimension of policy or happenstance. Nonetheless, the patterns of variation in policy and integration observed here can inform speculation about the influence of both policy and happenstance. The fact that there are differences in the social integration of immigrants in Canada compared to the United States gives rise to speculation about what could account for this difference. Is it the point system in the admissions policy of Canada that gives it this edge? Could it be the relatively lavish funding of language programs? Here, the comparison of Canada with Australia would suggest language programs. Australia and Canada use a similar point system in admissions, but Canada's language program is more extensive than Australia's. These speculations prompted by this crude comparison can be followed by more contextualized comparative studies that would inform the choice between these explanations.

Notes

1. The estimate of 35 percent comes from Nigel Charles, *Understanding British Citizenship Application Rates* (London: Home Office, 1997), as cited in Stephen Glover et al., *Migration: An Economic and Social Analysis* (London: Home Office, 2001). The estimate of 45 percent is the average ratio of the number naturalized in a given year and the number admitted in that year for 1998 through 2000.

2. The U.S. estimates come from an admissions cohort followed for twenty years (38.7 percent), and the ratio of naturalizations to admissions are from 1907 to 1990 (34 percent).

3. Timothy Hatton and Stephen Wheatley Price, "Migration, Migrants and Policy in the United Kingdom," Discussion Paper no. 81 (Bonn: Institute for the Study of Labour, December 1999). This high-mean education hides a bimodal distribution in which the foreign born have large numbers of highly educated and large numbers of persons with little education.

4. Heather Antecol, Deborah A. Cobb-Clark, and Stephen J. Trejo, "Immigration Policy and the Skills of Immigrants to Australia, Canada, and the United States," Claremont Colleges Working Papers in Economics (Claremont, Calif.: Claremont Institute for Economic Policy Studies, March 2000).

5. Antecol, Cobb-Clark, and Trejo, "Immigration Policy."

6. Informetrica Limited, *Canada's Recent Immigrants: A Comparative Portrait Based on the 1996 Census* (Ottawa: Citizenship and Immigration Canada, 2001).

7. Antecol, Cobb-Clark, and Trejo, "Immigration Policy."

8. Christian Dustmann and Francesca Fabbri, "Language Proficiency and Labour Market Performance of Immigrants in the UK," Discussion Paper no. 156 (Bonn: Institute for the Study of Labour, May 2000).

9. Antecol, Cobb-Clark, and Trejo, "Immigration Policy."

10. The intermarriage rate for the United States was computed with data taken from Amara Bachu, "Fertility of American Men," Population Division Working Paper no. 11, Fertility Statistics Branch (Washington, D.C.: U.S. Bureau of the Census, 1996).

Conclusion

This multinational review of immigration and immigration policies has demonstrated that there are few universals when it comes to this issue. But one important common tie among persons who opt to immigrate from anywhere to anywhere is the desire to improve their lives, for themselves and their children, to find better jobs, and to enjoy a higher standard of living. Having said that, we note that the composition of immigrant groups, and the expectations and policies of the host nations differ across societies. These differences are manifest in immigration policies that are relatively open and others that are extremely restrictive. The accommodations reached by immigrants and the host nations also vary across the nations discussed in the foregoing chapters. In some, the newcomers are integrated into the society very quickly, while in others they remain on the margin indefinitely. The only area in which there is virtual uniformity across nations is in the area of public opinion where a majority of citizens in all host nations feel that, in principle, immigration should be reduced.

This relative absence of universals regarding immigration suggests that the impact and social meaning of immigration has less to do with immigrants and immigration than it does with the response of the host nation. In nations that welcome immigrants, the immigrants will be absorbed relatively quickly without substantial negative consequences for the host society and often with considerable benefits for the receiving nation. In nations that keep immigrants on the margin of society, the newcomers will behave accordingly by not participating in the society in positive ways and by engaging in negative activities such as crime and dependency.

Immigration means that people change their residence. This movement causes disruption of existing social arrangements both in the sending nation and in the receiving nation. In this book, we examined the reaction of nations to this disruption and found that the impact and social meaning of immigration differs substantially across nations. If the disruption attendant to moving is universal but the repercussions of moving are not, then we must assume that some intervening process produces the differential impact of immigration observed across nations. That intervening process begins with immigration policy.

Immigration policies are an attempt to buffer the host society from the disruption that newcomers bring while getting from immigrants that which the receiving nations need. A host society that needs marginal labor would try to recruit younger immigrants, perhaps with special skills to serve those labor needs. They may also try to minimize the resulting disruption by restricting recruitment to those nations most culturally similar to the host nation. Nations configure their admission, control, and naturalization policies to achieve this balance between disruption and need. These policies set the tone for the interrelationship between the society and immigrants.

In some cases, the bargain is explicit as with guest workers who are recruited explicitly to work for a certain term and there is no promise or expectation for fuller participation in the host nation. In other cases, the screening is more subtle, as in those nations that employ point systems for admissions and where points are given for language facility and other characteristics of immigrants that make their presence in the host nation less disruptive.

Control policies also communicate the expectations of society to the immigrant. Policies that restrict where immigrants can work or live send the message that the newcomer is held in suspicion by the host society. The same is true for registration requirements. These contacts with immigration authorities raise the specter of deportation, and this uncertainty minimizes the investment that the newcomer can and should make in his or her new home.

Naturalization policies send the clearest message about the expectations of the host society for the immigrant. In nations like Japan (and until recently Germany) where it is virtually impossible to become a citizen, the message is clear: You are, and will always be, a visitor here.

Immigration policies, then, are a powerful determinant of the behavior and social impact of immigrants. We have seen in the preceding chapters that the social integration of immigrants is highest and negative activity lowest in immigrant nations relative to nonimmigrant nations. The more inclusive the immigration policy, the less disruptive and more beneficial immigration is to the society.

While immigration policies are central to setting expectations for immigrants, these policies, in turn, are influenced by other factors in society including the history of immigration. It would not be prudent, or even possible, for some nonimmigrant nations to simply adopt the immigration policies of immigrant nations. Even if it were politically feasible, it would probably lead to massive social disruption and anti-immigrant feeling. As we noted in earlier chapters, cultural homogeneity and relatively rigid institutional arrangements are mainstays of social control in many nonimmigrant societies. Introducing large numbers of persons with different cultural backgrounds who do not share the norms of the host society is likely to cause considerable disruption in these societies, much more than would occur in immigrant nations. Other social institutions must change in these nations before more inclusive immigration policies could be adopted.

There are several major institutional arrangements that support the accommodation of immigrants and that seem to distinguish immigrant from nonimmigrant nations. One of these institutional arrangements is the relative involvement of the government and the private sector in the assimilation of immigrants. In the nonimmigrant nations examined here, the government is heavily involved in efforts to accommodate newcomers. In immigrant nations, much of the accommodation is accomplished through self-help within the immigrant communities. Earlier arrivals assist newer arrivals. This privatization of immigration removes a potentially contentious issue from public debate and the costs of assimilation from the public budgets.

Changing this (and other) institutional arrangement is not trivial and not without its risks. Privatization of philanthropic and social service activities, for example, would be a huge step for most of the countries in question. It raises the prospects of inequity that may be at odds with the understanding of citizenship in these countries.

This respite may be short lived, however, in light of the demographic transition facing most industrialized nations. The fertility rate for the native population in the countries observed here is declining and life expectancy is increasing. The result of an aging population will be less workers supporting larger dependent populations. Japan provides the most dramatic example of this phenomenon. This, in turn, could result in substantial renegotiation of the social contract between citizens and their government in these social democracies. Benefits will need to be scaled back considerably, retirement will be delayed, and means tests will be applied to benefits formerly considered entitlements. Increasing immigration is another way to increase the productive population in these nations and to lessen the impact of demographic transition. Indeed, the age structure of the population in nonimmigrant nations is already older than that of immigrant nations, a fact largely due to the lack of immigration in the former. As such, the potential disruption resulting from demographic transition is of sufficient magnitude and the possible beneficial effects of immigration likely enough to make it worth considering substantial changes in social policies that would make immigration less problematic for these nations.

Index

Page numbers with *t* indicate tables.

aborigines: Australian naturalization and, 96; dictation test for immigration to Australia, 91
Adjustment Assistance Program, Canada's, 69
admission laws and rules: in cross-national comparisons, 4; social integration and, 263. *See also* point system, Canadian
Afghanistan, asylum seekers in U.K. from, 131
Africa: asylum seekers in U.K. from, 131, 132; Australian naturalization and, 96; Australian public opinion on immigrants from, 118, 118*t*, 119; British entry of Asian stock from, 125; dictation test for immigration to Australia from, 91; French rejections of asylum seekers from, 153; French residence permits for immigrants from, 155; immigrants to Australia from, 98; immigrants to Canada from, 57, 64; immigrants to France from, 147, 148, 149*t*, 167*t*, 169; immigrants to U.S. from, 21; student applicants to Great Britain from, 127; U.S. naturalized citizens from, 26
age: of Australian immigrants versus native populations, 103; of Canadian immigrants versus native populations, 70, 70*t*; Canadian immigration criteria on, 60*t*; structure in nonimmigrant nations, social policies and, 271
agricultural immigrants: in Great Britain, 127; Polish, in Germany, 171–72; in U.S., 15, 16. *See also* contract laborers, U.S. exclusion of; farm workers
Aid to Families With Dependent Children (AFDC), 36
airlines, Canadian penalties for transporting illegal passengers on, 58
Akbari, Ather H., 76
Albrecht, Hans-Jorg, 179–80
Algerians in France, 148, 149*t*, 150, 151; criminal involvement of, 160; naturalization of, 153; residence permits for, 155
Alien Decree, and foreigners residing in Germany, 172
Aliens Act (Germany, 1965), 173

Aliens Act (Great Britain, 1905), 123–28
Aliens Restrictions Act (Great Britain, 1919), 124
ambivalent nations, 219, 223–25; conflicted pluralism and, 221*t*; default pluralism and, 221*t*, 223–25; public opinion on immigrants and, 247
anarchists, U.S. exclusion of, 13
Anti-Terrorism and Effective Death Penalty Act (AEDPA) (U.S., 1996), 17
art visas, Japanese, 190, 191*t*
Ashcroft, John, 6
Asia: Australian public opinion on immigrants from, 118, 118*t*, 119; British public opinion on support for immigrants from, 142; dictation test for immigration to Australia from, 91; estimated net immigration to Great Britain, 1953–1962, 128*t*; immigrants in Canada from, 56, 64, 66; immigrants to Australia from, 90, 96, 98, 99*t*, 115; immigrants to France from, 147, 149*t*; immigration to Great Britain from, 124; immigration to Japan from, 189; refugees in France from, 152; student applicants to Great Britain from, 127; U.S. exclusion of immigrants from, 12; U.S. naturalized citizens from, 26
assimilation: government versus private support of, 271; social integration and, 251
assisted passage, Australian immigration and, 88, 90, 102
asylum seekers: applications in Great Britain by, 124, 130–32; British support for, 135; Canadian admissions of, 66–67; Canadian criteria for, 58, 61; in cross-national comparisons, 4; French rejections of, 153; French restrictions on, 151; in Germany, 173, 174, 176, 186; in Great Britain, unemployment among, 137; U.S. regulations on, 15, 17–18; U.S. visa allocations for FY 1995, 20*t*. *See also* refugees
Australia: annual admissions to, 212; British public opinion on immigrants from, 139, 140*t*; as choice for cross-national comparisons, 3; as immigrant nation, 211, 219; immigration policy openness versus public opinion in, 245, 246; incarceration ratio for immigrants and nonimmigrants, 230*t*; net immigration and population growth from 1788–1920, 88*t*; offense-specific stock incarceration rates by birth country, 232*t*; as Old Commonwealth nation, 124; U.S. immigrants from, 21. *See also* Old Commonwealth
Australia, immigrants in: average attitude toward, 246–47; birthplace by regions, 1989–1999, 100*t*; criminal involvement of, 110–13, 120, 231; drug offenses by nonimmigrants versus, 231; as entrepreneurs, 107–9; illegal, 212; intermarriage of, 110; internal regulations for, 215; language proficiency, 109–10; naturalization, 96–97, 101, 121n26, 215, 254; public opinion on, 113, 115–19, 120, 241–42; public opinion on non-European, 116*t*; public opinion on numbers admitted, 117*t*; public opinion on specific ethnic groups, 115*t*; screening of, 213, 214; social integration, 103–9; social integration in economic institutions, 255; social integration of, 217, 218, 219; stock and flow of, 97–102; on welfare, 109
Australia, immigrants to, 259, 261
Australia Bureau of Statistics: census on incarcerated native-born versus immigrants, 110
Australian immigration policies: admissions laws of, 90–96; controlled pluralism of, 222; dictation test for, 90, 91–92; dimensions of, 220*t*; eligibility components and settler arrival categories, for 1990–1991 and 1991–1992, 93*t*; entry permits for, 92;

historical background of, 87–90; integration policies, 102–3; major legislation on, 90; net by periods and annual averages, 89*t*; net by periods with annual averages and percentage distribution, 99*t*; policy oversight in, 216; program planning levels, 1991–1992 and 1992–1993, 94*t*
Australian-Jewish Welfare Society, 102
Australian miracle, 226n1
Austria-Hungary, U.S. immigrants from, 21

Bangladesh, asylum seekers in U.K. from, 131
birth rate, of Canadian immigrants, 71
borders, social integration and length of, 265
Bracero Program, U.S., 13; end of, 14
British Nationality Act (1948), 125
British Nationality Act (1981), 126, 129, 144
British Nationality and the Status of Aliens Act (1914), 125
British North American Act (1867), section 95, 55
British subjects: Australian naturalization and, 96; Canadian immigration criteria for, 56
Bureau of Immigration, U.S., 11
business immigrants: to Australia, 92; Canadian criteria for, 58, 59*t*. *See also* labor shortages; work visas and permits
Business Skills category, Australian, 93, 94
business travelers to U.S., 18

Cambodia, Japanese opinion on refugees from, 200
Canada: as choice for cross-national comparisons, 3; controlled pluralism of, 222; French immigrants from, 149*t*; as immigrant nation, 211, 219; incarceration ratio for immigrants and nonimmigrants, 230*t*; as Old Commonwealth, 124; U.S. immigrants from, 20; U.S. naturalized citizens from, 26. *See also* Old Commonwealth
Canada, immigrants in: age structure of native populations versus, 70, 70*t*; birth rate of, 71; country of origin and number of, 64*t*; criminal involvement of, 76, 80, 231; demographic and socioeconomic characteristics of, 70–76; dependency on government of, 75–76; drug offenses by nonimmigrants versus, 231; educational attainment, 71, 72*t*; ethnic composition of, 62, 63*t*, 64, 65*t*; flow from 1946–2000, 62*t*; gender of native populations versus, 70–71, 72*t*; illegal, 212–13; income by sources, 76, 77*t*; income by gender and immigration status, 1996, 75*t*; internal regulations for, 215; in labor force, 72–75; languages of, 72; marital status of, 71; net public treasury effect on nonimmigrant households by, 76, 79*t*; public opinion on, 80, 81*t*, 82, 241; social integration of, 217, 255, 259; stock and flow of, 61–67; taxpaying native-born versus taxpaying, 76, 78*t*
Canadian Act (1931), 56
Canadian immigration policies, 55–85; on annual admissions, 212; decentralized 246; dimensions of, 220*t*; historical background and major legislation, 55–61; on illegal immigrants, 69; on integration, 68–69; internal regulation of, 67; naturalization and, 67–68, 215, 254; point system of, 58, 59–61*t*, 61, 213–14; policy oversight in, 216; public opinion versus openness of, 245, 246
Caribbean, U.S. immigrants from, 20
carte de sejour temporaire (CST), 150. *See also* residence permits
Castro, Fidel, 14
Central America, U.S. immigrants from, 20

children born abroad to permanent residents, U.S. visa allocations for, 20*t*
Chile, refugees in France from, 152
China, Japanese public opinion on refugees from, 201
Chinese Exclusion Act (U.S., 1882), 12, 13
Chinese immigrants: Australian naturalization of, 101; Australian restrictions on, 120n 7; Canada's policies open to, 57; Canadian tax on, 55; labor shortage in France and, 147; to U.S., 20, 22
Chinese Immigration Act (Canada, 1923), 56
Chirac, Jacques, 6–7
citizenship: British laws on, 125, 126; criminal statistics and birth country versus, 229; immigration and U.S. laws on, 13; Japanese, 195. *See also* naturalization
Citizenship and Immigration Canada, 68; Refugee Branch of, 69
clandestine workers in Japan, 206n 4
Clinton, Bill, 17
Commission on Racial Equality, British, 135
common-law nations, internal regulations for immigrants in, 215–16
Commons, John R., 39
Commonwealth: British citizenship registration by citizens from, 132; British labor recruitment during WWII from, 124. *See also* Great Britain; New Commonwealth; Old Commonwealth
Commonwealth Immigration Act (British, 1962), 125, 129
Commonwealth Immigration Act (British, 1968), 125
community, immigration impact on, 5. *See also* social integration
comparative immigration: admissions and preferences, 212; dimensions of, 209–11, 220*t*; discretion for immigration authorities, 216–17; illegal immigration and, 212–13; immigrant nation policies, 219; internal regulation of immigrants, 215–16; naturalization, 215; policies across nations, 211–12; preferences and exclusions, 213–15. *See also* cross-national comparisons
Concessional Family category, Australian, 93, 95
conflicted pluralism, 221*t*, 223–25
contained pluralism, 221–22*t*, 225–26
contract laborers, U.S. exclusion of, 12. *See also* employment, arranged; employment-based immigrants; labor force
controlled pluralism, 219, 221*t*, 222–23
control policies, 215–16, 270; in France, 154–55; in Great Britain, 133–34; social integration and, 263–64; U.S., 15, 20*t*, 26–28
Convention Refugees, Canada, 61, 66, 67*t*, 84n 13
Cornelius, Wayne, 198, 205
crime by immigrants, 5; in Australia, 110–13; in Australia, by birthplace in 1971, 111*t*; in Australia, by birthplace in 1985, 112*t*; in Australia, by birthplace in 1992–1997, 112*t*; in Australia, incarcerated native-born versus, by offense, 113*t*; in Australia, offense-specific incarceration rates by birth country, 114*t*; in Australia, restrictions on, 91; in Canada, 76, 80; deportation from U.S. and, 28; exclusion from U.S. and, 12; in France, 159–64, 169; in France, 1991 incarcerations, 161*t*; in France, annual rates including or excluding immigration offenses, 163*t*; in France, by nationality, 1995, 162*t*; in France, by offense, 1993, 162*t*; in France, estimated offenses by citizenship and crime type, 1991, 159*t*; in France, loss of citizenship for, 154; in France, police charges including or excluding immigration offenses, 163*t*; in Germany, 179–82, 186; in Germany, by age and gender,

182*t*; in Germany, by offense type, 181*t,* 183; in Great Britain, 137–39; in Japan, 198, 200, 200*t*; in U.S., 39–44, 53n 44; in U.S., by citizenship status and offense in, 41*t*
crime comparisons across countries, 227–38; complexities and limitations of, 227–30; cultural homogeneity and, 236; exclusiveness policies and, 234–35; "immigrant" definition and, 235; immigration policies enforcement and, 235–36; incarceration ratio for immigrants and nonimmigrants, 231*t*; incarceration ratios, 230*t*; rates of, 230–34; selectivity policies and, 236–37; social integration policies and, 236–37
Criminal Alien Report, U.S., 41–42
cross-national comparisons: characterization of, 4–5; choices for, 3–4. *See also* comparative immigration
Cuba: refugees to U.S. from, 14, 217, 218; U.S. immigrants from, 20; U.S. public opinion on immigrants from, 45
cultural activity visas, Japanese, 190, 193*t*
cultural homogeneity: criminal comparisons across countries and, 236; of immigrant groups, perceived threat of, 265–66
cultural integration: criminal comparisons across countries and, 236–37; social integration and, 252
culturally unassimable, Canadian criteria for, 55
Current Population Survey (U.S.), foreign born and immigrants in, 24

Declaration of Independence, U.S. immigration policy and, 11
Decret no. 81-405 (France, 1981), 151
default pluralism, 221*t,* 223–25
demographic factors, Canadian point system on, 60–61*t*
denial rate for citizen applicants in U.S., 26
dependency: of asylum seekers in Great Britain, 131; immigration impact on, 5; social integration and, 260*t*. *See also* income support, for U.S. immigrants; unemployment; welfare
dependent visas, Japanese, 190, 194*t*
deportation: of Japanese immigrants, 197–98; of legal immigrants from U.S., 27–28
designated activity visas, Japanese, 190
Designated Refugees, Canadian, 61, 66, 67*t,* 84n 13
d'Estaing, Valéry Giscard, 147, 168, 243
dictation test, Australian, 90, 91–92; naturalization and, 96
Dillingham Commission, 12, 39
diplomatic visas, Japanese, 190, 191*t*
direct immigration policies, definition of, 4
Displaced Persons Act (U.S., post WWII), 13
Distinguished Talent category, Australian, 93
diversity immigrants, 19; social integration and, 251; U.S. regulations on, 16, 17; U.S. visa allocations for FY 1995, 20*t*
Dovey Committee, on criminal involvement by Australian immigrants, 110
drug offenses: of immigrants and nonimmigrants, 231; by immigrants in Australia, 113, 120; by immigrants in France, 159*t,* 160, 169; by immigrants in Germany, 180, 181, 183; by immigrants in Great Britain, 138–39; by immigrants in Japan, 200; by immigrants in U.S., 40–41, 43–44; incarceration ratio of immigrants and nonimmigrants for, 231*t*; sojourner residents and, 229. *See also* crime by immigrants

Earned Income Tax Credit, U.S., 36, 38
earnings, average weekly: of Australian immigrants, 107; of full-time Australian employees by

birthplace, 107*t*. *See also* incomes, average
economic immigrants: Canadian admissions by year, 66*t*; Canadian Designated and Open Occupation List, 58; Canadian flow of, 64; seeking U.S. admission, 11. *See also* employment-based immigrants; entrepreneur immigrants
economic institutions, social integration and, 254–56
education: for British immigrants, 134, 137; Canadian immigration criteria on, 59*t*; for French immigrants, 158, 158*t*; for German immigrants, 178, 179; for U.S. immigrants, 33, 36, 38
educational institutions: immigration impact on, 5; social integration and, 256, 260*t*
Egypt, Canada on immigrants from, 57
El Salvador: estimated U.S. illegal immigrants from, 29, 29*t*; U.S. protected status for undocumented immigrants from, 17
Employer Nomination Scheme, Australian, 93
employment, arranged: Canadian immigration criteria on, 60*t*. *See also* contract laborers, U.S. exclusion of
employment-based immigrants: post-WWI in France, 147. *See also* work visas and permits
employment-based immigrants in Great Britain: average income and employment rates for, 135–37; under First Commonwealth Immigration Act, 125; under Immigration Act of 1971, 126, 127; indefinite residence status in 1996 for, 129; policies for control of, 133–34; during WWII, 124
employment-based immigrants in U.S.: naturalization rates for, 26*t*; occupational status of, 34–35*t*; regulations on, 16, 19; visa allocations for FY 1995, 20*t*. *See also* contract laborers, U.S. exclusion of
engineering visas, Japanese, 190, 192*t*
England. *See* Great Britain
English-speakers: among immigrants in Canada, 72, 73*t*; among immigrants in Great Britain, 137; among immigrants in U.S., 30, 33*t*; Australian criteria for, 95; Australian dictation test and, 91; Australian Independent Business Skills category and, 94; British naturalizations of, 133; British work permits for, 127; Canadian point system on, 60*t*
entertainment visas, Japanese, 190, 193*t*
entrepreneur immigrants: in Australia, 107–9; in Australia, employed immigrants versus, 108*t*; Canadian criteria for, 58; to Great Britain, 127; U.S. regulations on, 16. *See also* economic immigrants; employment-based immigrants
entry permits, Australian, 92
Espenshade, Thomas J., 40
"Ethnic Minorities, Crime, and Criminal Justice in Germany" (Albrecht), 179–80
Europe: asylum seekers in U.K. from, 132; Australian public opinion on immigrants from, 118, 118*t*, 119; British labor recruitment during WWII from, 124; immigrants in Australia from, 90, 98, 99*t*, 102; immigrants in Canada from, 56, 66; immigrants in France from, 149*t*; immigrants in Great Britain from, 132; immigrants in U.S. from, 20, 21, 22; U.S. public opinion on immigrants from, 45
European Community (EC): British public opinion on immigrants from, 139, 140*t*; French immigrants from, 148, 150–51
European Economic Community (EEC): German regulations for labor from, 173
European Social Charter, French immigrants and, 151
exclusion: criminal involvement and policies of, 234–35; U.S. regulations

on, 13, 19. *See also* deportation; quotas
extended voluntary departures, U.S. regulations on, 17

families, immigration impact on, 5
families of Canadian citizens: Canadian admission priorities for, 58; Canadian admission by year, 66*t*; Canadian point system on, 61*t*; Canadian regulations on, 56; flow of, 64
Family Migration category, Australia, 93, 94
family reunion immigrants, Australia, 92, 101, 106
family reunion immigrants, France, 148, 151
family reunion immigrants, Germany, 173, 174
family reunion immigrants, Great Britain, 126–27, 129, 134, 144
family-sponsored immigrants, U.S.: naturalization rates for, 26*t*; occupational distribution of, 34–35*t*; occupational status of, 34–35*t*; regulations on, 16, 19; U.S. immigration regulations on, 16; visa allocations for FY 1995, 20*t*
farm workers: post-WWII Canadian regulations on, 56. *See also* agricultural immigrants; contract laborers, U.S. exclusion of
Federal Republic of Yugoslavia. *See* Yugoslavia
felony rates: for immigrants versus total U.S. population, 42–43, 42*t*. *See also* crime by immigrants
fertility rates: of British immigrants, 137; of French immigrants and native-born, 156, 157*t*; of German immigrants and native-born, 177–78; social integration and, 258–59, 260*t*; social policies, age structure and, 271
Fifteenth Amendment, U.S., on voting rights, 51–52n1
First Commonwealth Immigration Act (British, 1962), 125
Foran Act (U.S., 1885), 12
France: as ambivalent nation, 219, 223–26; annual admissions to, 212; as choice for cross-national comparisons, 3; cultural homogeneity in, 266; immigrants in Canada from, 56; incarceration ratio for immigrants and nonimmigrants, 230*t*; police statistics in, 228. *See also* Le Pen, Jean-Marie
France, immigrants in: annual rates of police matters including or excluding immigration offenses, 163*t*; average attitude toward, 246; control policies for, 154–55; criminal involvement by nationality, 1995, 162*t*; criminal involvement by offense, 1993, 162*t*; criminal involvement of, 159–64, 231; criminal involvement of citizens versus, 233, 233*t*; demographic and socioeconomic characteristics of, 156–59; drug offenses by nonimmigrants versus, 231; estimated criminal offenses by citizenship and crime type, 1991, 159*t*; fertility rates of nonimmigrants versus, 157*t*; illegal, 148, 154, 155–56, 212, 213; incarcerations in 1991, 161*t*; internal regulations for, 215, 216; naturalization, 153–54, 215, 254; police charges including or excluding immigration offenses of, 163*t*; public opinion on, 164–68, 243; public opinion on particular groups of, 167*t*; in schools, 158*t*; social integration in economic institutions, 255; social integration of, 217, 261–62; stock and flow of, 153
French immigration policies, 211–12; dimensions of, 220*t*; evolution of, 1921–1990, 149*t*; historical background and major legislation, 147–53; preferences in, 214
French language, speakers of: among Canadian immigrants, 72, 73*t*; Canadian point system on, 60*t*

Gallaby, Frank, 102–3
general eligibility immigrants to Australia, 92
general visas, Japanese, 190
German immigration: dimensions of, 220*t*; historical background and major legislation, 171–74; policy oversight in, 217; preferences in, 214
Germany: annual admissions to, 212; anti-immigration sentiment and policies in, 171; asylum seekers in, 131; as choice for cross-national comparisons, 3; contained pluralism in, 225–26; cultural homogeneity in, 266; incarceration ratio for immigrants and nonimmigrants, 230*t*; naturalization of Australian immigrants from, 101; as nonimmigrant nation, 211, 219; U.S. immigrants from, 21
Germany, immigrants in: average attitude toward, 246; criminal involvement by age and gender, 182*t*; criminal involvement by offense type, 181*t*; criminal involvement of, 179–82, 231; criminal involvement of citizens versus, 233, 234*t*; demographic and socioeconomic characteristics of, 177–79; drug offenses by nonimmigrants versus, 231; employment distribution of nationals and, 180*t*; illegal, 212–13; internal regulations for, 215, 216; naturalization of, 176–77, 186, 215; public opinion on, 183, 184*t*, 184–85, 244; public opinion toward particular groups of, 185*t*; social integration of, 217, 218–19, 255, 262; stock and flow of, 174–76
Giscard d'Estaing, Valéry, 147, 168, 243
Glover, Stephen, 137
good neighbor councils, Australian immigrant integration and, 102
Great Britain: as ambivalent nation, 219, 223–24; annual admissions to, 212; asylum seekers in, 130–32; Australian immigrants from, 90, 98, 99*t*; Australian public opinion on immigrants from, 118, 118*t*, 119; as choice for cross-national comparisons, 3; citizenship in, 125; criminal act definitions in, 228; cultural homogeneity in, 266; "school leaving" in, 253
Great Britain, immigrants in: average attitude toward, 246, 247; Canadian heterogeneity, 55–56; change in stock of, 1984–1990, 133*t*; criminal involvement of, 137–39, 231; drug offenses by nonimmigrants versus, 231; educational participation, 267n3; employment distribution of nationals and, 136*t*; illegal, 134, 212; incarceration ratio for nonimmigrants and, 230*t*; internal regulations for, 215; naturalization, 132–33, 215, 254, 266n1; policies for control of, 133–34; public opinion on, 139–43, 242–43; social integration of, 217, 218, 255, 261; stock and flow of, 128–29; victimization by ethnic group, 138, 138*t*
Great Britain's immigration policies, 144–45, 211–12; dimensions of, 220*t*; historical background and major legislation, 123–28; public opinion versus, 245; race-based preferences in, 214–15; social and policy integration of, 134–37; U.S. immigrants from, 21
Greece: German immigrants from, 175; naturalization of Australian immigrants from, 101; nonspecific German work permits for immigrants from, 174
Guatemala, estimated U.S. illegal immigrants from, 29, 29*t*
guest-worker policies, 270; U.S. consideration of, 2–3. *See also* agricultural immigrants; contract laborers, U.S. exclusion of; labor shortages

H-1B temporary visas, for skilled foreign laborers in U.S., 16
Haiti: asylum seekers in U.K. from, 131; U.S. public opinion on immigrants from, 45
Hansen, Marcus, 11
Hart-Celler Act (U.S., 1965), 14
Hazelhurst, Kathleen, 111
Hollifield, James, 198, 205
Hong Kong: British restrictions on immigration from, 124–25, 144; Canadian refugees from, 66; U.S. immigrants from, 22. *See also* New Commonwealth
Host Program, Canada's, 69
housing, for German immigrants, 179
humanitarian immigrants: Australian, 94, 101; Canadian regulations on, 58–59
humanities and international services visas, Japanese, 190, 192*t*
Hungarian Uprising (1956), refugees to U.S. after, 14, 19

illegal immigrants in Canada, 11, 69, 212–13
illegal immigrants in France, 155–56, 169, 223; naturalization of, 154; post-WWII, 148
illegal immigrants in Great Britain, 134
illegal immigrants in U.S., 15, 28–29, 41–42, 212; criminal involvement in Los Angeles, 40; estimates by country of birth in 1980, 29*t*; estimates of criminal involvement by, 42, 43; during FY 1990, 24; incarceration rates for, 41; social welfare for, 38–39
illegal immigration: comparisons of, 212–13; in immigrant versus nonimmigrant nations, 211
Illegal Immigration Reform and Immigrant Responsibility Act (IRIRA) (U.S., 1997), 17–18
immigrant nations: characteristics of, 209–11; conflicted pluralism, 221*t*, 223–25; contained pluralism, 221–22*t*, 225–26; controlled pluralism, 219, 221*t*, 222–23; default pluralism, 221*t*, 223–25; immigration policy in, 219; immigration policy oversight, 216–17; laissez-faire pluralism, 219, 221*t*, 222–23. *See also* ambivalent nations; nonimmigrant nations
immigrants: goals for, 269; perceived threats from, 1, 265–66
immigrant self-help groups: assimilation assistance by, 271; U.S., 38. *See also* nongovernmental organizations
Immigration Act (Canada, 1923), 55
Immigration Act (Canada, 1952), 57
Immigration Act (Canada, 1976), 57–58
Immigration Act (Great Britain, 1971), 125–26, 129
Immigration Act (U.S., 1917), 12
Immigration Act (U.S., 1921), 12–13
Immigration Act (U.S., 1990), 16, 24
Immigration Advisory Council (of Australia), study on immigrants' criminal involvement, 110
Immigration and Nationality Act (U.S., 1952), 13–14
Immigration and Nationality Act (U.S., 1976), 14
Immigration and Naturalization Service (U.S., INS), 15; Criminal Alien Report, 41–42
Immigration Control and Refugee Recognition Law (ICRRL) (Japan, 1993), 189–90
immigration policies, 270–71; criminal comparisons across countries and, 236; in cross-national comparisons, 4; social integration and, 262. *See also* ambivalent nations; comparative immigration; immigrant nations; nonimmigrant nations
Immigration Reform and Control Act (U.S., 1986), 15; visa allocations for FY 1995, 20*t*
Immigration Restriction Act (Australia, 1901), 90–92
Immigration Settlement and Adaptation Program (ISAP), Canada's, 68–69

"Impact of Immigration on Canada's Treasury, circa 1900" (Akbari), 76
implementation, immigration policy, 4
incarceration rates. *See* crime by immigrants
incomes, average: economic institution integration and, 255, 260*t*. *See also* earnings, average weekly
income support, for U.S. immigrants, 33, 36, 38. *See also* dependency; welfare
Independent Business Skills category, Australian, 94
independent immigrants to Australia, 92, 93, 95
India: British public opinion on immigrants from, 139, 140*t*; British restrictions on immigration from, 124–25, 126, 144; estimated net immigration to Great Britain, 1953–1962, 128*t*. *See also* New Commonwealth
indirect immigration policies, definition of, 4
individual economic enterprise: U.S. immigrants seeking, 11. *See also* economic immigrants; employment-based immigrants; entrepreneur immigrants
Indochinese Refugee Resettlement Program (U.S., 1975), 14
instruction visas, Japanese, 190, 192*t*
integration policies: Australian, 102–3; Canadian, 68–69; United States, 33, 36, 38–39. *See also* social integration
intermarriage: between Australians and immigrants, 110; between French and immigrants, 156; between Germans and immigrants, 177; between Japanese and immigrants, 205; social integration and, 257–58, 260*t*
Internal Security Act (U.S., 1950), 29
intracompany transfer visas, Japanese, 190, 192–93*t*
investment and business management visas, Japanese, 190, 191*t*
Iran, U.S. public opinion on immigrants from, 45
Ireland: Australian immigrants from, 90, 98; Australian public opinion on immigrants from, 118, 118*t*, 119; British immigrants from, 132; U.S. immigrants from, 21
Israel, immigrants to, 87, 119
Italy, U.S. immigrants from, 21

Japan: annual admissions to, 212; as choice for cross-national comparisons, 3; criminal immigrants in Canada from, 80; cultural homogeneity in, 265–66; as nonimmigrant nation, 211, 219, 225, 226; preferences in, 215; Vietnamese refugees in, 197
Japan, immigrants in: criminal involvement of, 198, 200, 200*t*, 231; deportation of, 197–98; drug offenses by nonimmigrants versus, 231; estimates of visa overstayers by nationality, 1990–1993, 199*t*; illegal, 212; incarceration ratio for nonimmigrants and, 230*t*; internal regulations for, 216; naturalization, 215, 254; numbers of, 196–97; public opinion on, 200–205, 244–45; social integration of, 217, 251, 255
Japanese immigration policies: dimensions of, 220*t*; historical background and major legislation, 189–90, 195–96; residence statutes and authorized activity, 191–95*t*
Japanese Nationality Law (1950), 195
job prestige, social integration and, 260*t*
job training, in immigrant versus nonimmigrant nations, 210–11
Johnson Act (U.S., 1921), on quotas, 12–13
journalism visas, Japanese, 190, 191*t*
judicial review, U.S. deportation procedures and, 28

King, Mackenzie, 56–57
Korea: Japanese immigrants from, 226; U.S. immigrants from, 20; U.S. public opinion on immigrants from, 45

Kosovars, as asylum seekers in Great Britain, 130

labor force: of Australian native-born and foreign-born by birthplace, 104*t*; distribution of German immigrants and nationals in, 180*t*; French immigrants in, 158, 168; German immigrants in, 178, 179*t*, 186; participation of Australian immigrants, 103; social integration and participation in, 254–56, 260*t*. *See also* employment-based immigrants
labor shortages: immigrants to Australia and, 92; immigrants to Germany and, 171–73; immigrants to Japan and, 202–4, 205. *See also* guest-worker policies
laissez-faire pluralism, 219, 221*t*, 222–23
language facility: of immigrants in Australia, 109–10; social integration and, 257, 260*t*
language instruction: in immigrant versus nonimmigrant nations, 210–11; for newcomers to Australia, 102, 103; for newcomers to Germany, 178, 186; for newcomers to Great Britain, 134
Language Instruction for Newcomers to Canada (LINC), 69
Latin America: immigration to Japan from, 189, 226. *See also* South America
Lebanon: naturalization of Australian immigrants from, 101; refugees in France from, 152
Lee, Matthew T., 40
legal aliens: in cross-national comparisons, 4. *See also* illegal immigration
legal and accounting services visas, Japanese, 190, 192*t*
Le Pen, Jean-Marie, 6–7, 147, 168, 243
literacy: Australia's dictation test, 90–91; U.S. on, 12. *See also* education
loggers, post-WWII Canadian regulations on, 56
London, Herbert, 115
Los Angeles, Calif., criminal immigrants in, 39–40

Malta, Canadian immigrants from, 56
Manpower and Immigration Council Act (Canada, 1967), 57
Martin, Philip, 171, 198, 205
Martinez, Ramiro, 40
McCarran-Walters Act (U.S., 1952), 13–14
medical care, for U.S. immigrants, 33, 36
medical histories: Australian exclusion due to, 91; U.S. exclusion and, 13
medical services visas, Japanese, 190, 192*t*
mental health services, for German immigrants, 179
mental incapacities: Australian restrictions on, 90; Canadian immigration and, 55
Mexico: estimated U.S. illegal immigrants from, 29, 29*t*; U.S. immigrants deported back to, 28; U.S. immigrants from, 20, 22; U.S. naturalized citizens from, 26; U.S. public opinion on immigrants from, 45
Middle East: Australian public opinion on immigrants from, 118, 118*t*, 119; Canadian immigrants from, 64
Migrant Education Program, Australian, 102
Migrant Selection System, Australia, 92
Migration and Refugee Assistance Act (U.S., 1960), 14
military service, citizenship in France and, 154
Miller, John, 26
miners, post-WWII Canadian regulations on, 56
Ministry of Citizenship and Immigration, Canada, Designated and Open Occupation List, 58
Ministry of Justice, France, residence permits from, 155
Ministry of Justice, Japan: change in status reports to, 206; permanent

resident status application to, 190, 195–96, 205
Ministry of Labor, France, work permits from, 155
Muller, Thomas, 40
multiculturalism: Australian immigration policy and, 103; U.S. immigrants on, 50

National Asylum Support Service, British Home Office's, 135
National Crime Victimization Survey, on criminal immigrants in U.S., 40
National Front Party, France, 168, 243. *See also* Le Pen, Jean-Marie
Nationality and Citizenship Act (Australia, 1903), 96–97
National Prisoners Survey, Australia, 110–11
National Quota Act (U.S., 1924), 13
nativity, criminal statistics and citizenship versus, 229
Naturalization and Citizenship Act (Australia, 1948), 96
naturalization: in Australia, 101, 121n 26; Australian requirements for, 96–97; in Canada, 67–68; comparative, 215; in France, 153–54, 168–69; in Germany, 176–77, 186; in Great Britain, 132–33; in immigrant versus nonimmigrant nations, 210; in Japan, 195–96; patterns across nations, 253–54, 260*t*; policies on, 270; social integration and, 263, 264; U.S. approvals for, 26; U.S. requirements for, 24–25; in U.S., by class of admission, 26*t*; in U.S. for FY 1991 by birth country, 27*t*
Netherlands: asylum seekers in, 131; naturalization of Australian immigrants from, 101
New Commonwealth: British antidiscrimination legislation in support of, 135; British public opinion on immigrants from, 142–43; immigration to Great Britain, 128*t*, 129*t*; restrictions on immigration to U.K. from, 132, 135. *See also* Great Britain
New Zealand: British public opinion on immigrants from, 139, 140*t*; immigrants in Australia from, 101; immigrants in U.S. from, 21; as Old (British) Commonwealth, 124. *See also* Old Commonwealth
noneconomic institutions: immigration effects on, 1–2; variations in international data on, 2. *See also* social integration
nongovernmental organizations: Canadian grants for immigrant integration to, 68–69. *See also* immigrant self-help groups; private philanthropic organizations, U.S. immigrants and
nonimmigrant nations, 209; age structure and social policies in, 271; contained pluralism, 221–22*t*, 225; immigration policies adoption by, 270–71; nonpluralism, 222*t*, 225–26; policy oversight in, 216–17. *See also* ambivalent nations; immigrant nations
nonpluralism, 222*t*, 225–26
nonspecific work permits, for German immigrants, 173–74
Non-White Immigration and the "White Australia" Policy (London), 115
North America, immigrants in Canada from, 66
Numerical Assessment System, Australian, 92–94

occupational institutions, immigration impact on, 5. *See also* employment-based immigrants; entrepreneur immigrants
occupations of Australian immigrants: average distribution for 1979–1983, 105*t*; distribution of, 103, 105–6, 106*t*; restrictions on, 91
occupations of Canadian immigrants, 72–75; by age and gender, 73, 74*t*; education and skill levels by age and

gender, 73–75, 74*t*; point system criteria on, 59*t*
occupations of immigrants: in France, 158–59; in Germany, 175*t*; social integration and, 255–56
Office for the Protection of Refugees and Stateless Persons (OFPRA), France, 152
Office of National del' Immigration (ONI), France, 148
Office of Refugee Resettlement, U.S., 14–15, 218
Office of U.S. Coordination for Refugee Affairs, 14–15
official business visas, Japanese, 190, 191*t*
Ogden, Philip E., 154
Oklahoma City bombing (1996), U.S. regulations on terrorist groups after, 17
Old Commonwealth, 124. *See also* Great Britain
One Nation Party, Australia, 118
open immigration policies, conjecture for, 2

Pakistan: asylum seekers in U.K. from, 131; British public opinion on immigrants from, 139, 140*t*; British restrictions on immigration from, 124–25, 144; estimated net immigration to Great Britain, 1953–1962, 128*t*. *See also* New Commonwealth
Passel, Jeffrey S., 42
patrials: British naturalization of Irish, 133; Immigration Act (Great Britain, 1971) on, 126
permanent entry permits, Australia, 92
Personal Responsibility and Work Opportunity Reevaluation Act (PWORA) (U.S., 1996), 17
personal suitability, Canadian point system on, 60*t*
Philippines: naturalization of Australian immigrants from, 101; U.S. immigrants from, 20
physical incapacities, Canadian immigration and, 55. *See also* medical histories
pluralism, social integration and, 251. *See also* conflicted pluralism; contained pluralism; controlled pluralism
Plyer v. Doe (U.S.), on public education for undocumented immigrants' children, 38
point system, Canadian, 58, 59–61*t*, 61, 213–14
Poland, German agricultural laborers from, 171–72
Polish ex-servicemen in U.K. and Italy, Canadian regulations on, 56
political activities and ideologies, U.S. exclusion and, 13
Polynesia: Australian naturalization and, 96; dictation test for immigration to Australia from, 91
Portugal: immigrants in Germany from, 175; immigrants in Great Britain from, 132
Preferential Family category, Australian, 93, 95
president, U.S., refugee flow authority for, 15
preuniversity study visas, Japanese, 190, 193*t*
private philanthropic organizations, U.S. immigrants and, 38. *See also* immigrant self-help groups; nongovernmental organizations
professorship visas, Japanese, 190, 191*t*
prostitutes: Australian restrictions on, 91; Japanese entertainment visas and, 190; U.S. exclusion of, 12
public opinion: about immigrants and immigration policy, 5–6; average, toward immigrants, 246–47, 248; British, on particular groups, 1991, 141*t*; and comparative consensus about immigrants, 248; cross-national comparisons and, 245–49; of foreign-born adults on U.S. and U.S. immigration policies, 49–50; on

immigrants in Australia, 113, 115–19, 241–42; on immigrants in Canada, 80, 81*t*, 82, 83, 241; on immigrants in France, 164–68, 167*t*, 243; on immigrants in Germany, 183, 184*t*, 184–85, 185*t*, 244; on immigrants in Great Britain, 139–43, 242–43; on immigrants in Japan, 200–205, 244–45; on immigrants in U.S., 44*t*, 45*t*, 47*t*, 44–50, 239–41; immigration policy consistency and, 247, 248; immigration policy openness versus, 245–46; size of immigrant group versus majority population and, 248; social distance between immigrants–majority population and, 247

Quota Act (U.S. 1921), 12–13
quotas: German, 172–73; public opinion and U.S. setting of, 246; for refugees to U.S., 14–15; U.S. regulations on, 13–14, 16–17, 19, 214. *See also* exclusion

Race Relations Act (Great Britain, 1965), 135
Race Relations Act (Great Britain, 1968), 135
Race Relations Act (Great Britain, 1976), 135, 139
racially unassimable, Canadian immigration and, 55
Refugee Act (U.S., 1980), 14–15
refugees: to Australia, 92, 94, 95, 97; to Australia, post-WWII integration of, 102; to Canada, post-WWII regulations on, 56; Canada's Convention or Designated, 61, 66, 67*t*, 84n 13; Canadian admissions by year, 66*t*; Canadian admissions of, 66–67; Canadian government-sponsored and privately sponsored, 58; Canadian public opinion on, 241; Canadian six-month determination system, 58; in cross-national comparisons, 4; French restrictions on, 151–52; to Germany, nonspecific work permits for, 174; to Great Britain, unemployment among, 137; to Great Britain during 1999, 131; to Great Britain escaping Nazi Germany, 128; Japanese opinion on, 200–201, 205; UN Convention on (1951), 14; U.S. applications and admissions by selected nationality for FY 1991, 24*t*; U.S. visa allocations for FY 1995, 20*t*; to U.S., 14. *See also* asylum seekers
relatives of Canadian citizens. *See* families of Canadian citizens
relatives of U.S. citizens. *See* family-sponsored immigrants, U.S.
religion visas, Japanese, 190, 191*t*
research visas, Japanese, 190, 192*t*
Resettlement Assistance Program, Canada's, 69
residence categories, Japanese, 190
residence permits: for immigrants to France, 148, 150, 154–55; for immigrants to Germany, 173, 175–76
residency requirements: in immigrant versus nonimmigrant nations, 210; in U.S., 11
restrictive immigration policies, conjecture for, 2
Richards, Martin, 138
Roper Center, University of Connecticut, 44–45, 44*t*

Samual, T. J., 76
San Diego, Calif., criminal immigrants in, 40
Schuck, Peter H., 18
seasonal agricultural workers (SAW), legal immigrant status for U.S., 15, 16. *See also* agricultural immigrants
September 11, 2001 terrorist attacks, U.S. immigration policy and, 6
service provider organizations (SPOs), language instruction for Canadian immigrants by, 69. *See also* nongovernmental organizations
settlement houses, U.S., 38
Settlement Service, Canada's, 68

short-term visit visas, Japanese, 190
skilled foreign laborers, U.S. temporary visas for, 16. *See also* employment-based immigrants
skilled labor visas, Japanese, 190, 193*t*
Skill Migration category, Australian, 93, 94, 101
social context of immigration, 4–5
social indicator data, cross-national comparisons using, 3–4
social institutions, defining impacts on, 5–6
social integration, 251–67; comparative, 217–19, 259, 260*t*, 261–62; crime, dependency and, 269; criminal comparisons across countries and, 236–37; cross-national cultural integration patterns, 256–59; cultural integration and, 252; dimensions of, 252; economic institutions, 254–56; happenstance, 264–66; of immigrants in Australia, 103–9; immigration policy and, 262; naturalization, 253–54; patterns across nations, 253–56; perceived threat of immigrant groups and, 265–66; social structural integration and, 252–53; strategies for inclusion and, 251. *See also* integration policies
social security funds: in Germany, immigrants' contributions to versus benefits from, 178, 181*t*, 186. *See also* Supplemental Security Income (SSI)
social structural integration, 252–53
sojourner residents: criminal statistics and, 229; temporary authorization for refugees in France, 152
Somalia, asylum seekers in U.K. from, 131
South America: U.S. immigrants from, 20. *See also* Latin America
Spain: immigrants to Germany from, 175; nonspecific German work permits for immigrants from, 174
Special Assistance category, Australian, 94
special eligibility immigrants to Australia, 92–93; occupational distribution of, 106
specific work permits, for German immigrants, 173–74
Sri Lanka, asylum seekers in U.K. from, 131
Steinberg, Allen, 39
students, rights for admission to U.K., 126, 127
Supplemental Security Income (SSI), U.S. restrictions for legal immigrants to, 17. *See also* social security funds
Survey of Inmates of State Correctional Facilities, U.S. Bureau of Justice Statistics, 40

Taguchi, Sumikazu, 195
Taiwan, U.S. immigrants from, 22
Task Force Report on Refugee Status Determination (Canada, 1981), 61
Taustino-Santos, R., 76
Technical Intern Training Program, Japan, 195
temporary entry permits, Australia, 92
temporary sojourn authorization, for refugees in France, 152
temporary visas: Japanese, 190, 193*t*; U.S. visitors who overstay, 28–29
terrorist groups, U.S. regulations on, 17
Texas, criminal immigrants in, 40
tourists to U.S., instigation of removal procedures against, 18
training visas, Japanese, 190, 193–94*t*
transit visas, Japanese, 190
transportation to Australia, 88, 90, 120n5
Tsuda, Takayuki, 196, 197
Turkey: asylum seekers in U.K. from, 131; Canada on immigrants from, 57; immigrants in France from, 149*t*, 169; immigrants in Germany from, 174, 175

Uganda, asylum seekers in U.K. from, 131
unemployment: compensation for immigrants to U.S., 36; of foreign-born versus native-born Australians,

103; of foreign-born versus native-born Germans, 178; social integration and, 255, 260*t*. *See also* dependency; income support, for U.S. immigrants
Uniform Crime Reports, on criminal immigrants in U.S., 40
United Kingdom. *See* Great Britain
United Nations: Convention on Refugees (1951), 14, 128; *Definition of Refugees,* 94; Educational, Scientific, and Cultural Organization study on Australian attitudes on ethnic groups, 115, 115*t*
United States: annual admissions to, 212; Australian immigrants from, 99*t*; as choice for cross-national comparisons, 3; criminal immigrants in Canada from, 80; "drop outs" in, 253; French immigrants from, 149*t*; as immigrant nation, 211, 219; immigration policy openness versus public opinion in, 245, 246; police statistics in, 228
United States, immigrants in: average attitude toward, 246; control policies for, 15, 20*t*, 26–28; criminal involvement of, 39–44, 53n44, 231; criminal involvement of citizens versus, 234*t*; demographic and socioeconomic characteristics of, 30–33; drug offenses by nonimmigrants versus, 231; educational status of, 30, 32*t*; English-speaking, 30, 33*t*; illegal, 28–29, 29*t*, 212, 213; incarceration rates by citizenship status and offense, 40–41, 41*t*; incarceration ratio for nonimmigrants and, 230*t*; intermarriage rate, 267n10; internal regulations for, 215; leading "sender" states, 1820–1989, 22*t*; marital status and gender distribution by age, 30, 31*t*; naturalization rates by class of admission, 26*t*; naturalizations, 24–26, 254, 267n2; naturalizations for FY 1991 by birth country, 27*t*; occupational status and average income of, 31, 33, 37*t*; occupational status of, 30, 34–35*t*; percentage distribution by last residence, 23*t*; permanent residence visa allocations, 20*t*; public opinion on, 44*t*, 44–50, 239–41; public opinion on increases or decreases in, 47*t*; refugee applications by selected nationality, 24*t*; social integration of, 217–18, 255, 261; stock and flow of, 19–24; U.S. public opinion of, by ethnicity, 45, 45*t*
university study visas, Japanese, 190, 193*t*
unrestricted immigration policies, 209–10
unskilled laborers, U.S. exclusion of, 12
unspecified visas, Japanese, 190
USA Today/CNN poll, on U.S. public opinion of immigrants by ethnicity, 45*t*
U.S. citizens, Canadian regulations on, 56
U.S. Constitution: Fifteenth Amendment on voting rights, 51–52n1; immigration policy and, 11
U.S. immigration policies: dimensions of, 220*t*; foreign-born adults on, 49–50; FY 1821–1995, 25*t*; historical background and major legislation, 12–19; on integration, 33, 36, 38–39; laissez faire nature of, 219, 222; policy oversight in, 216; population increase by component of change, 1810–1989, 21*t*; public opinion on, 48–49; public opinion on restrictions in, 48; quotas, 213, 214; residency requirements for naturalization, 11; Sept. 11, 2001 terrorist attacks and, 6

Vietnam: immigrants in France from, 147; Japan and refugees from, 189, 197; Japanese opinion on refugees from, 200, 201; naturalization of Australian immigrants from, 101; refugees to U.S.

from, 217, 218; U.S. public opinion on immigrants from, 45
visas: U.S. preference list for, 14; U.S. regulations on nonfamily immigrants, 16. *See also* work visas and permits
vocational skills: Canadian immigration criteria on, 59*t*. *See also* employment-based immigrants

war brides, post WWII Australian, 97
War Brides Act (U.S., post WWII), 13
welfare: for Australian immigrants, 102, 103, 109; for British immigrants, 134; California's restrictions on, 38; Canadian immigrant's eligibility for, 69; Canadian immigrants on, 75–76; for German immigrants, 179, 186; immigration impact on, 5; U.S. restrictions for legal immigrants to, 17. *See also* dependency; income support, for U.S. immigrants
West Indies: British public opinion on immigrants from, 139, 140*t*; British public opinion on support for immigrants from, 142; British restrictions on immigration from, 144; immigration to Great Britain from, 124, 128–29, 128*t*. *See also* New Commonwealth
Woodrow, Karen, on illegal immigrants in U.S., 42
work experience. *See* business immigrants
working holiday admissions, British, 127
work visas and permits: for immigrants to France, 148, 154–55; for immigrants to Germany, 173–74, 175, 176; for immigrants to Japan, 190, 191–93*t*. *See also* employment-based immigrants

Yugoslavia: asylum seekers in U.K. from, 131, 132; naturalization of Australian immigrants from, 101; refugees in Germany from, 175

About the Authors

James P. Lynch is a professor in the Department of Justice, Law, and Society at the American University in Washington, D.C. He received his doctorate in sociology at the University of Chicago in 1983. Professor Lynch has done extensive work in the area of crime statistics with a special emphasis on victimization surveys. He has coauthored the book *Understanding Crime Incidence Statistics* (1991), with Albert D. Biderman. He has also published numerous articles on the cross-national comparisons of crime and social control. His most recent work explores the interrelationship between marginal groups and crime and the role of punishment in social control.

Rita J. Simon is a sociologist who earned her doctorate at the University of Chicago in 1957. Before coming to American University in 1983 to serve as dean of the School of Justice, she was a faculty member at the University of Illinois, at the Hebrew University in Jerusalem, and the University of Chicago. She is currently a university professor in the School of Public Affairs and the Washington College of Law at American University.

Professor Simon has authored twenty-eight books and edited seventeen including *Adoption across Borders* (2000), with Howard Altstein, *In the Golden Land: A Century of Russian and Soviet Jewish Immigration* (1997), *The Ambivalent Welcome: Media Coverage of American Immigration* (1993), with Susan Alexander, and *New Lives: The Adjustment of Soviet Jewish Immigrants in the United States and Israel* (1985).

She is currently editor of *Gender Issues*. From 1978 to 1981, she served as editor of the *American Sociological Review* and from 1983 to 1986 as editor of *Justice Quarterly*. In 1966, she received a Guggenheim Fellowship.